Playful Palette's

Beginner's Art

Book One (ages 5-6)

by

Joel Gwidt

Copyright 2022
Playful Palette Publications and Joel Gwidt
Lessons from Playful Palette are reproducible for 'in home' use only

About Playful Palette

As public schools cut art education programs, children are finding it increasingly difficult to tap into their creativity. Instead of creativity flourishing, it is being suppressed with regulated projects and simple crafts in order to comply with downsized curriculums.

The mission of Playful Palette is to counter this effect by helping to raise generations of children that value the creativity, the passion, and the power of art.

About Our Philosophy

One thing we have to be reminded of is that art is a discipline much like learning to play an instrument or sport. It can be fun, but it does take practice and discipline along with a basic understanding of artistic principles.

Many students, parents, and teachers look at art class as just a fun time to make pretty pictures. We are taught to let the children "be creative" and do whatever they want in art. This may be fun for kids for a while, but it leads to a loss of interest and an eventual feeling that they never had the talent to draw or paint.

Playful Palette hopes to escape this mentality and give children a solid art foundation to advance upon.

So Why Learn Art?

Art classes don't just benefit creativity. They can help build confidence, commitment, patience, and a sense of accomplishment. The creative process also can have a relaxing and comforting affect on children.

The fine arts can also help children academically. During a research experiment through the National Endowment of the Arts and the Department of Health and Human Services, children were split into two groups. One group had a curriculum with art, while the other had a curriculum without art. The results of the study showed that students who had programs in art, along with their other courses, fared much better academically than students who were deprived of art.

"Children who possess broad background knowledge, especially in fine arts, learn new things more readily than those that lack it."

Pollee Freier, teacher and speaker

About the Author

Joel Gwidt, founder of Playful Palette, utilizes his expertise in both art and early childhood development to create a unique learning environment. With more than 10 years of experience working with children in an educational environment, Joel has found that they learn best through active participation, thought-provoking subjects, and creative projects.

After teaching children in the school system, Joel started working with artists of all ages by creating the Playful Palette. Helping kids nurture their artistic side, students of the Playful Palette have grown to not only excel in art but also foster an interest in creating art well past the class.

Joel holds a Bachelor of Fine Arts with an emphasis in painting and a minor in sculpture and art history from the University of Wisconsin-Stevens Point. His art has been displayed in New York City, London, New Orleans, Wisconsin and the Kansas City Metro Area. He is an active participant of the "Now Showing Program" sponsored by The Arts Council of Metropolitan Kansas City, and he shows regularly at other events and galleries in the area.

Art Supplies

What art supplies you will need for the art lessons in this book

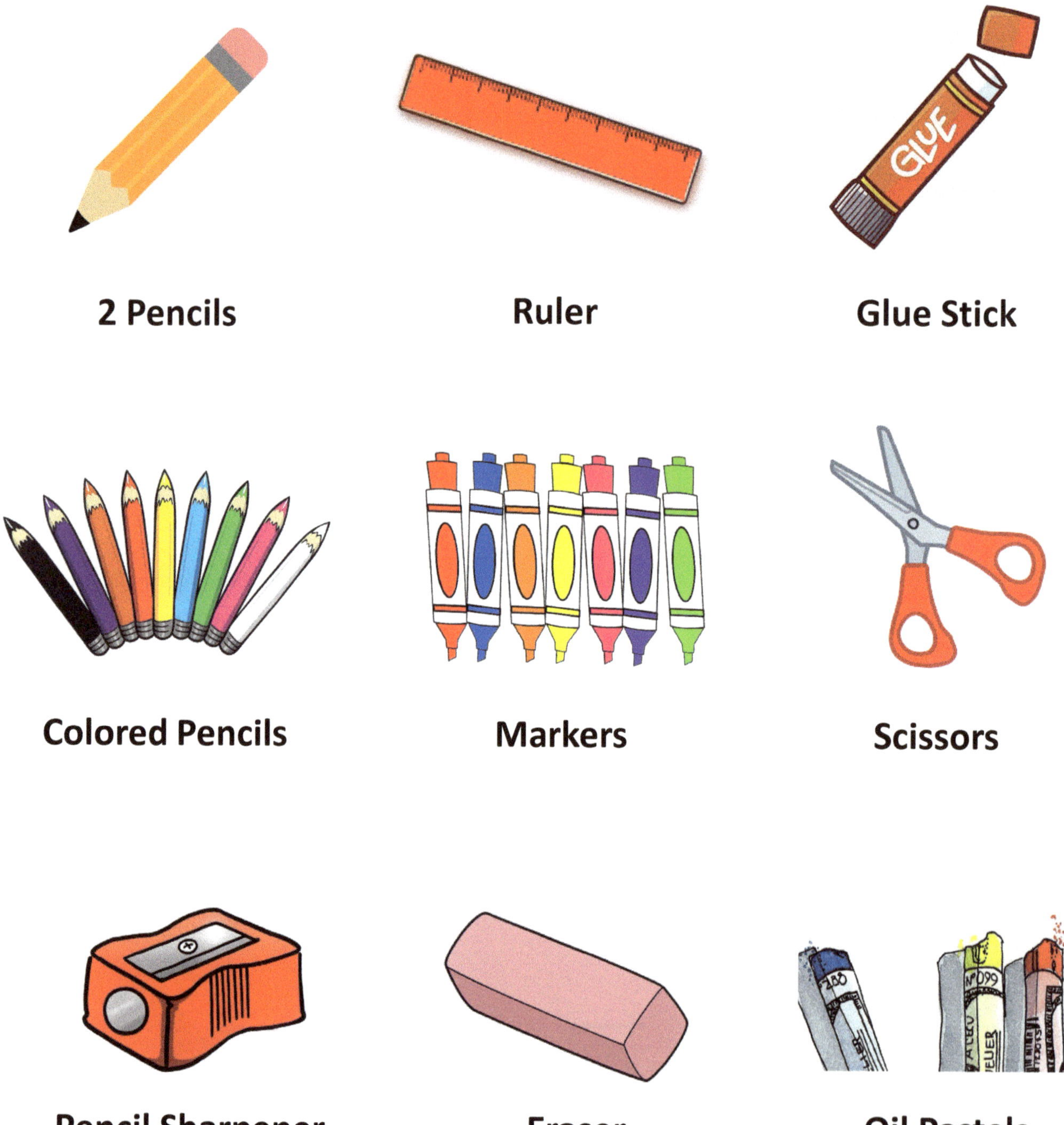

Art Supplies

How to take care of your art supplies

Always keep your pencil sharp but not too sharp. You don't want it to be so sharp as to hurt you. When drawing with a pencil, do not press too hard on your paper or you may not be able to erase it. Always draw lightly.

Same as your pencil, you will want to keep these always sharpened and ready to use. When drawing with a pencil, do not press too hard on your paper or you may not be able to erase it. Always draw lightly.

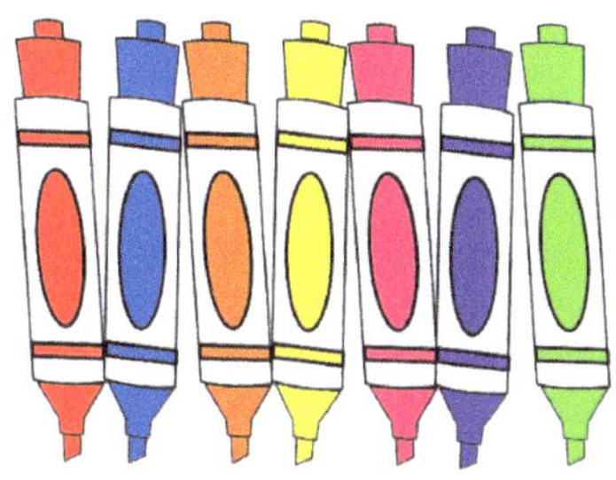

When you use markers, do not press very hard on the paper. This will ruin the tip of your marker. Always draw in smooth, slow strokes when using markers. When you are finished, make sure the cap is on tightly by hearing it click when you put it on.

Art Supplies

How to take care of your art supplies

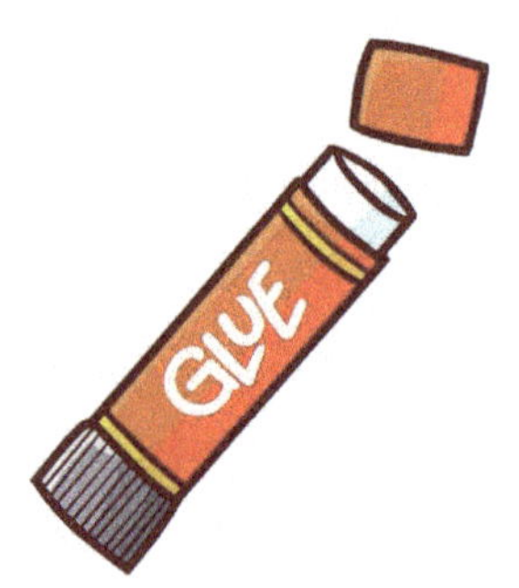

Do not press too hard when using your glue stick. This will smoosh the glue. You don't need a lot of glue to glue something in place so don't put too much on. When finished, always make sure the cap in on tightly or your glue will dry out.

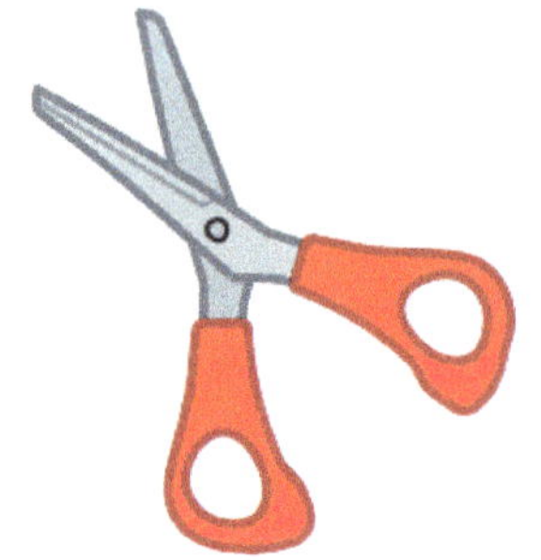

Be careful when using scissors. Keep your thumb in the top hole and two fingers in the bottom hole. Always cut with the scissors pointing away from you. If you need to make a curved cut, turn the paper not the scissors.

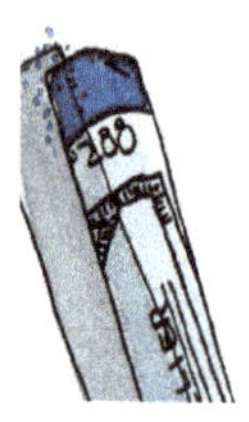
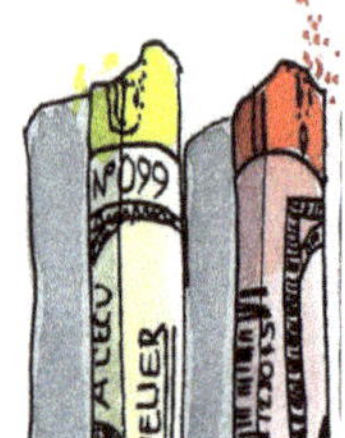

Oil Pastels can be messy! When using them, try not to rub your hand across the paper or it will smear and get your hand dirty. They are also fragile so do not press too hard on the paper or they will break. It might be good to have a paper towel ready. Sometimes, if you mixed the colors on the paper, it will transfer onto the stick. You can easily wipe the stick clean.

Art Lessons

What you will find in each lesson

Art is much like learning to play an instrument. You don't learn to play the piano but banging on the keys and eventually playing Beethoven. It takes practice and instruction. Much like learning to play the piano, you cannot learn art by just scribbling on paper. You learn little tools and tips along the way that will help you develop your drawings into something more, something artistic!

Each Playful Palette lesson consists of a variety of instructions, exercises, projects, and Art History lessons that will give you the tools to build up your artistic talents. We start off with simple exercises and build up from what we've learned.

You'll find these in each lesson

1. Introduction to the art lesson
2. Several exercises that go over the topic of each lesson
3. Two projects that go over the skills learned in the exercises
4. Step by Step instructions for each Project
5. An Art History Lesson that goes over information learned
6. Short game or questions about what was learned in the lesson

The most important thing to remember when working on each lesson is to have fun with it. If you have trouble or finding a particular lesson difficult, don't get frustrated with it. Just keep trying and practicing. All artists need to practice no matter how good they are

About this book

This book will guide you through some of the basics in learning art. It will provide step by step instructions on how to better your drawings. Playful Palette wants you to be able to learn the tools needed in order to draw confidently on your own and be proud of the artwork you do.

Some lessons may seem easy, but they are there to help you practice skills that you can immediately use in your own work. Other lessons may seem a little more difficult, but the instructions will hopefully help you through it all.

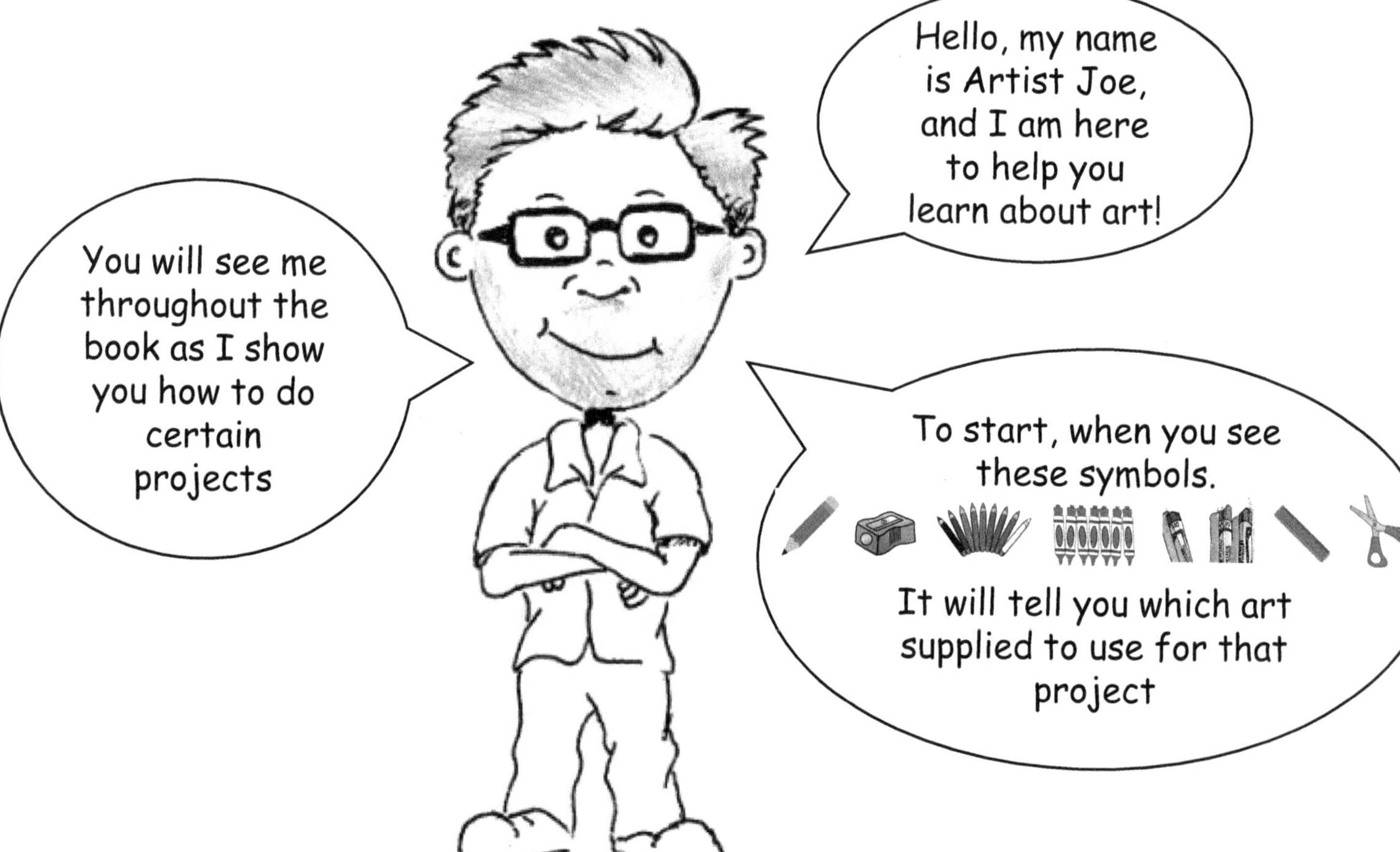

Table of Contents

UNIT 1 Shapes

Lesson 1.1 Identifying Shapes

In this first lesson, we will go over shapes. Shapes play an important role in art. With shapes, we can form all types of items we see everyday. We can take one object and break it down into several different shapes.

Let's start out by identifying the main shapes we will be practicing with.

- **Circle**
- **Square**
- **Triangle**
- **Rectangle**
- **Oval**
- **Heart**
- **Diamond**
- **Start**

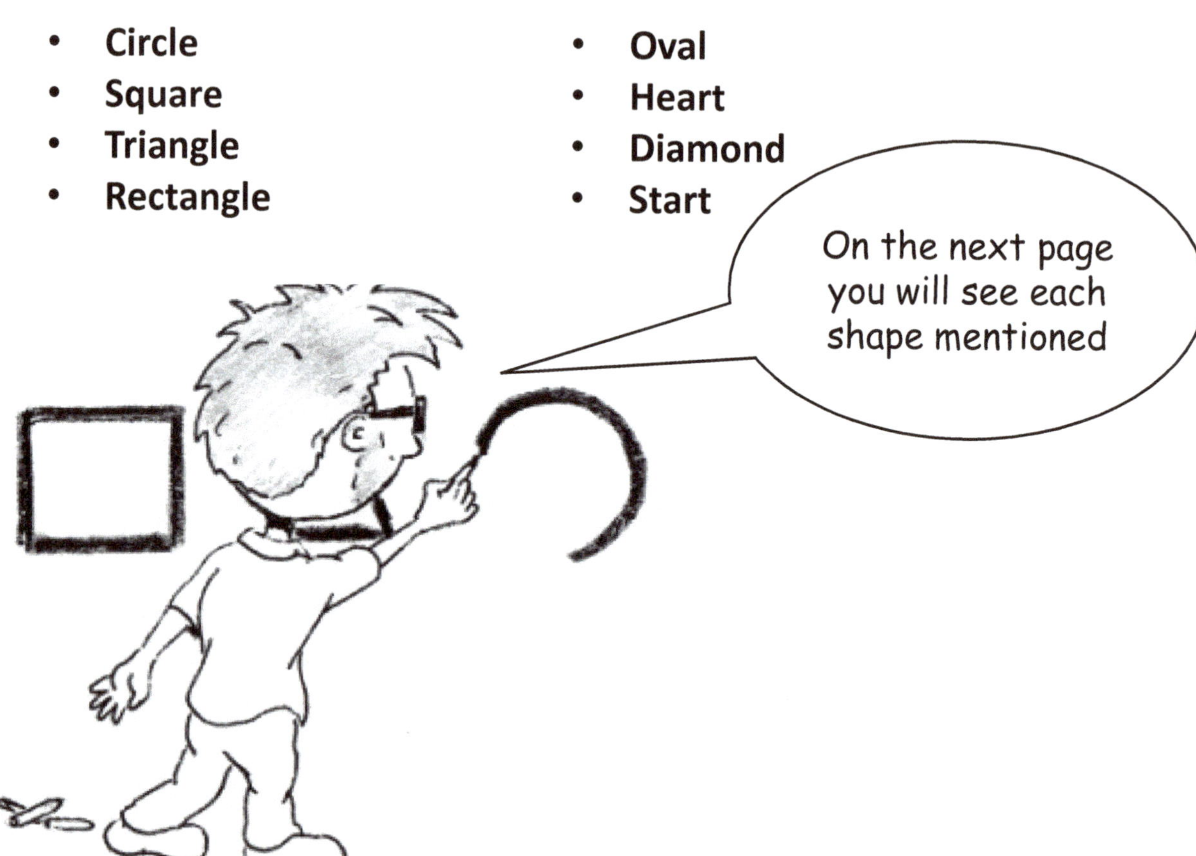

In this lesson, you will need pencils, colored pencils, pencil sharpener, and markers. Look for the icon next to each project to determine what to use

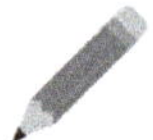 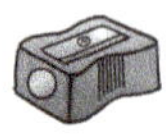 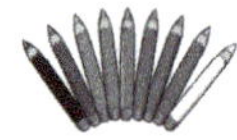 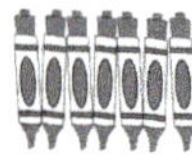

Here are the basic shapes we will start off with. In later lessons and instructional books, we will go over more complex shapes.

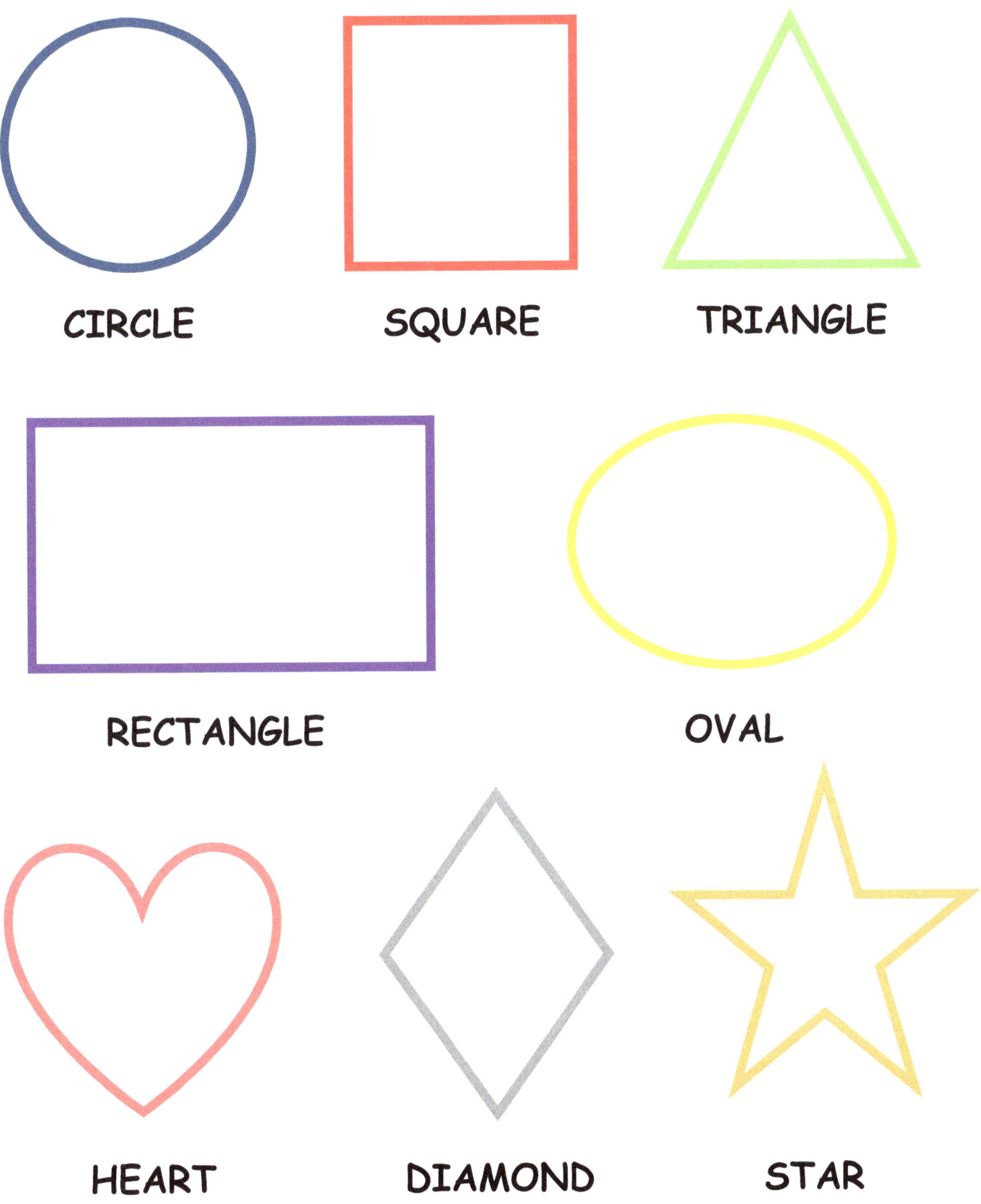

Exercise 1

Trace the Shapes

Trace the first two shapes and then practice on shape on your own

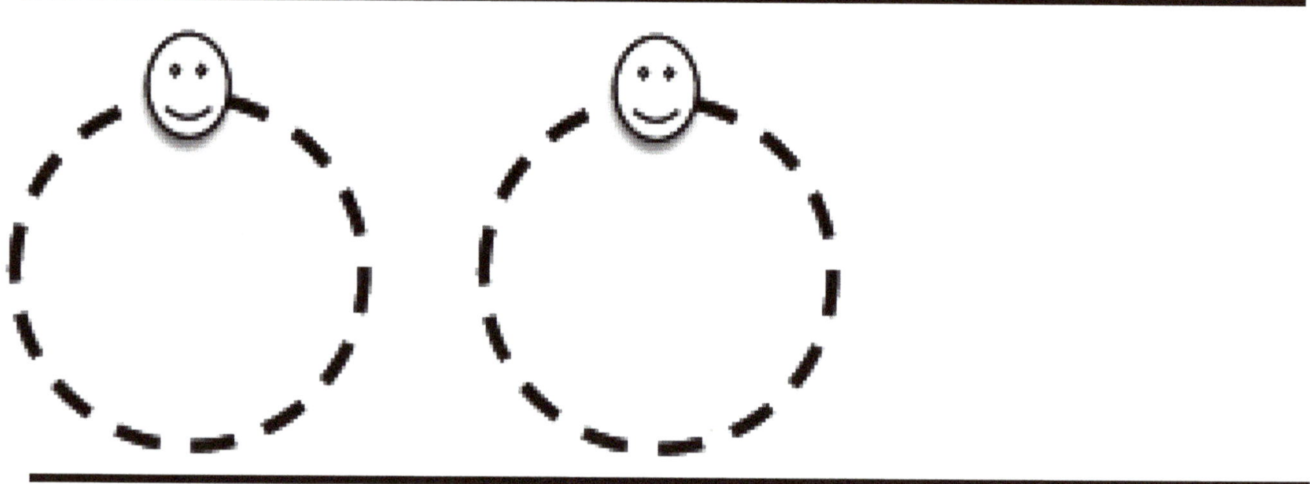

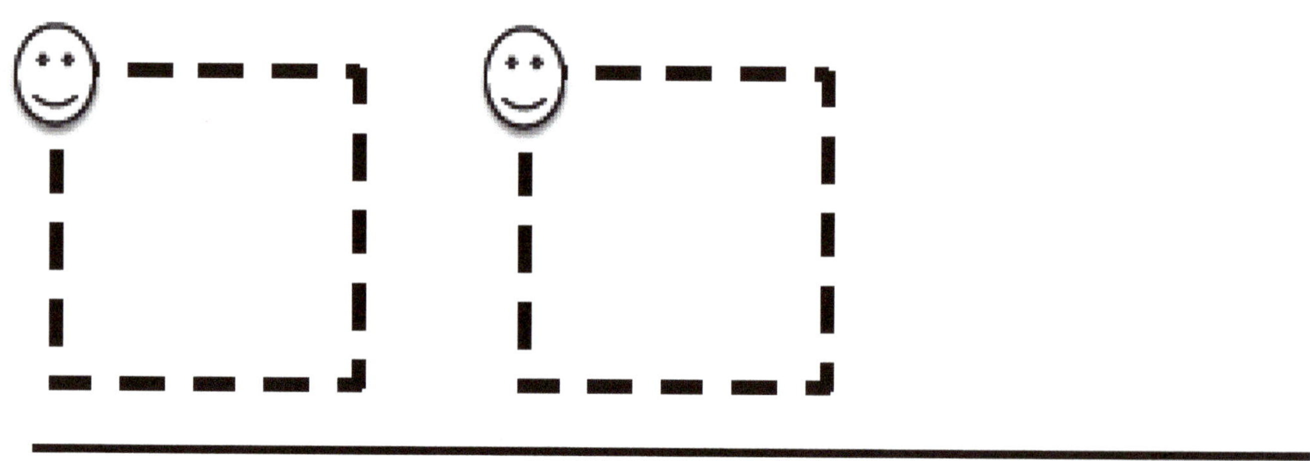

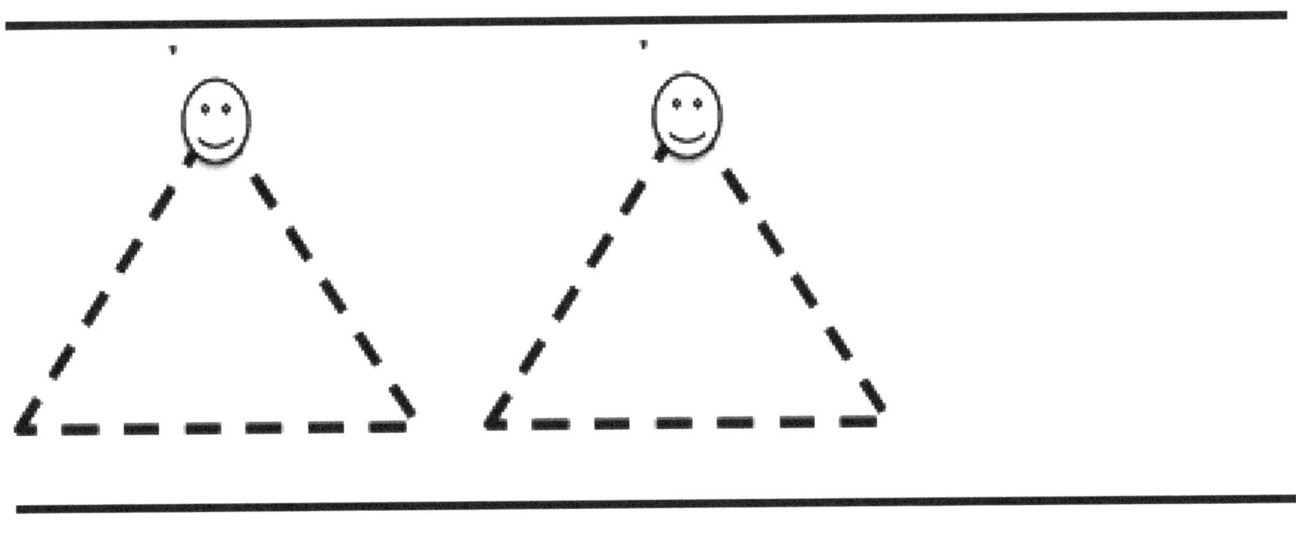

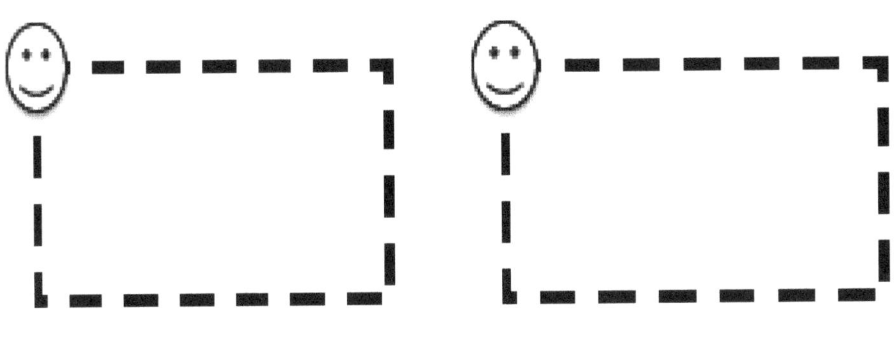

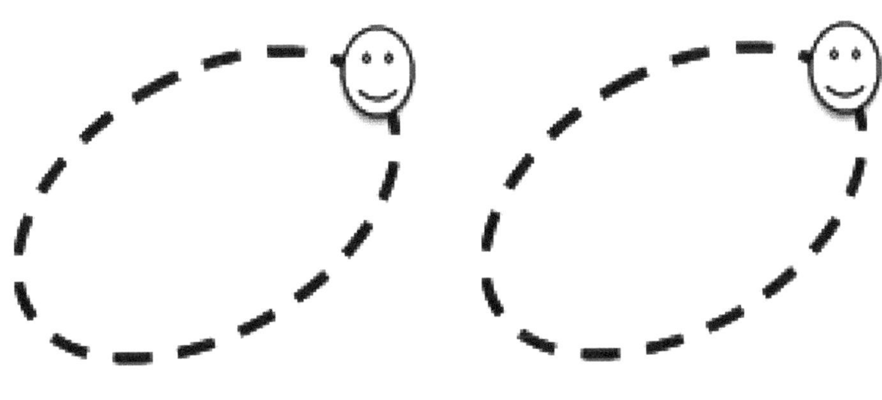

Practice on your own

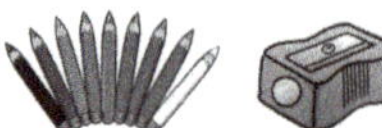

CIRCLE

SQUARE

TRIANGLE

RECTANGLE

OVAL

Exercise 2

Trace the Shapes

Trace the first two shapes and then practice on shape on your own

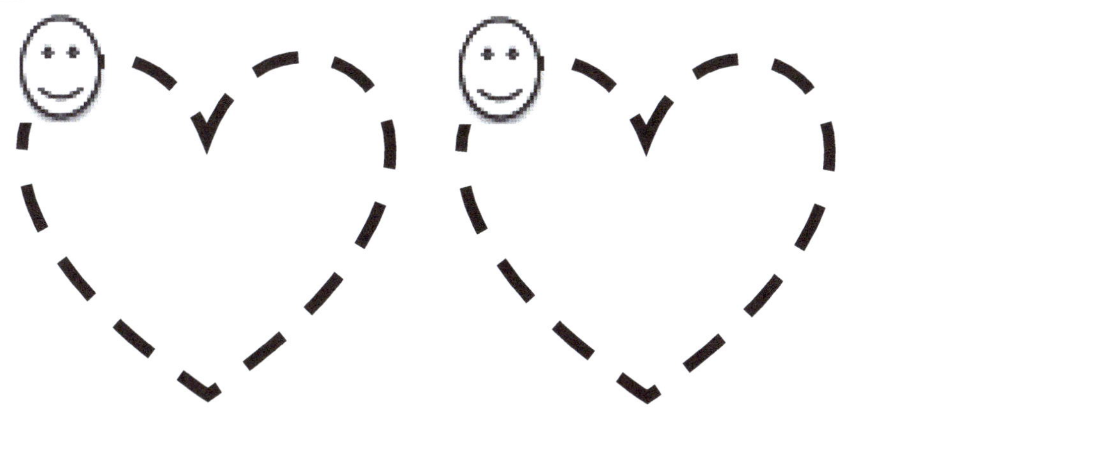

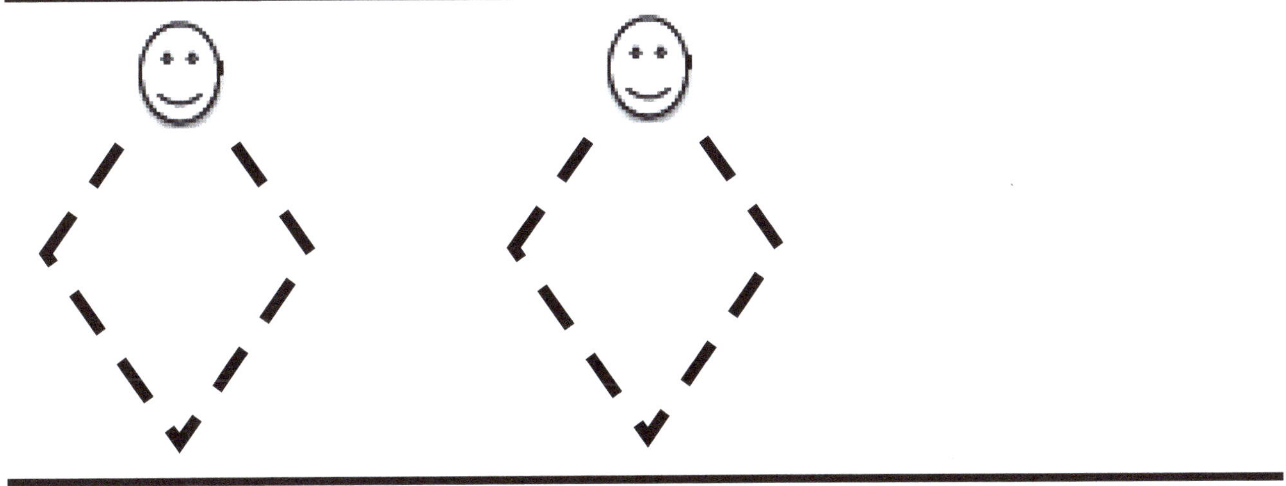

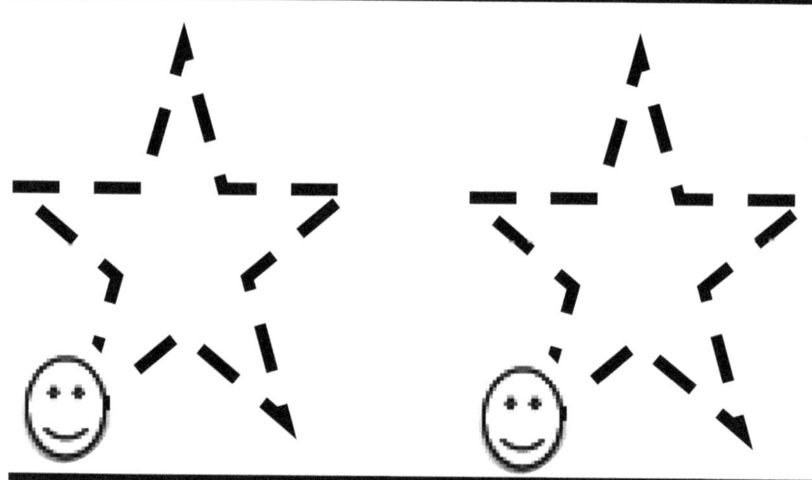

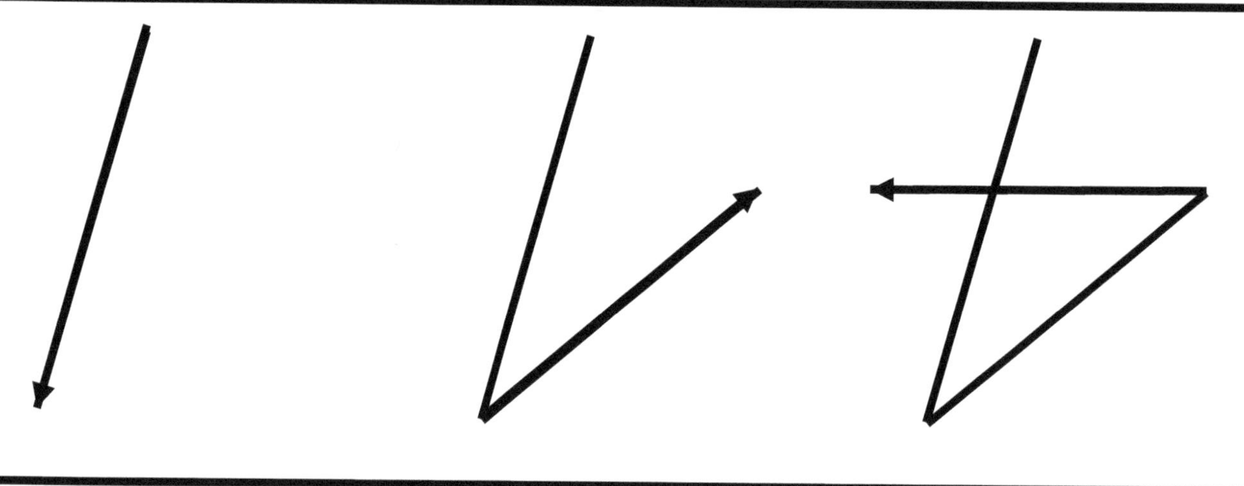

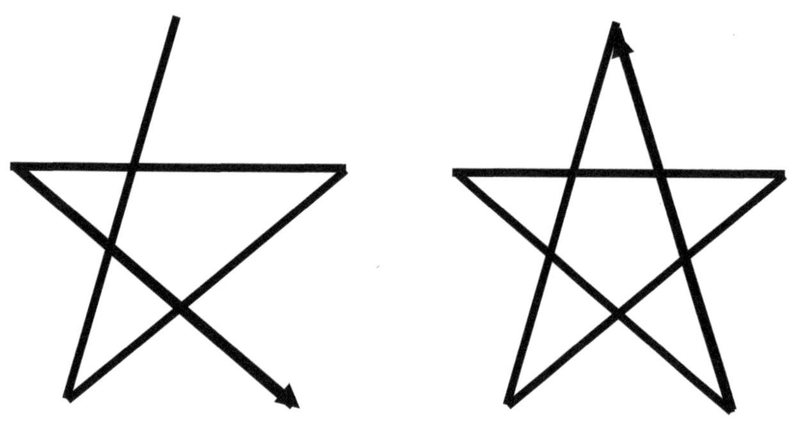

Practice on your own

HEART

HEART

DIAMOND

STAR

STAR

Project 1

Artist Joe wants to build a house, but he is having trouble with reading the blueprint. He doesn't know what shapes to use to build it.

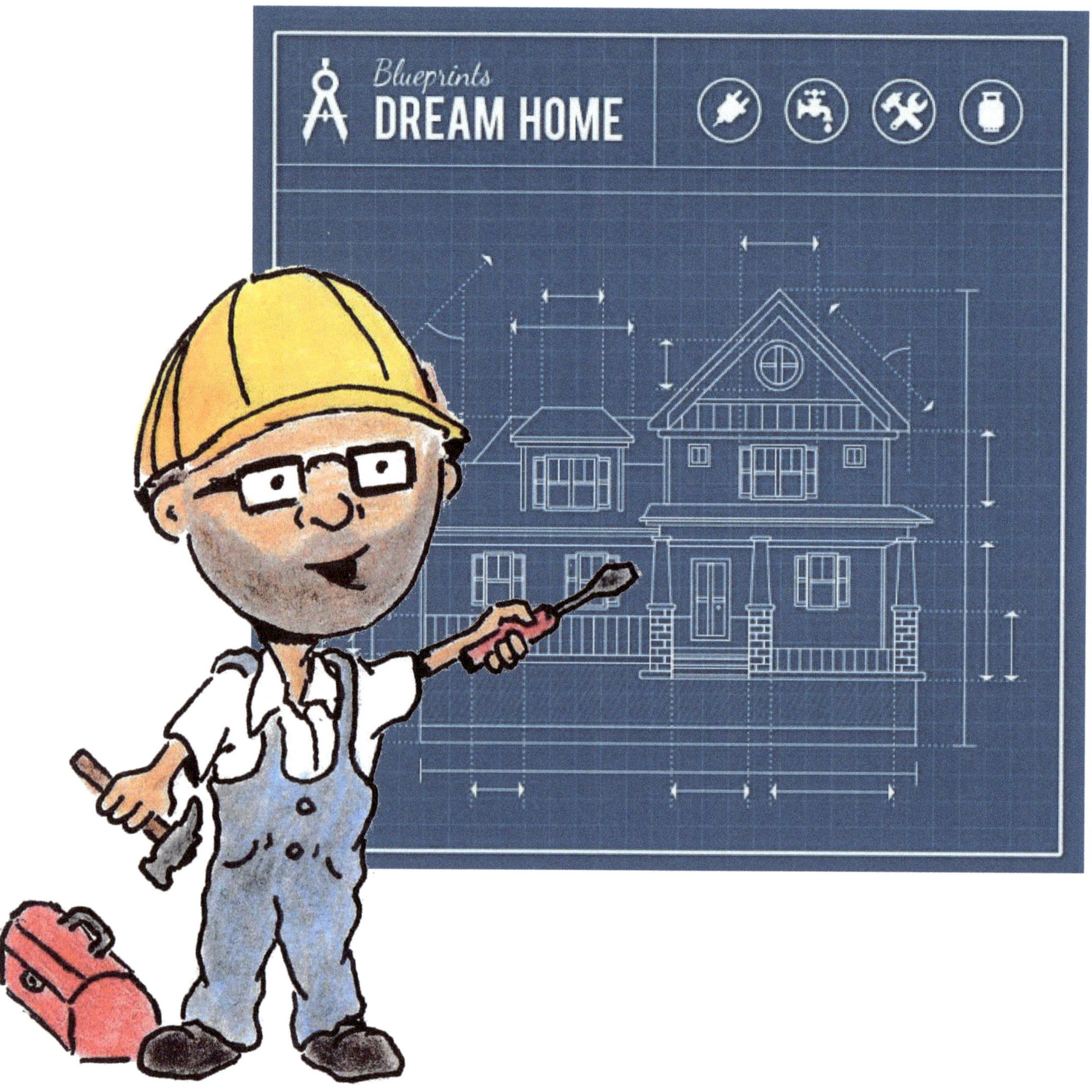

Project 1

Now that we have identified common shapes, we will begin to put those shapes together to form objects. Here is an example you can try.

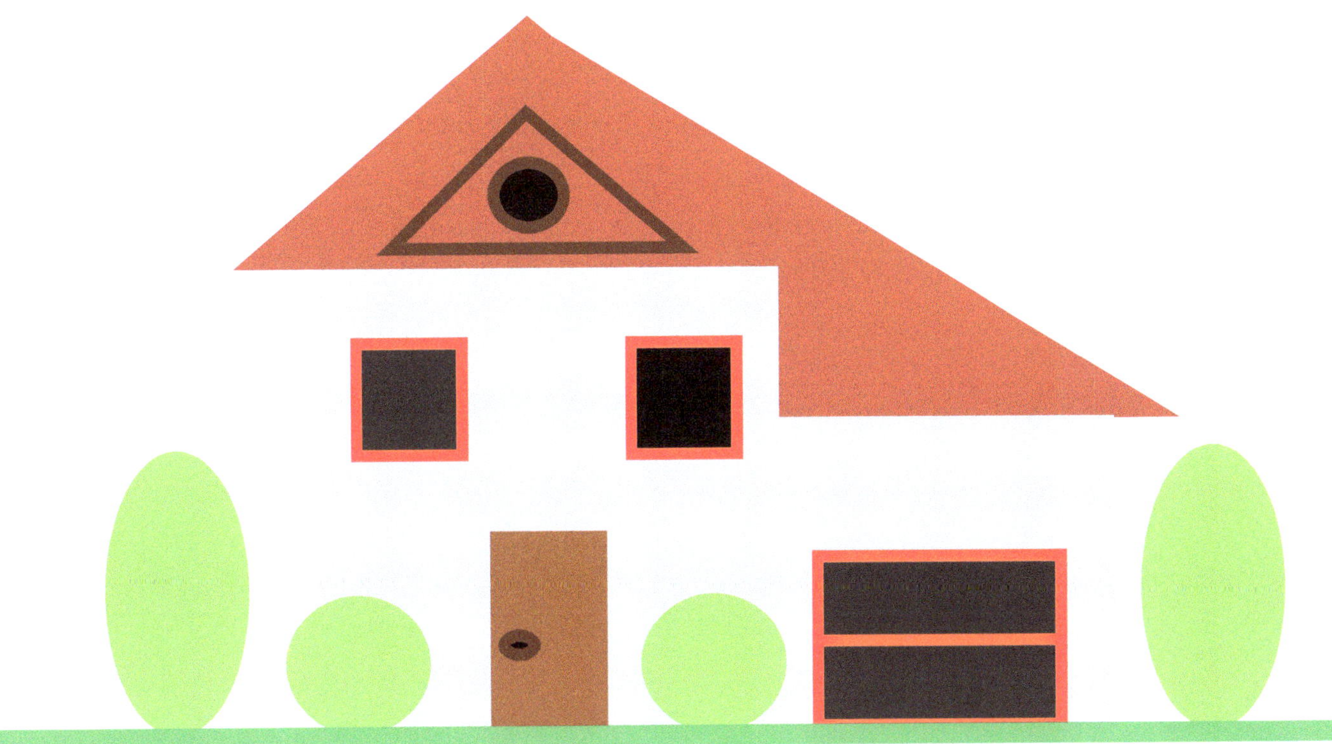

What shapes do you see? How many shapes can you find that make up the picture?

Do you see how some shapes are on top of each other. When using shapes to draw objects, you may need to erase a side or part of the shape, so it fits with the object you are drawing.

On the next page, draw your own house. Try to figure out how your house looks like. Does it have a garage? How many windows does it have. Does it have a pointed roof or a flat roof? Are there bushes or trees in front of it? Try to get your picture to look like your house as much as possible.

Project 1

Draw your house in the space provided. Draw with your pencil first and then color it in with markers

Remember to sign your name to your work

Art History Lesson One

Each lesson we will go over some Art History that follow what we have learned in each lesson. During this lesson, we identified certain shapes, practiced drawing those shapes, and learned how to use those shapes to create certain things.

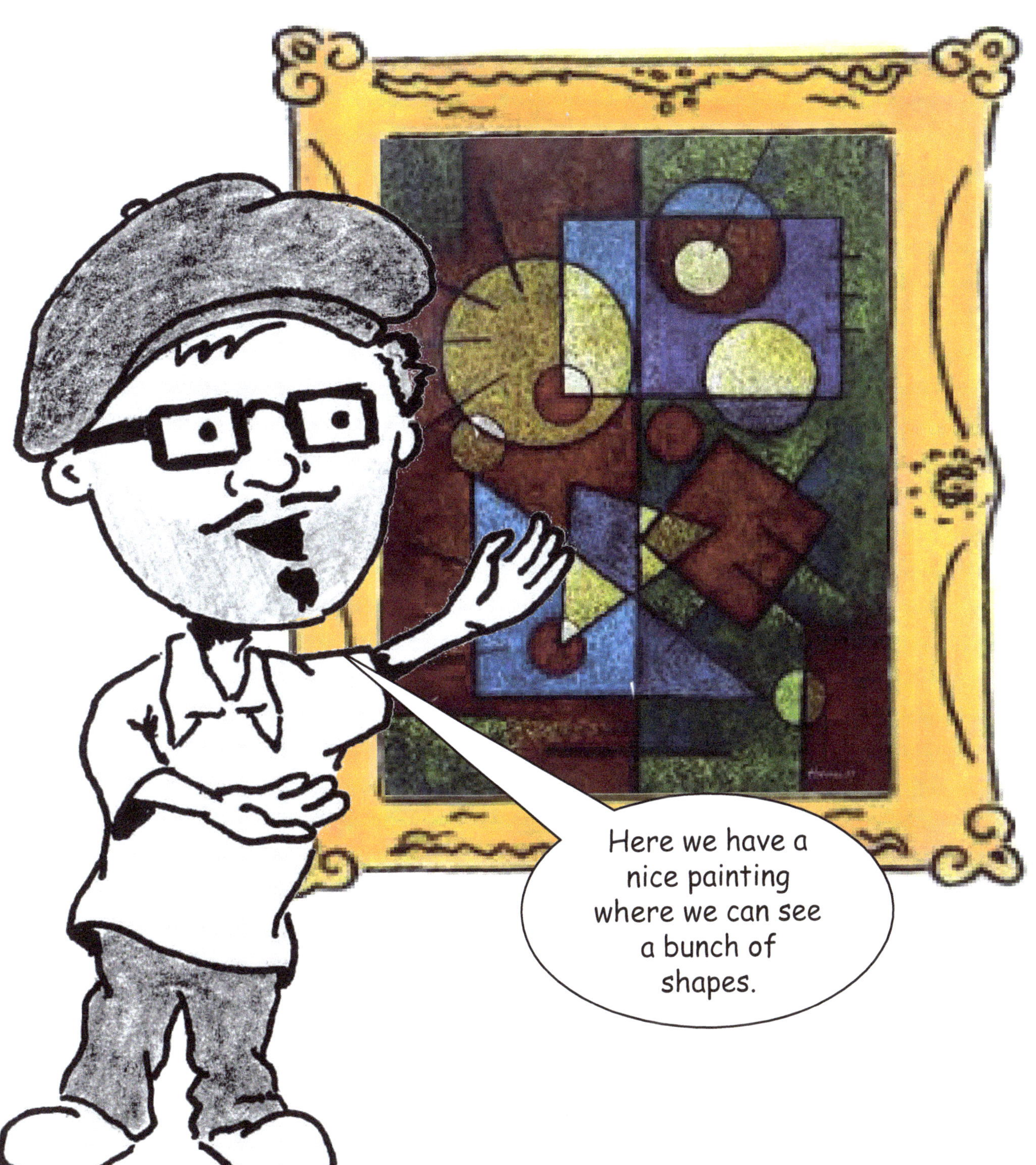

Harman

In the painting by the artist Harman titled 'Geometric in Colors', what shapes do you see? How many Circles can you spot? How about Squares, Rectangles, and Triangles. Do you see how the artist overlapped the shapes?

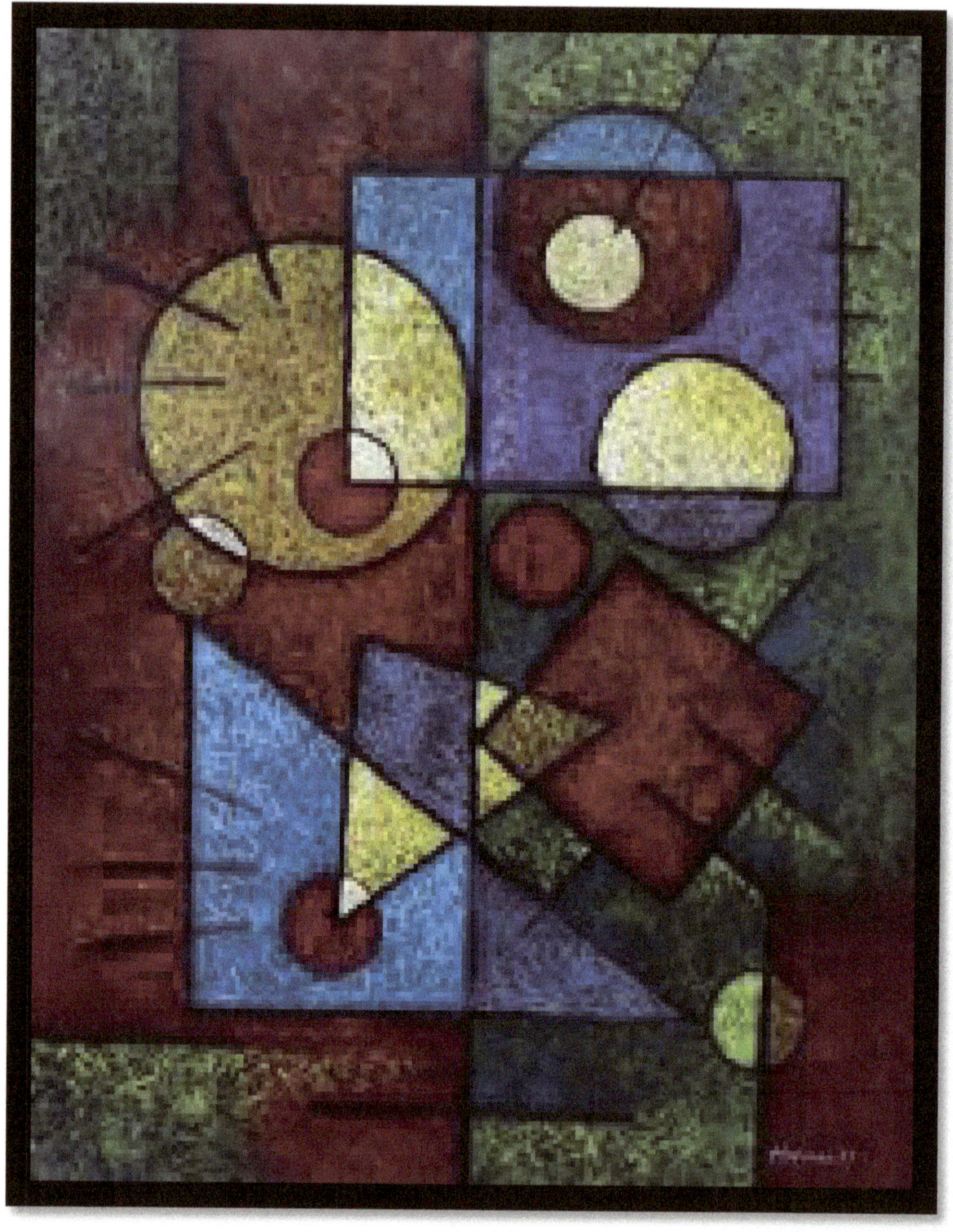

Does the image look like anything to you? Use your imagination to try to figure out what it might look like. When you look at some art, it may not look like anything at all. Sometimes you must be creative and try to imagine what the artist was trying to paint

Art History Project 1

Draw a picture similar to the painting we just saw by Harmon. Use the shapes you learned to make a unique picture. You can overlap the shapes and then color them using your markers. You can outline the shapes in black.

Remember to sign your name to your work

Chapter Fun

Try to find all the words in word box. They can be up and down, sideways or diagonal.

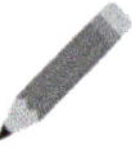

Shapes

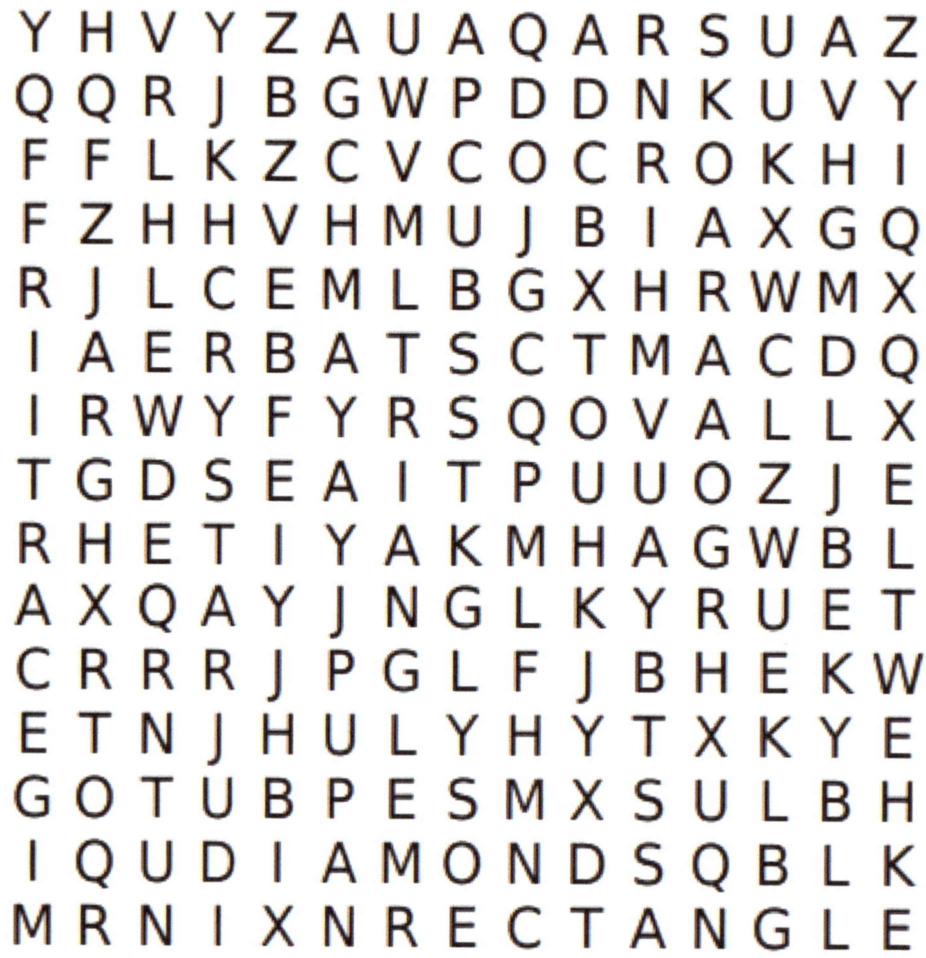

Rectangle	Triangle	Diamond	Square
Circle	Heart	Oval	Star
Draw	Trace		

UNIT 2 Lettering

Lesson 2.1 Capital and Lowercase letters

In this second lesson, we are going to learn about lettering. There are many times where artist use words in their artwork, so it is a good thing to practice how to write letters correctly. We will look at different ways we can create letters and practice writing them on our own.

First, we will practice.

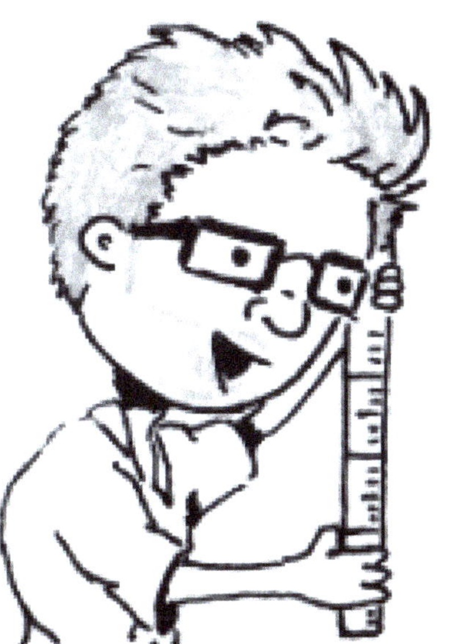

In this lesson, you will need pencils, pencil sharpener, eraser and markers. Look for the icon next to each project to determine what to use

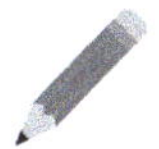 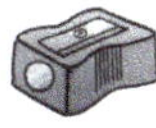 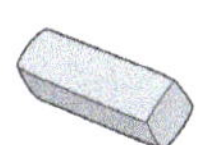 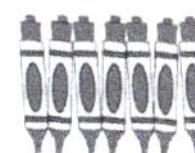

We will go over how these lines are use when writing both Capital letters and Lowercase letters. The top solid line is used for the very top of the letter and the bottom solid line is used for the very bottom of the letter. The middle-dotted line is used for the center and shows us were the middle section of the letter goes as in the B and the E.

A B C D E

Practice writing your name below in all capital letters. Make sure you are following the lines provided. We will practice the whole alphabet in Capital Letters on the next page.

Now we will practice lowercase letters. The middle, dotted line is used for the very top of the letter and the bottom solid line is used for the very bottom of the letter. The top, solid line is used for letters that have a neck and the bottom, dotted line is used for letters that have a tail.

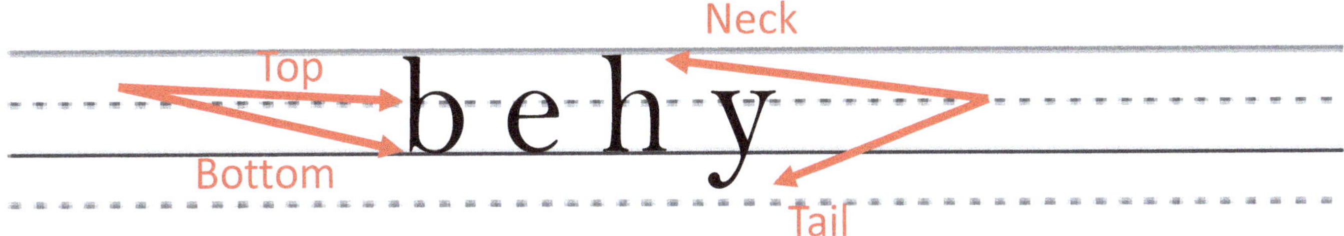

Below is the full alphabet in lowercase letters. You can practice below

a b c d e f g h i j

k l m n o p q r

s t u v w x y z

Exercise 1

Practice writing Capital and lowercase letters.

A B C D E F G H I

J K L M N O P Q

R S T U V W X Y Z

Exercise 2

Practice writing letters in a different way

There are many ways to write letters. When it comes to art, you can choose how you want your letters to look like.Below are some different ways.

I am learning how to write letters!
I am learning how to write letters!
I am learning how to write letters!
I am learning how to write letters!

Practice below writing different letters (both Capital and lowercase. You can also try different ways to write the letters as shown above. More practice lines on page 147

Lesson 2.1 Block Letters and Pixel Art

Next, we will look at how to write block letters. Block letters are used many times when creating posters. We will first start out by using a grid to write letters. A grid is a set of squares that are the same size. Our letters may not be perfect, but you should be able to read what it says. What does the word below say?

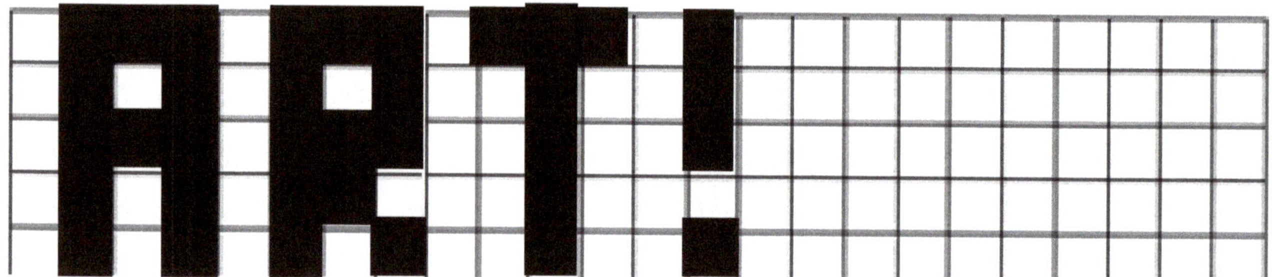

The way we wrote this word is like how they made video games a long time ago. By using little squares of color, they would create a character or image. This was called 8-bit or Pixel art. Later in this chapter we will practice this.

Exercise 1

Practice writing block letters

When writing letters in this grid, the letters should be 5 squares high and 3 squares long. Some letters like I may be shorter and some letters like M or W will be longer as seen in the image below.

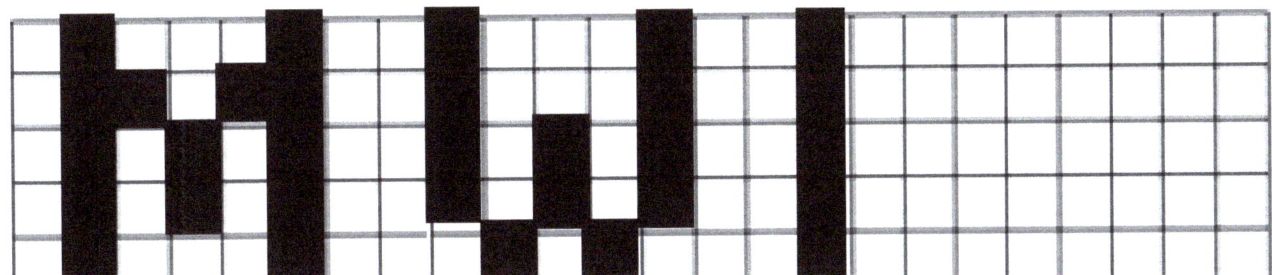

See if you can figure out how to draw each letter. If you have a longer name, use the other grids below to finish. If not, use those grids to write another word with different letters.

Project 1

Create an 8-bit piece of art 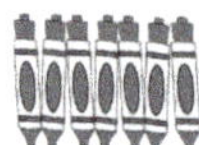

Uh oh, looks like Artist Joe has been playing with his computer and pixelated himself!

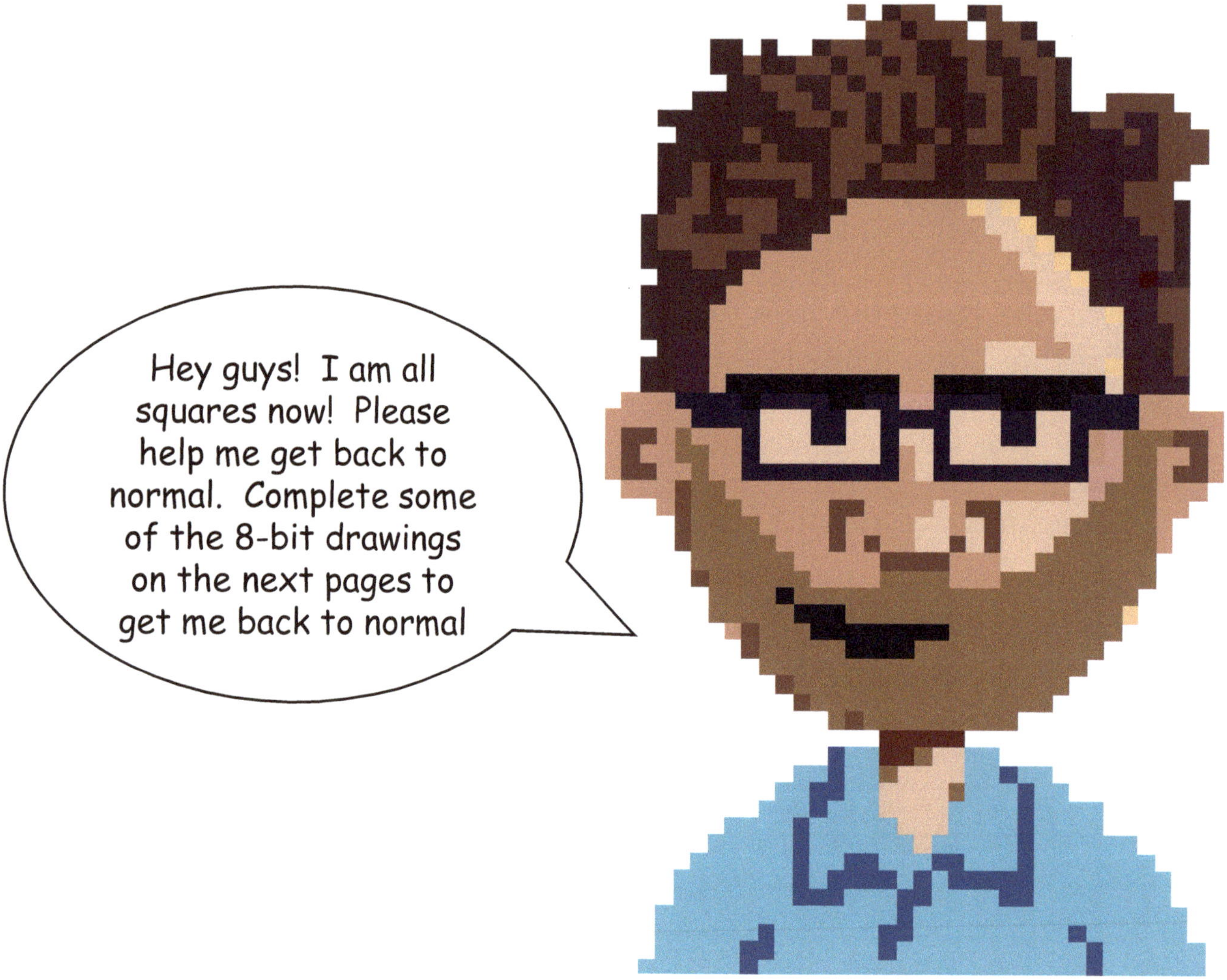

Hey guys! I am all squares now! Please help me get back to normal. Complete some of the 8-bit drawings on the next pages to get me back to normal

On the next two pages are examples of 8-bit images you can create using your markers. The grids are on the following pages. For the 1st grid, choose and easy design to draw. On the 2nd grid, you can either choose an easy or difficult design. On the 3rd grid, try to create your own by choosing something around the house. When doing these, make sure you count out the number of squares correctly before coloring it in. There are more grids at the back of the book (Pages 148-150) if you want to practice more

Project 1

Create an easy 8-bit piece of art 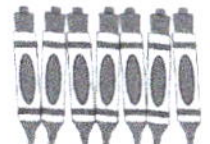

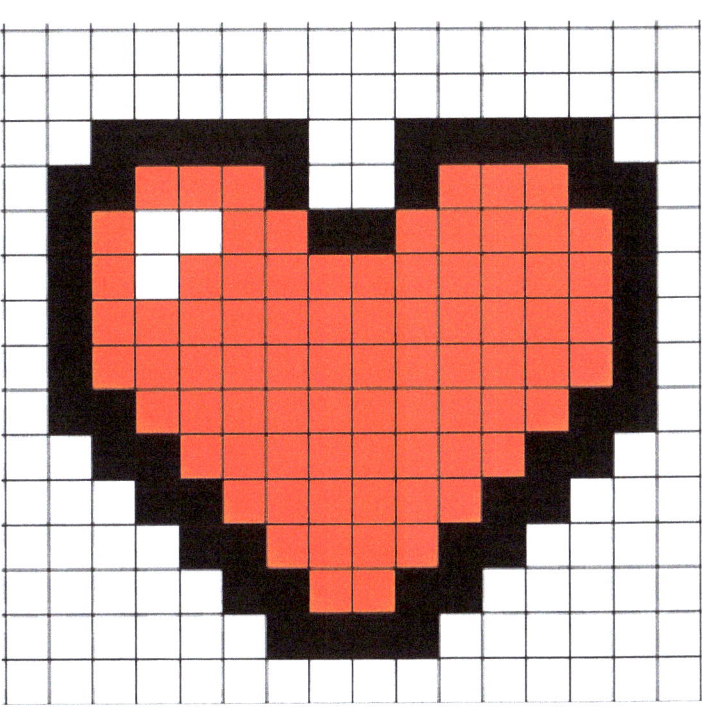

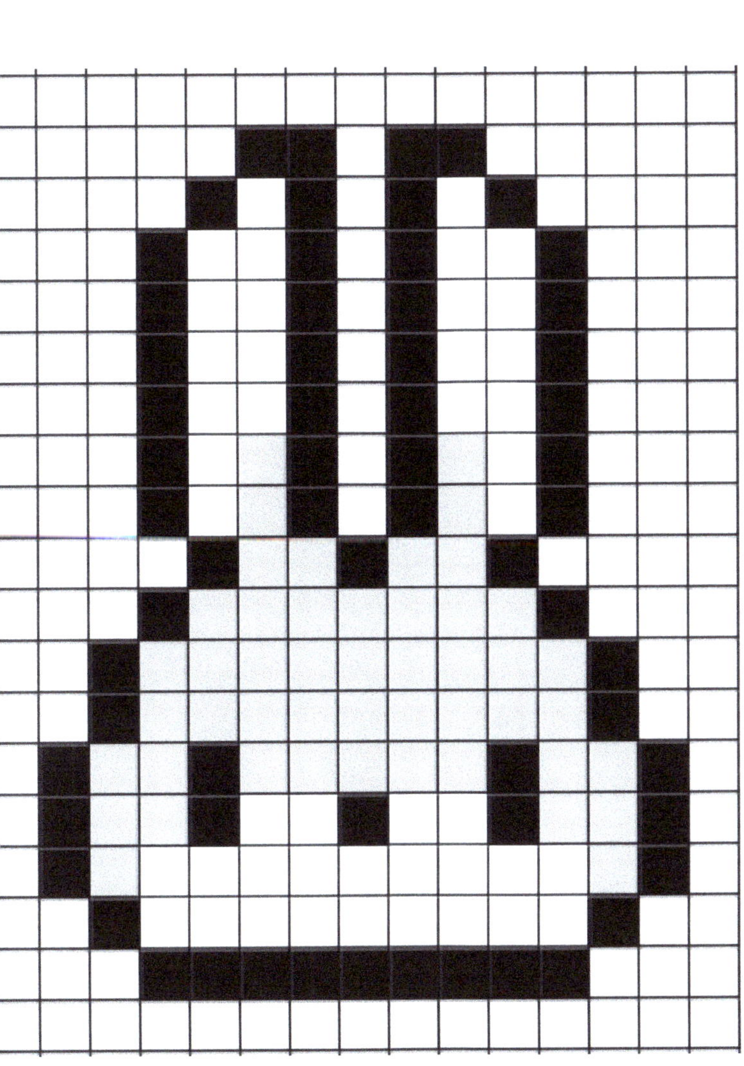

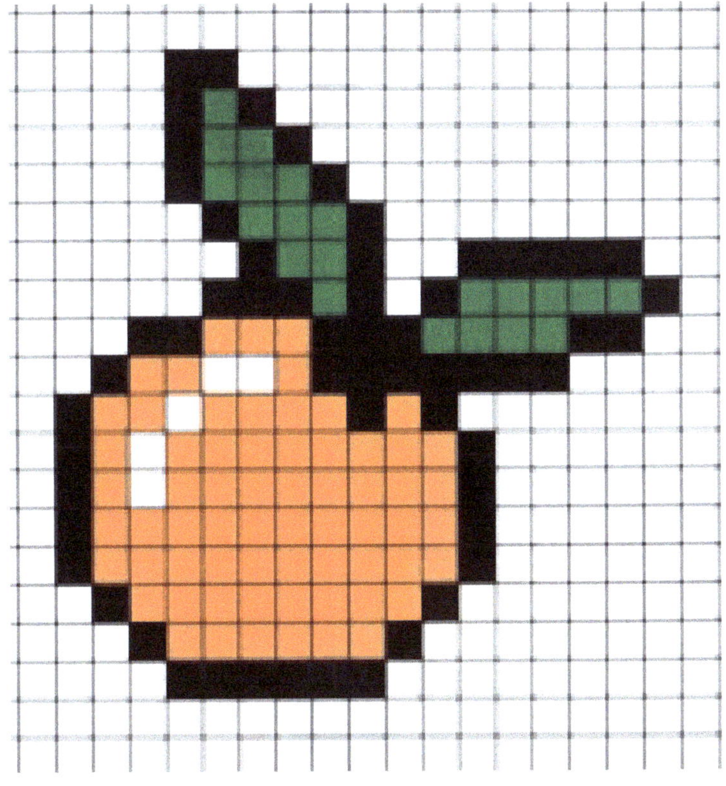

Project 1

Create a difficult 8-bit piece of art

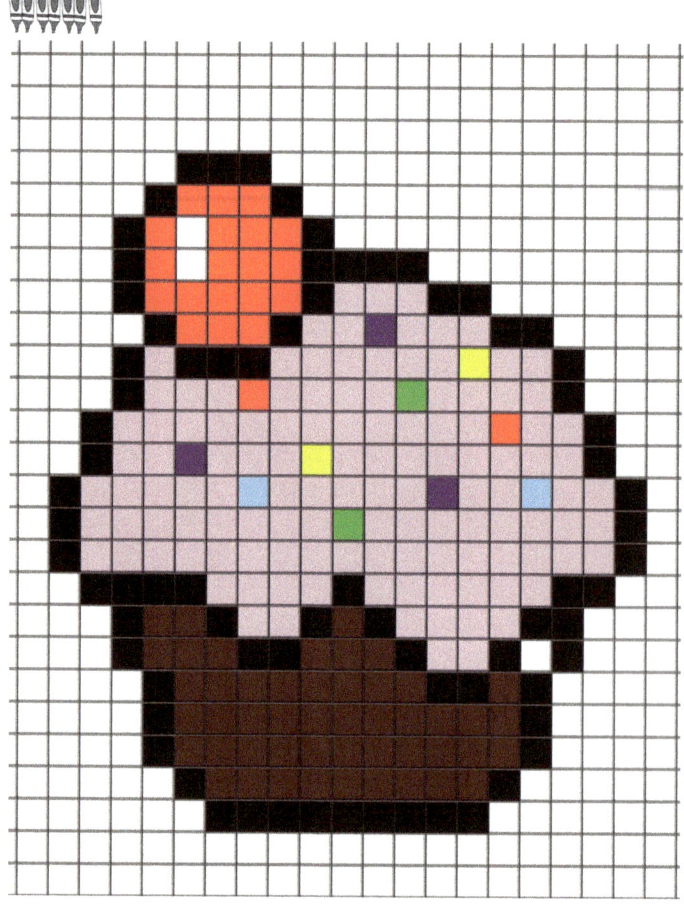

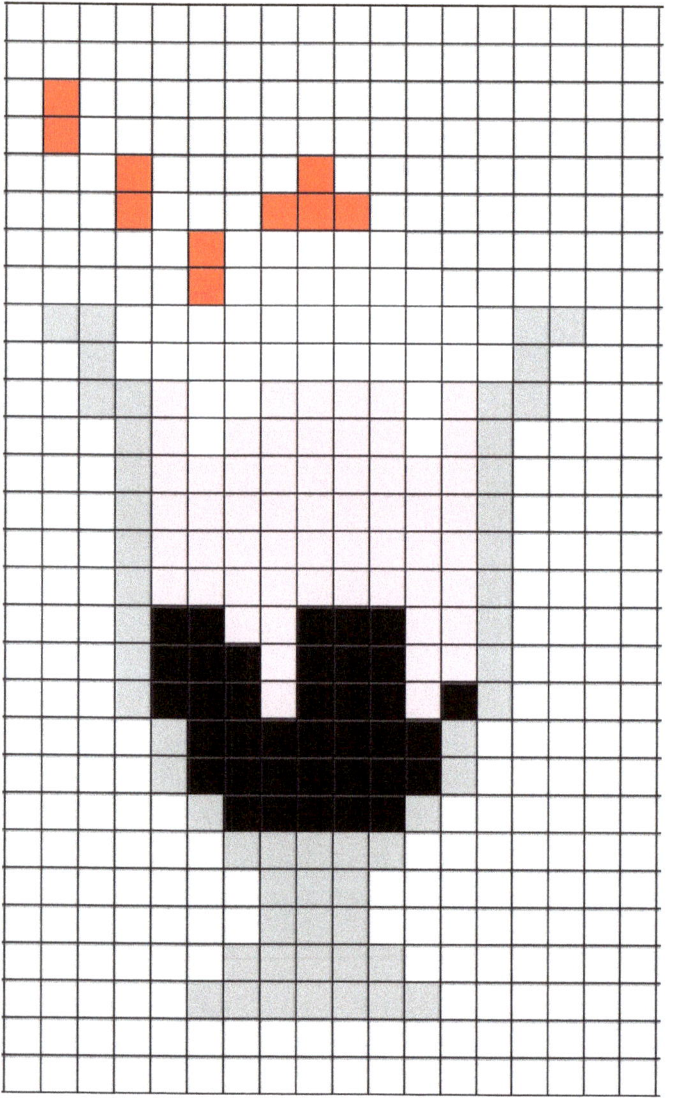

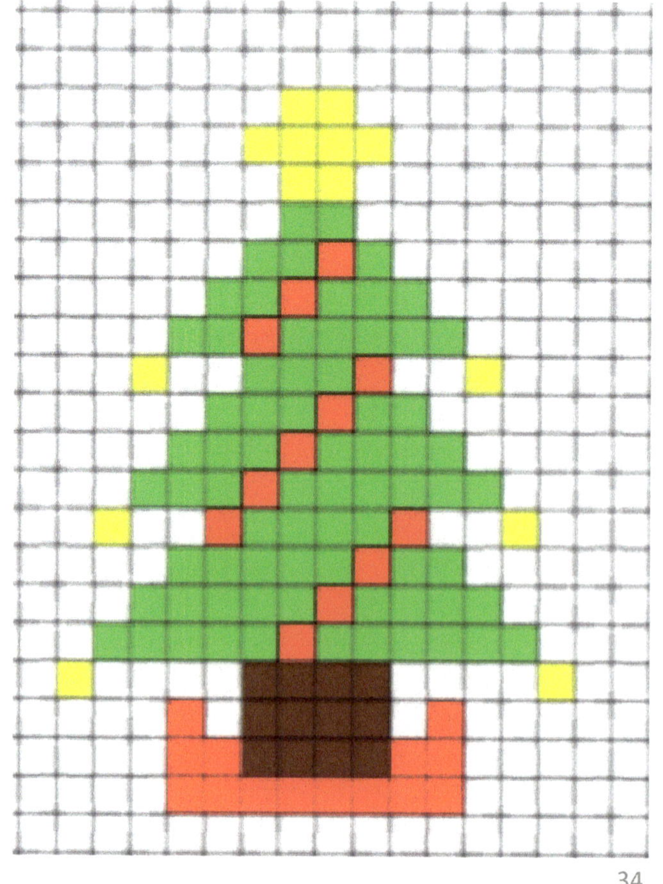

Use one of the **easy** images and fill in the correct squares with the correct color

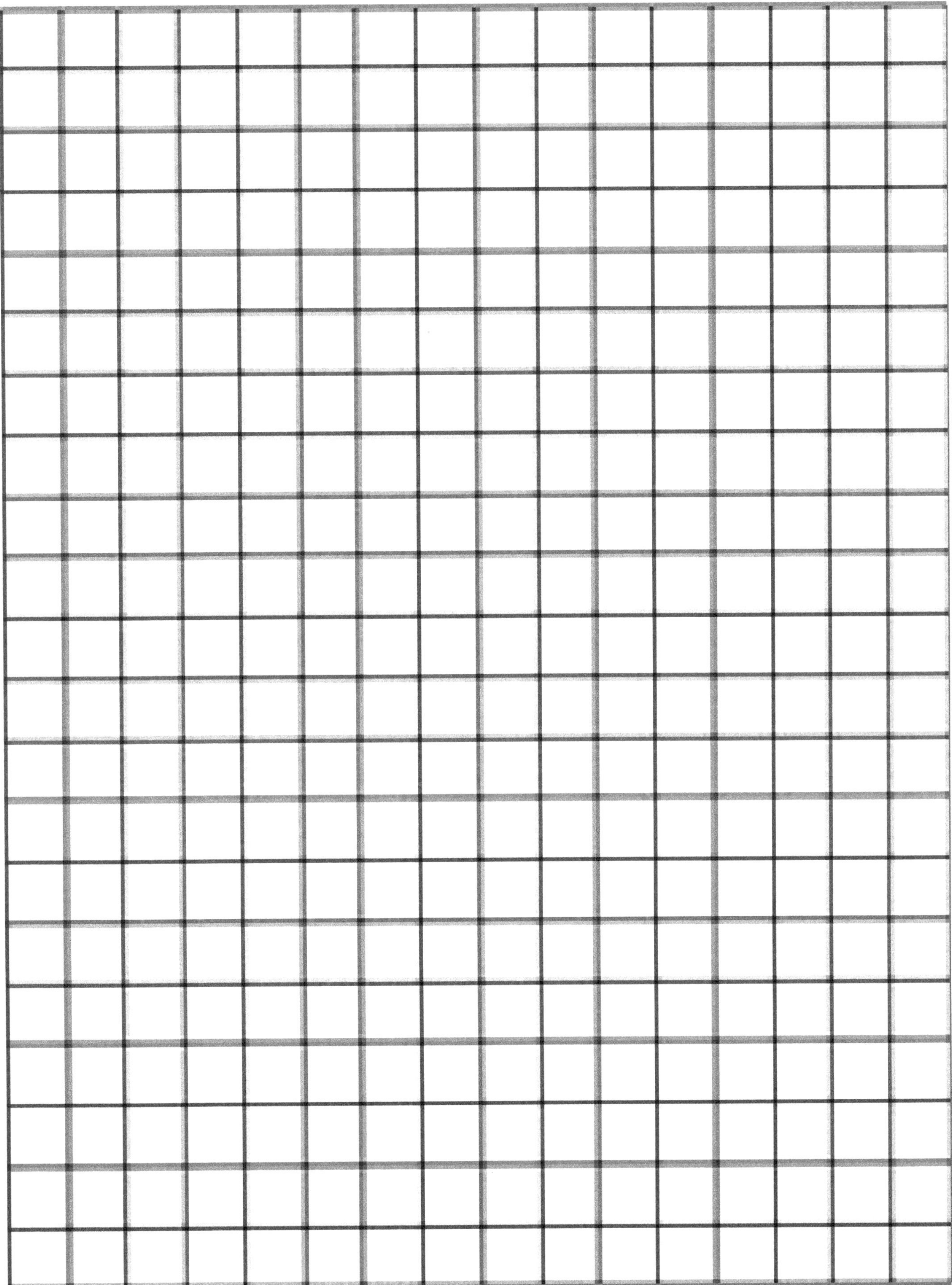

Use one of the **difficult** images and fill in the correct squares with the correct color

Try to create your own 8-bit image from an object you have at home

Art History Lesson Two

Each lesson we will go over some Art History that follow what we have learned in each lesson. During this lesson, we learned about lettering and different ways we can draw the letters

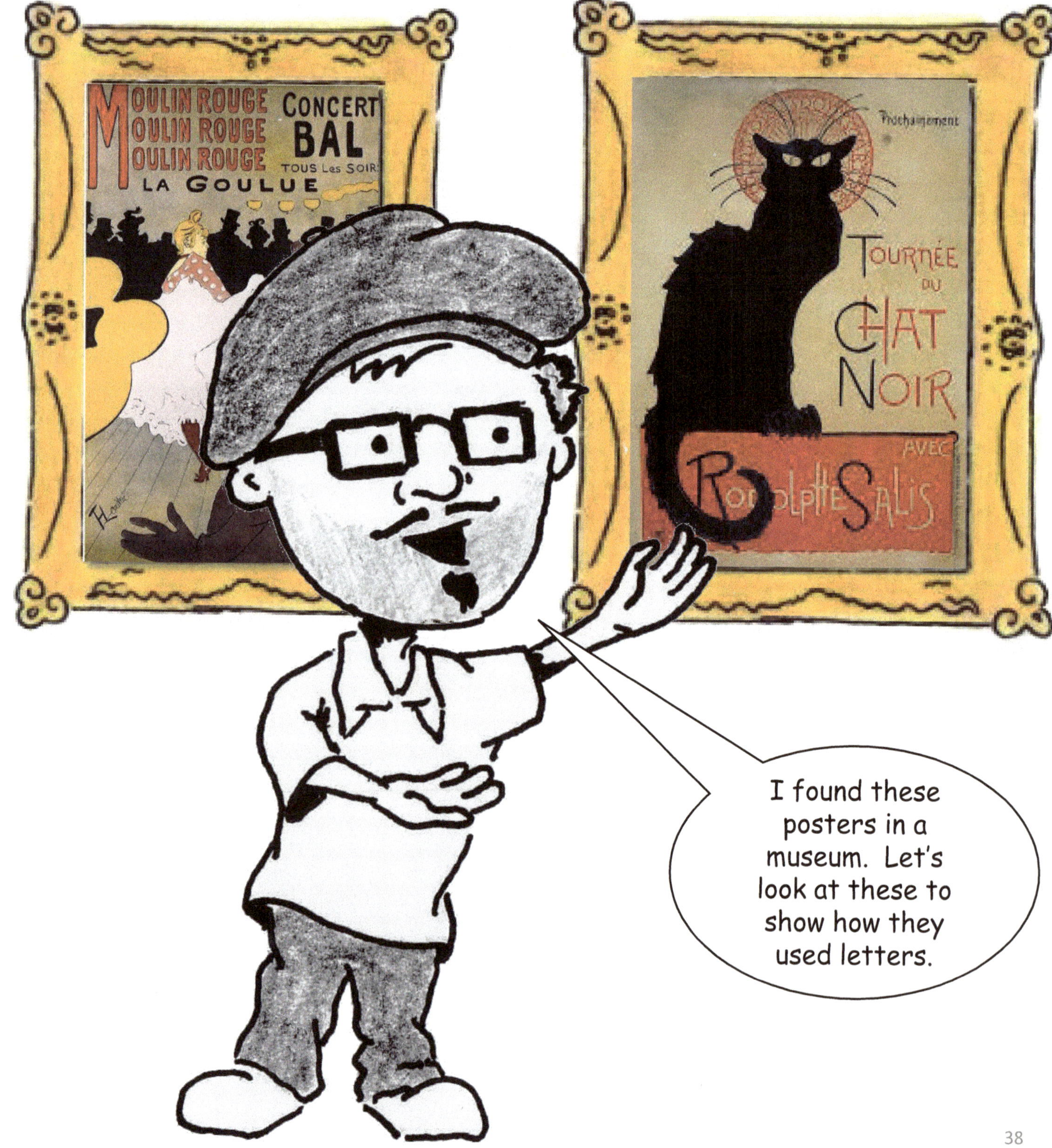

Henri de Toulouse-Lautrec

Let's look at some artwork and see how lettering was used. Below is a poster from 1891 made by the French artist Henri de Toulouse-Lautrec titled "Moulin Rouge"

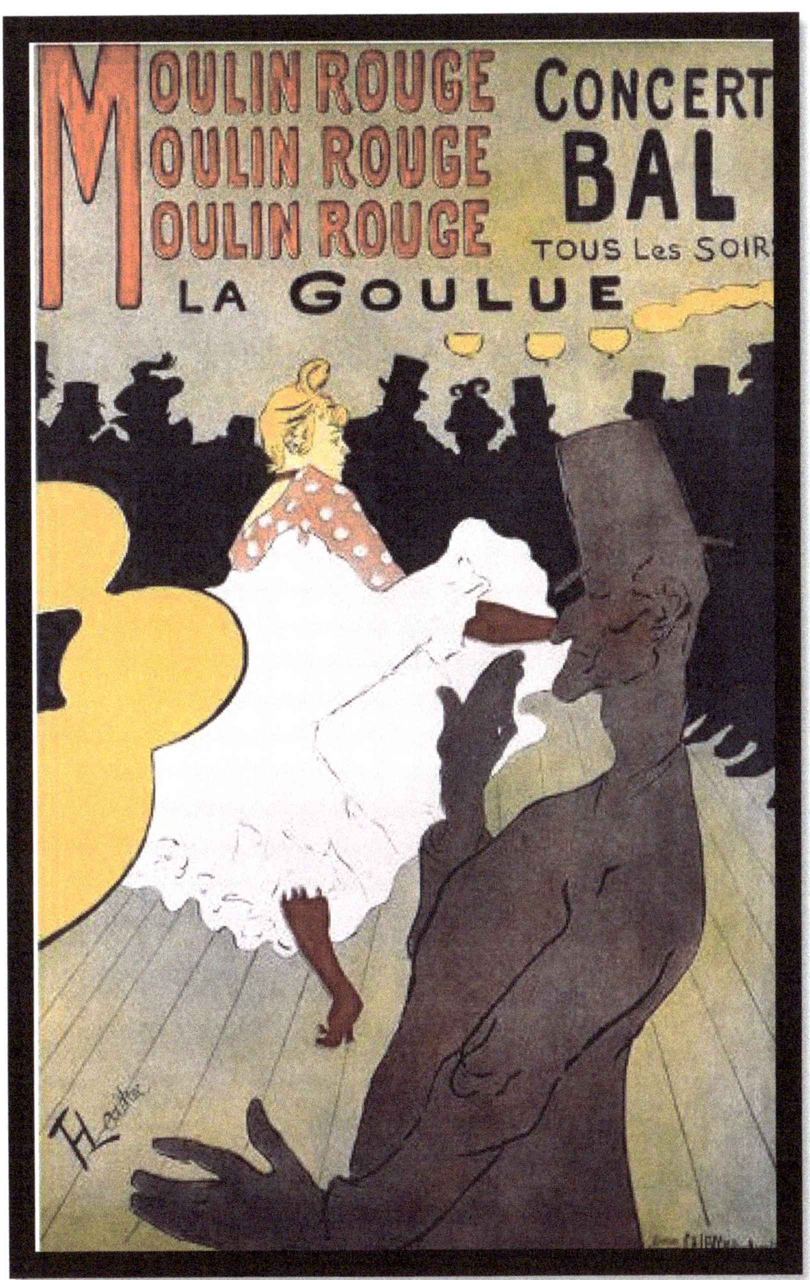

Do you see how he didn't use the same type of letters for each word? In some, he used all capital letters and in some he used both capital and lowercase letters. Some letters are thick, and some are thin. Do you see how he wrote Moulin Rouge 3 times but only used one M? What other things do you see about his lettering.

Let's look at another poster by Henri de Toulouse-Lautrec titled "Tournee du chat noir " which, in English means "The Black Cat Tour". Look at the different lettering he did for this poster compared to the previous one. How is it different?

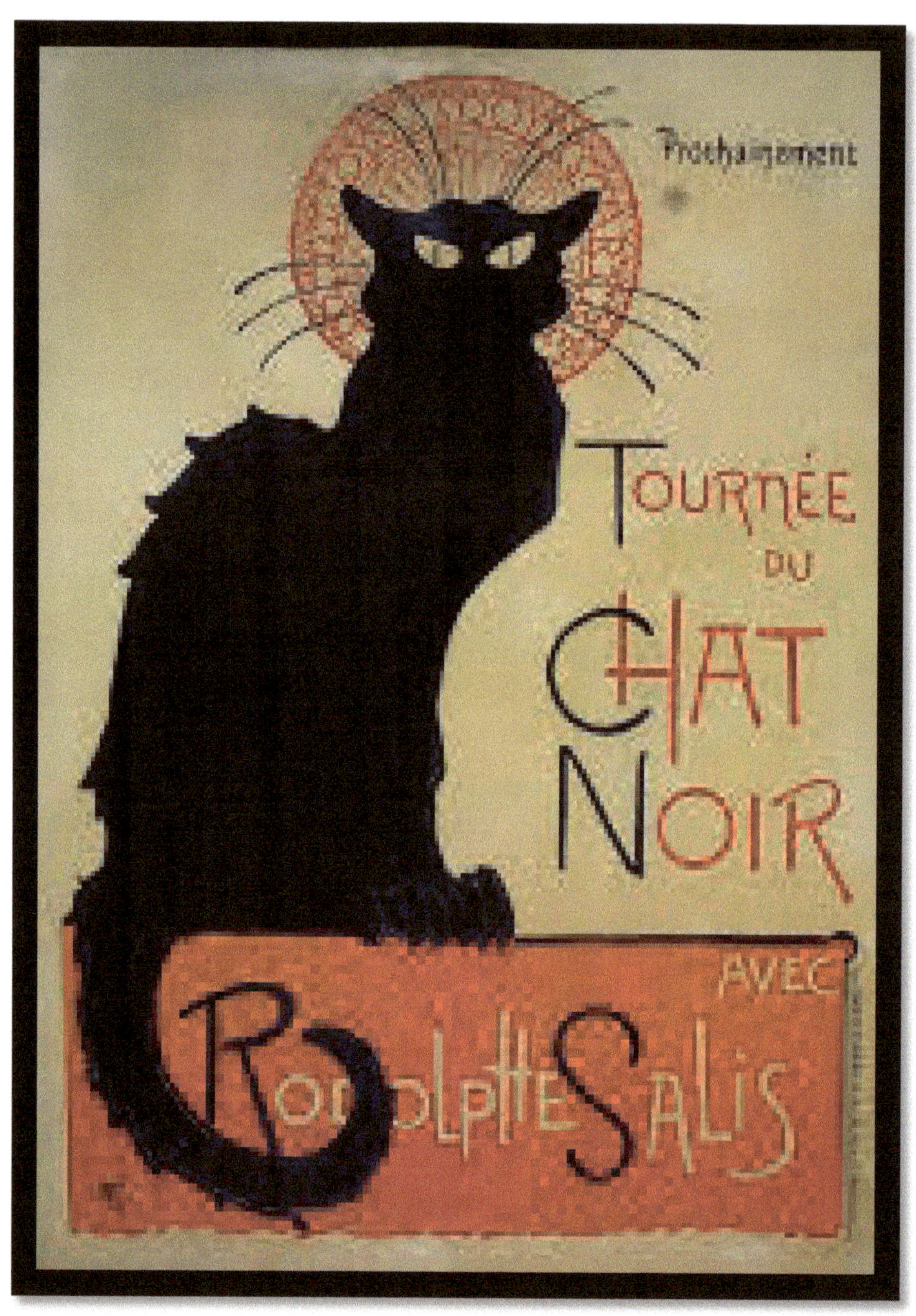

On the next page, design your own poster with different styles of lettering. You can draw a picture of something you like; sports, toys, video games, a place, whatever you want. Try to add several words that describe it using different types of letters.

Art History Project

Draw a poster of something you like, using words to describe it. Try to color in the whole square.

Remember to sign your name to your work

Chapter Fun

Match the style of letters in group A with the same style in group B 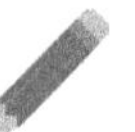

Box A	Box B
ABCDE	FGHIJK
ABCDE	FGHIJK
ABCDE	FGHIJK
ABCDE	FGHIJK
ABCDE	FGHIJK
ABCDE	FGHIJK
ABCDE	FGHIJK
ABCDE	FGHIJK
ABCDE	FGHIJK

UNIT 3 Colors

Lesson 3.1 Primary Colors

In this lesson, we will begin working on colors. We can change the way a drawing looks or feels by what colors we choose. We can make something look cold or warm depending on the color. Colors may seem like an easy thing to learn but, as you move through the courses, you will find that learning how to use colors correctly can be quite challenging.

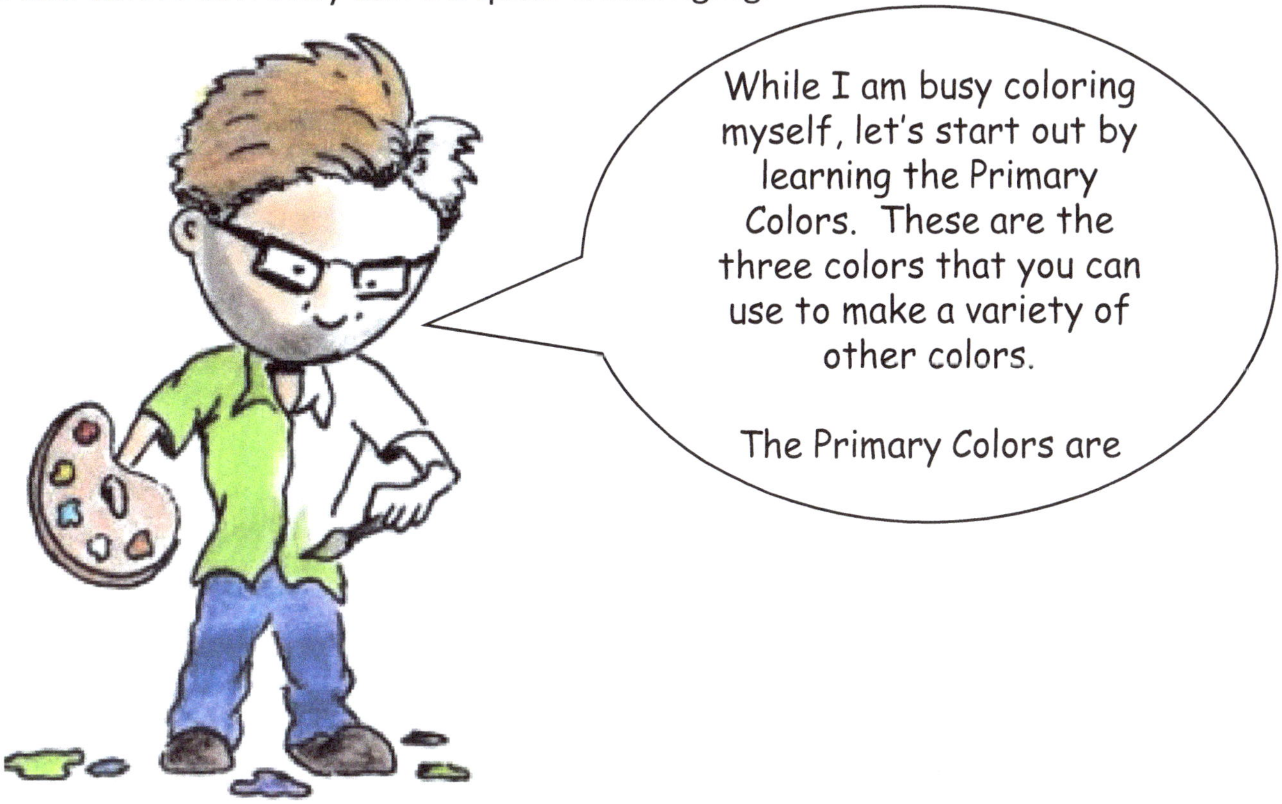

While I am busy coloring myself, let's start out by learning the Primary Colors. These are the three colors that you can use to make a variety of other colors.

The Primary Colors are

RED YELLOW BLUE

In this lesson, you will need pencils, markers, colored pencils, pastels, and a ruler. Look for the icon next to each project to determine what to use

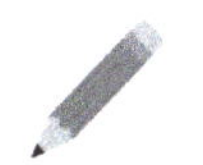
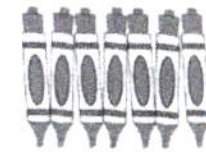
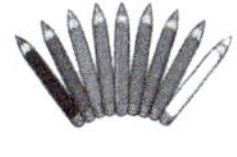
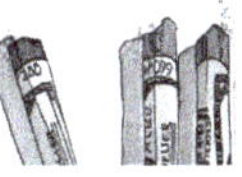
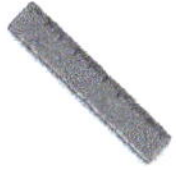

Now that we know the Primary Colors, let's create our first Color Wheel. The Color Wheel is like a pizza with different slices. Each slice represents a different color. Since you can create many, many colors with the three Primary Colors, the Color Wheel can be quite a large looking pizza.

Here is the basic Primary Color Wheel.

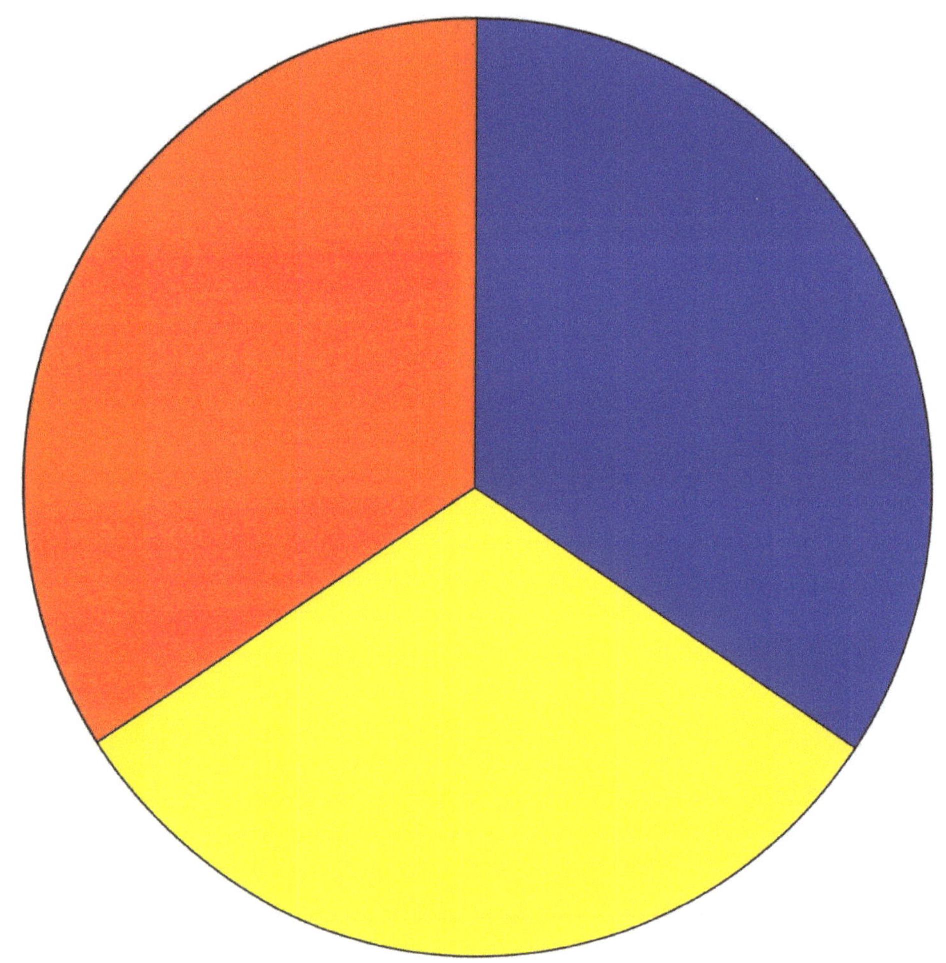

On the next page, we are going to create our own Color Wheel. Let's try with different materials

Exercise 1

Fill in the Primary and Secondary colors in each Color Wheel below

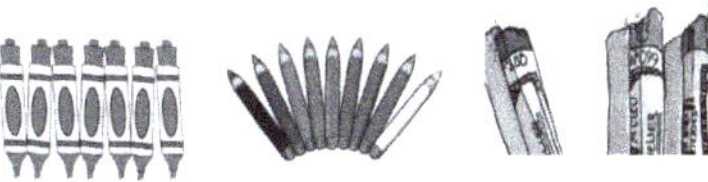

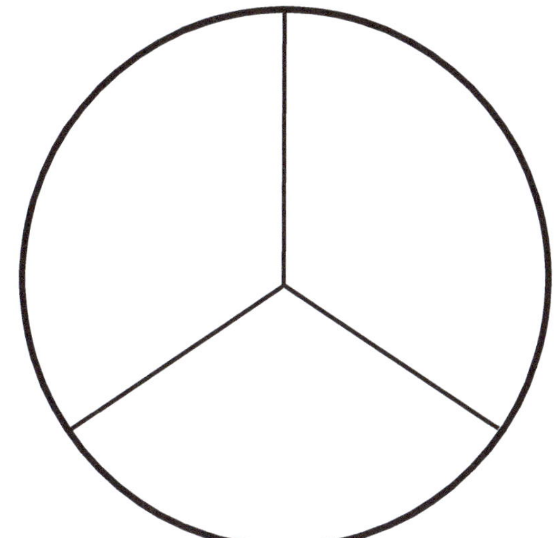

Fill in this Color Wheel with your Markers

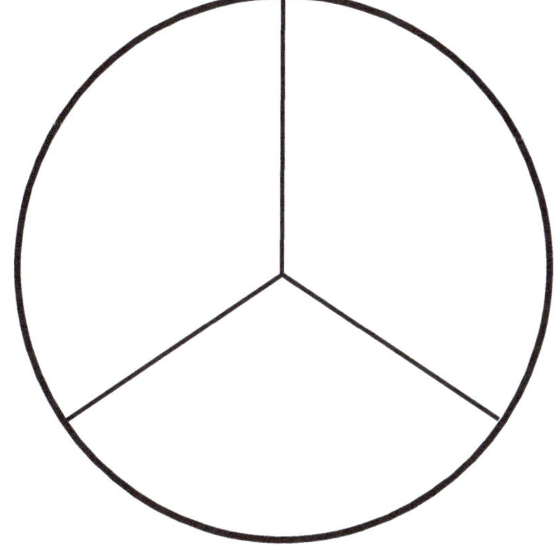

Fill in this Color Wheel with your Colored Pencils

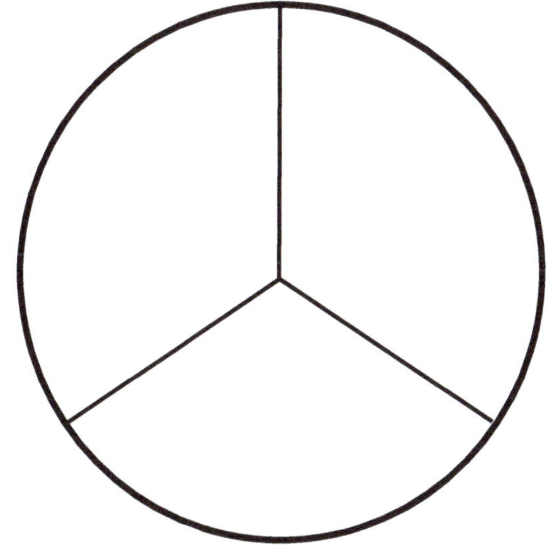

Fill in this Color Wheel with your Oil Pastels

Lesson 2.2 Secondary Colors

Now that we have our basic Color Wheel, we are going to build it and add three new colors. These three colors will be called the Secondary Colors. The Secondary Colors come from mixing two of the three Primary Colors.

Let's start by learning how to make these colors

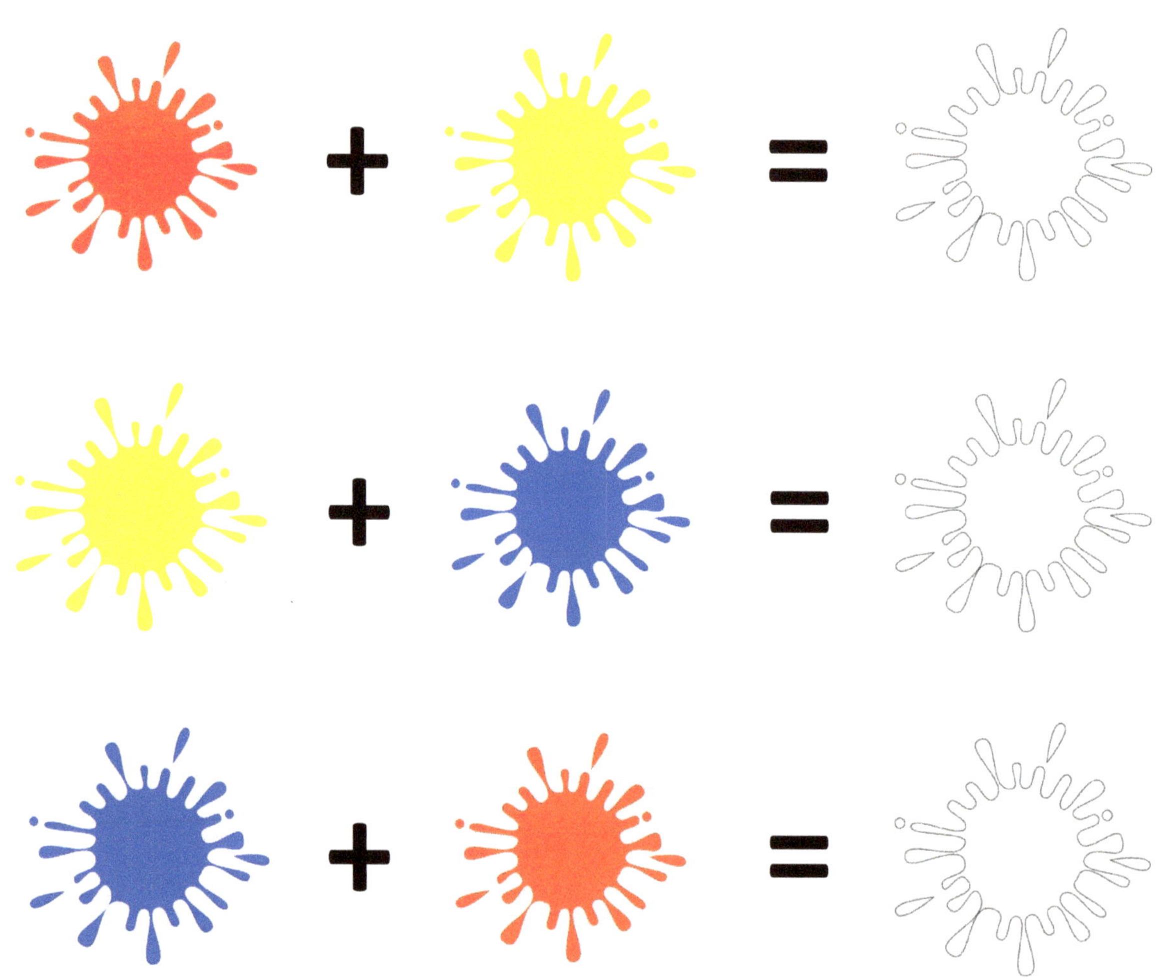

In a few pages, we are going to create our own Color Wheel. Let's try with different materials

Let's take a look at what our Color Wheel looks like when we add in the Secondary Colors.

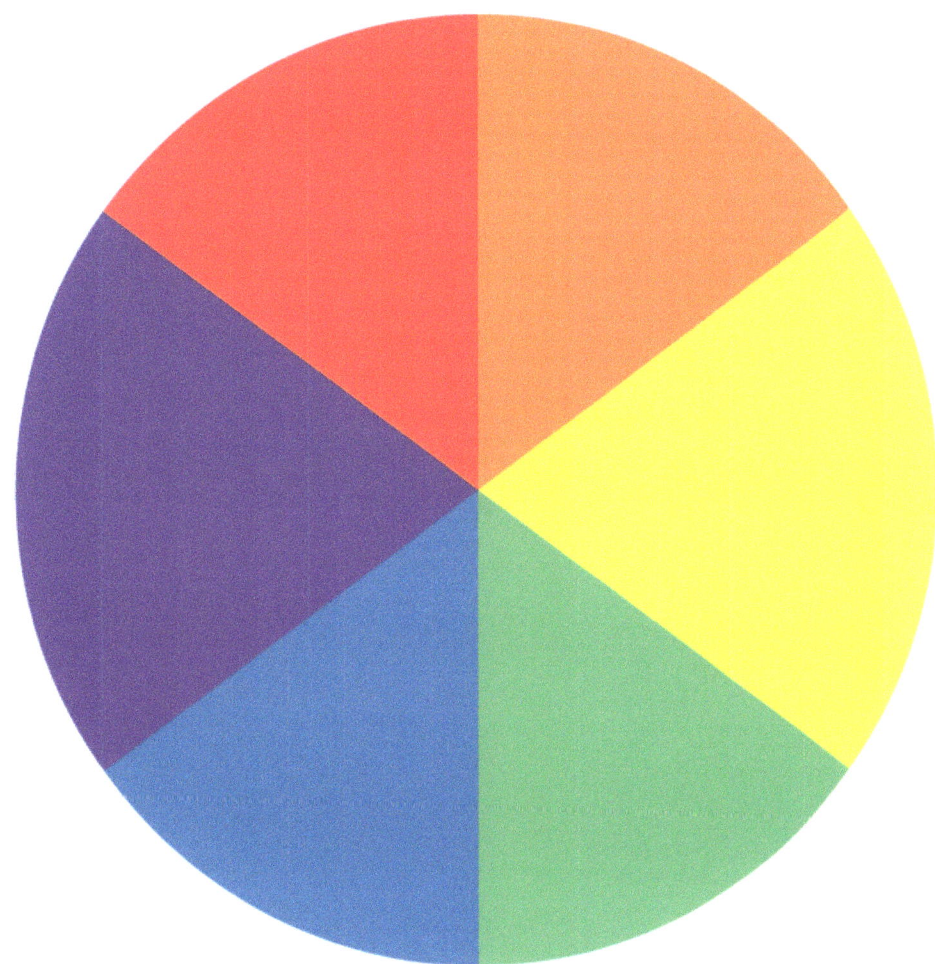

Do you see how the color in between the Primary Colors is the color that is created?

What if we unrolled the Color Wheel, what would we have? Let's take a look

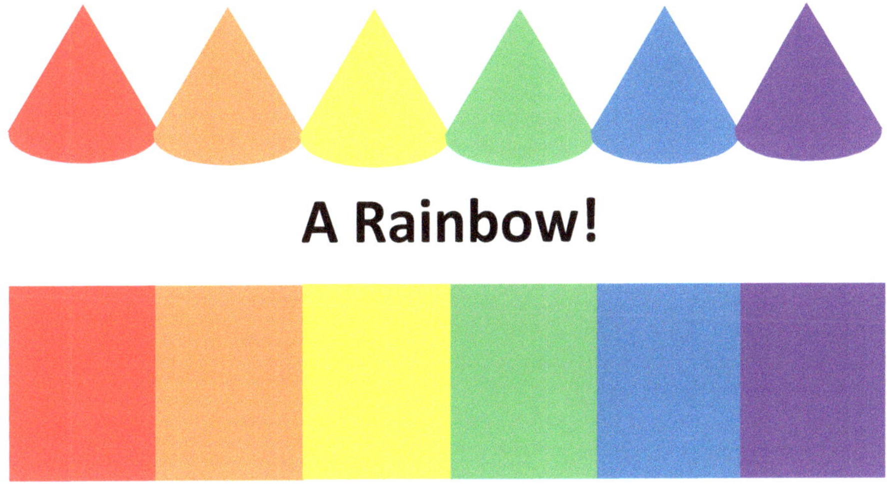

Exercise 2

Fill in the Primary and Secondary colors in each Color Wheel below

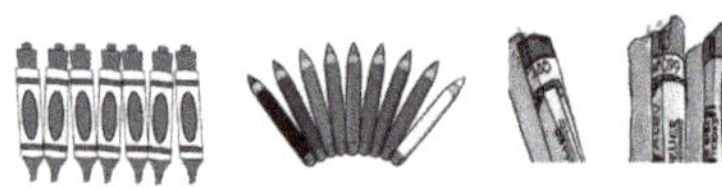

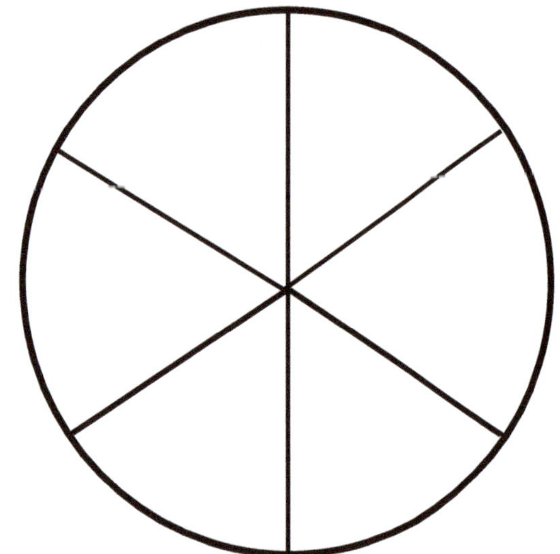

Fill in this Color Wheel with your Markers

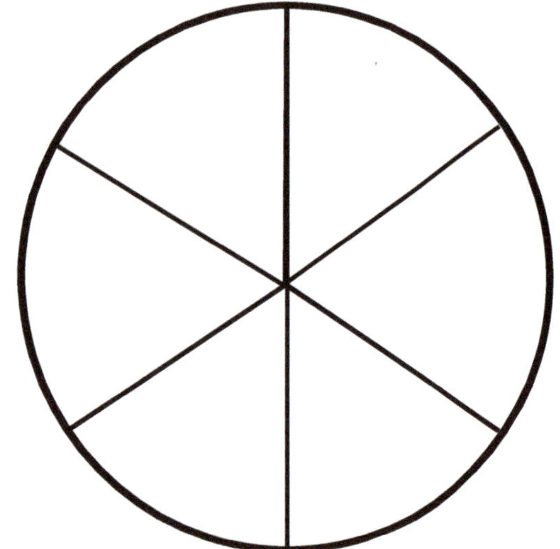

Fill in this Color Wheel with your Colored Pencils

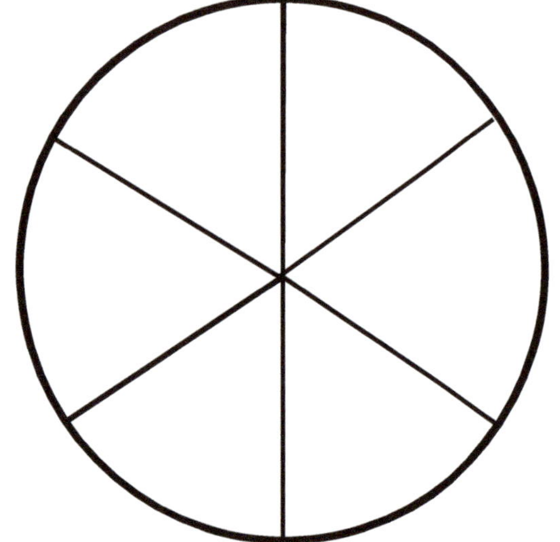

Fill in this Color Wheel with your Oil Pastels

Lesson 2.2 Blending Colors

Now that we have our basic Color Wheel, we are going to build it and add three new colors. These three colors will be called the Secondary Colors. The Secondary Colors come from mixing two of the three Primary Colors.

Let's start by learning how to make these colors by blending the two together. We will mostly use our pastels at first. When mixing colors with pastels, always put the darker color down first and do this softly. If you press too hard, the lighter color will have trouble mixing with it and it won't look correct.

Making Orange

Start by making soft marks of red

Then go over the red with a little bit harder marks of Yellow

Making Green

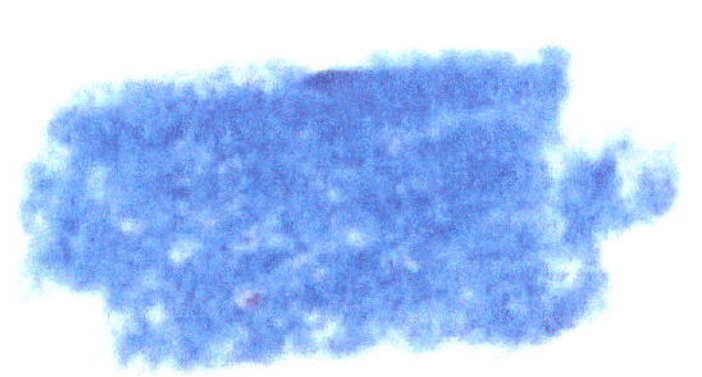

Start by making soft marks of blue

Then go over the red with a little bit harder marks of yellow

Making Purple

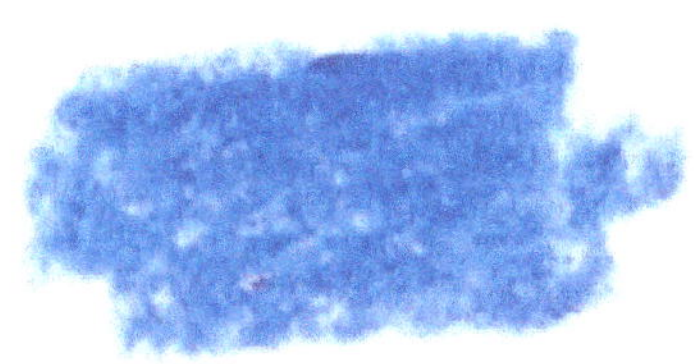

Start by making soft marks of blue

Then go over the red with a little bit harder marks of red

Exercise 3

Mix your own Secondary Colors using your pastels. You can try a couple times.

Make Orange

Make Green

Make Purple

Exercise 4

Now let's use the skills we learned to create this Color Wheel with both Primary and Secondary Colors using our pastels. More Color Wheels can be found on page 151 - 152.

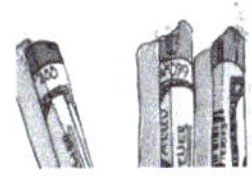

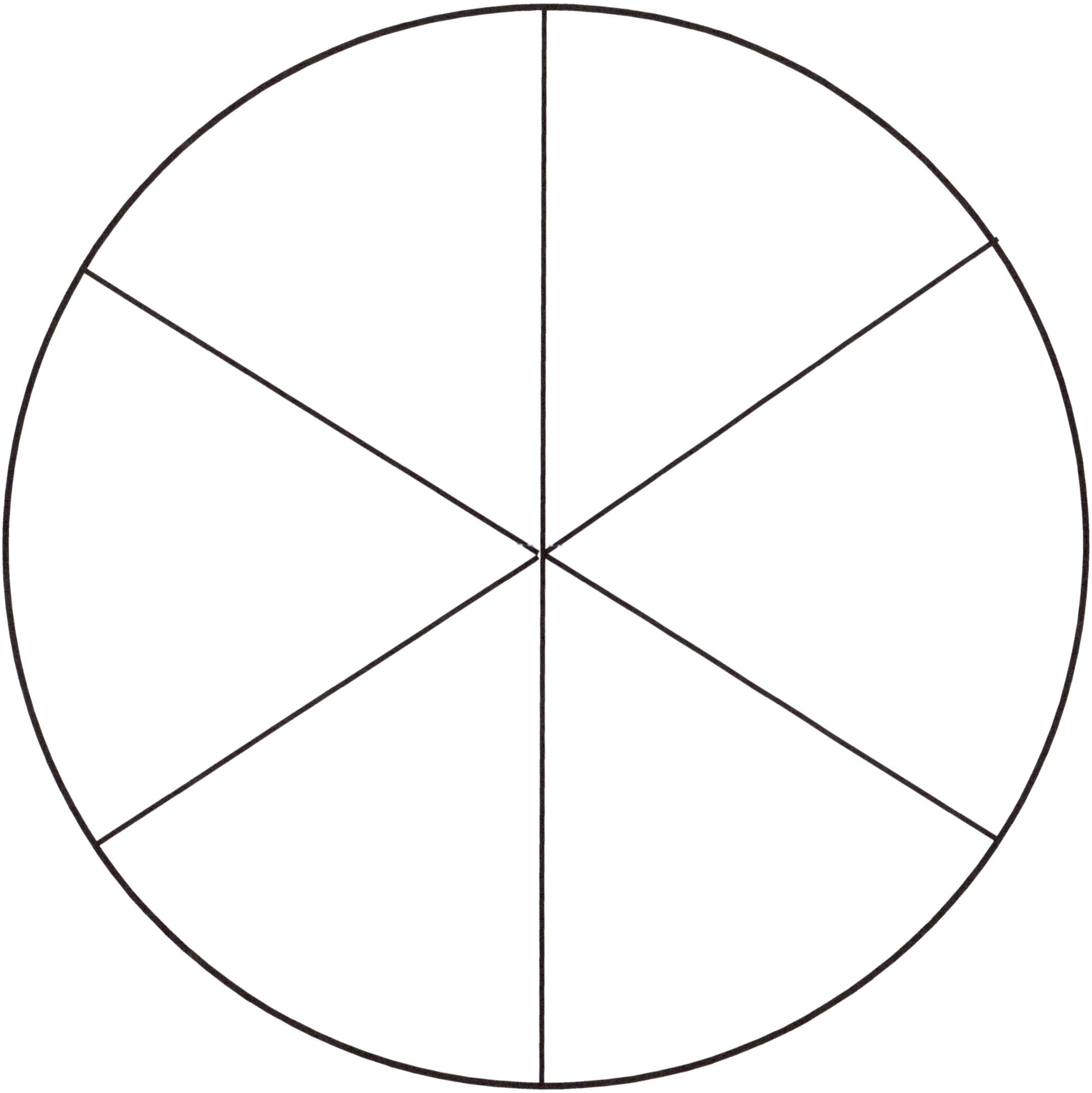

Exercise 4

Now that we have practiced mixing colors, let's use in when coloring a picture.

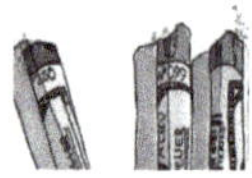

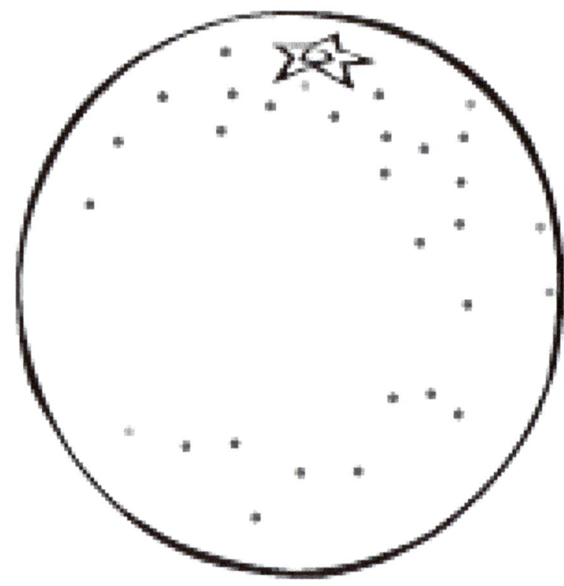

Make the Orange, Orange

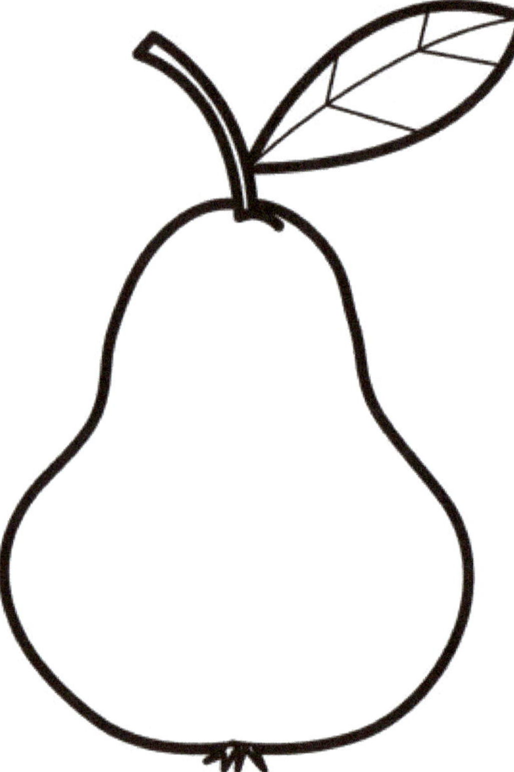

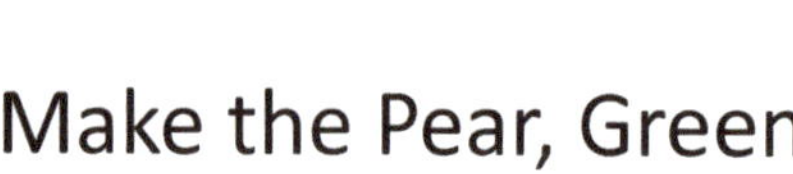

Make the Pear, Green

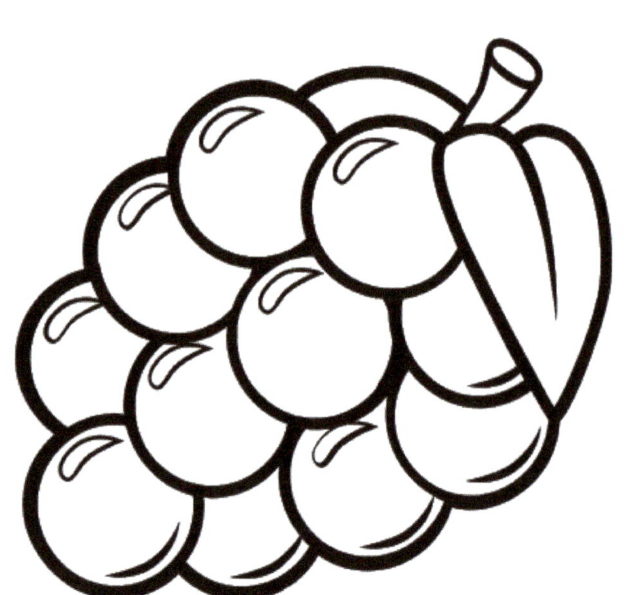

Make the Grapes, Purple

Art History Lesson Three

Each lesson we will go over some Art History that follow what we have learned in each lesson. During this lesson, we identified both the Primary and Secondary Colors

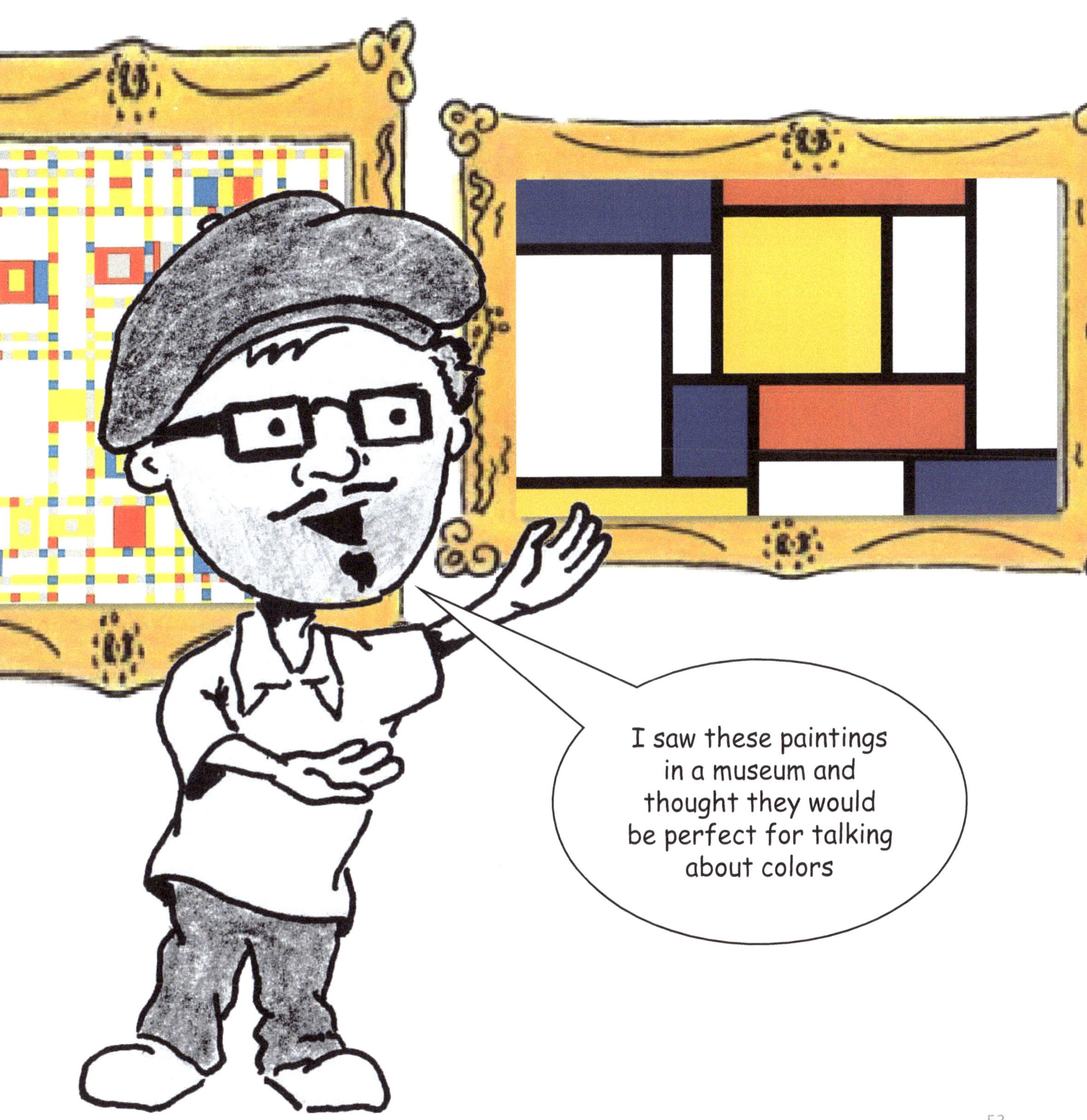

Piet Mondrian

Now, let's look at some artwork and see if we can see how the artist used colors in their work. In this painting by the artist Piet Mondrian, what colors did he use? Identify the colors.

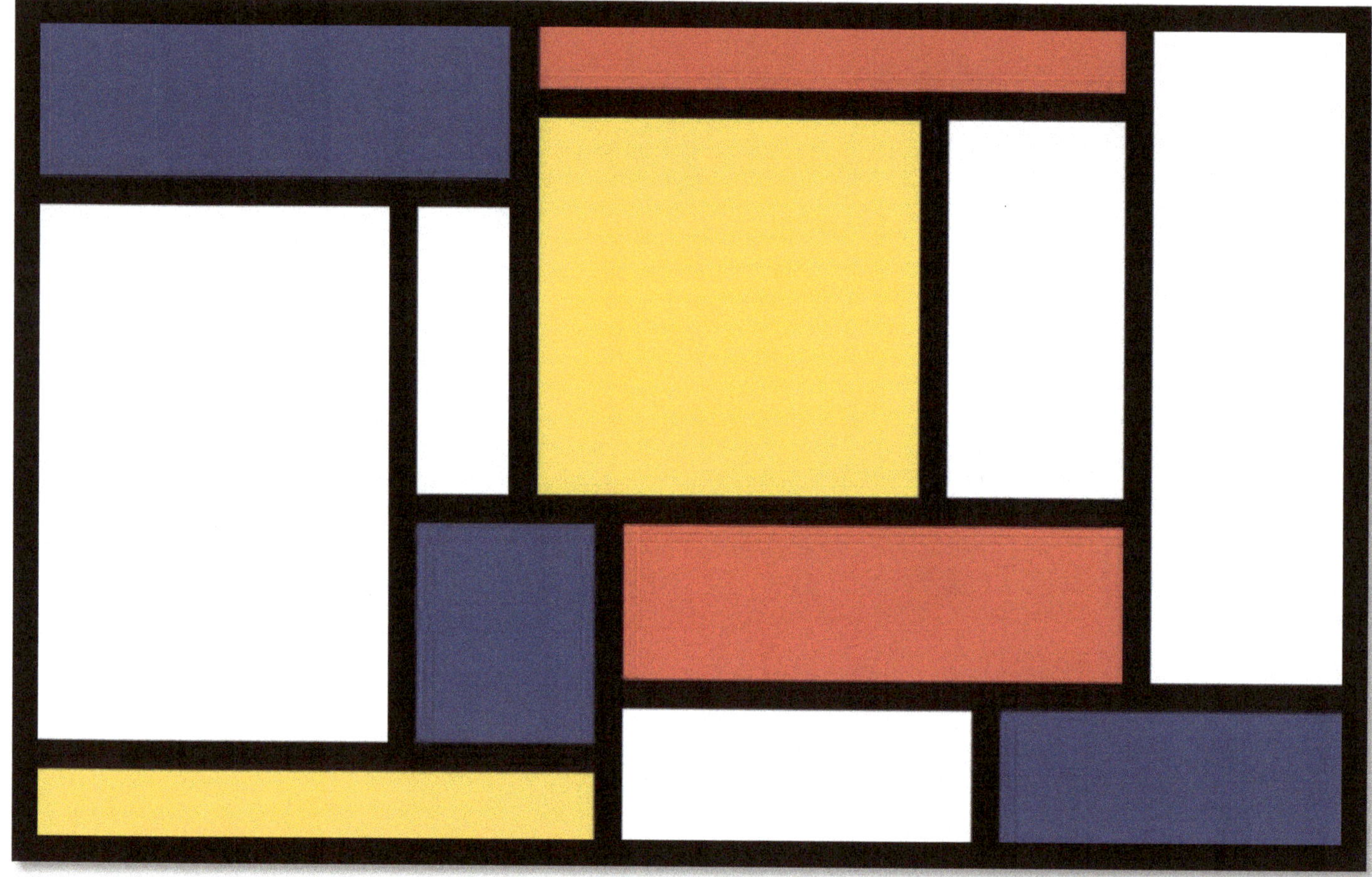

As you can see, he used squares and rectangles of different colors to create this painting. Do you like the painting? Does the image look like anything to you? Use your imagination to try to figure out what it might look like. When you look at some art, it may not look like anything at all. Sometimes you must be creative and try to imagine what the artist was trying to paint

Here is another painting by Mondrian titled "Broadway Boogie Woogie". Broadway is a section of New York City that can be very busy with cars and people. Boogie Woogie is a style of music that can make you get up and dance.

From this painting below, what do you think the artist was trying to show? What could all the small squares represent? Other than the primary colors, what other colors does he use?

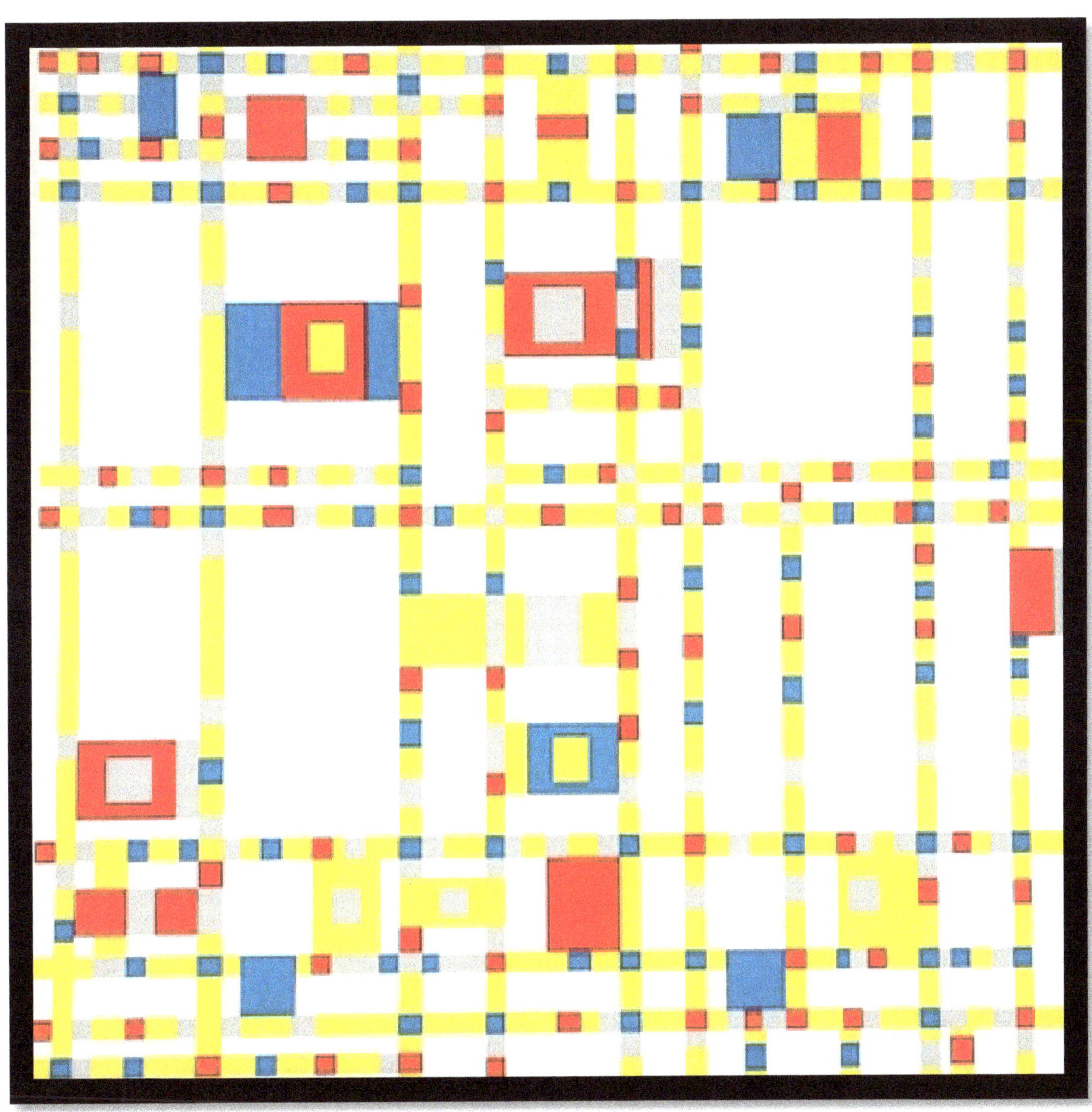

Maybe the small squares represent people or cars and the yellow lines could be roads. The larger squares could then be buildings. If you think of it like that, does it look like a busy place? Do you start to imagine it moving quickly?

Art History Project

Make your own Mondrian Painting in the space below using Markers. Try not to copy it from the picture you've seen, try to make your own. You may need a ruler for this Exercise.

Remember to sign your name to your work

Chapter Fun

Complete the Crossword puzzle using the clues below 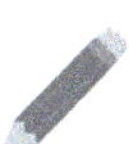

Colors

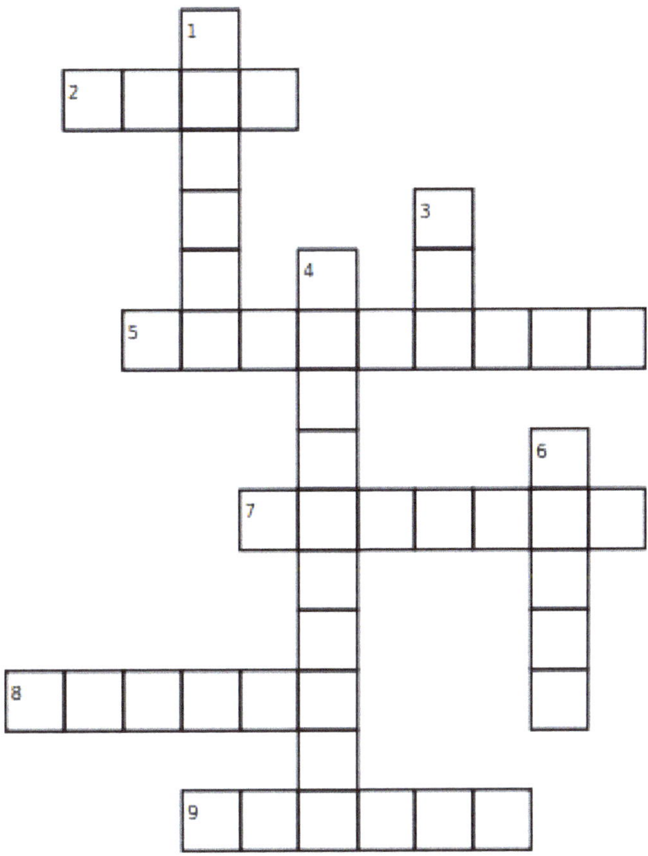

Down:

1. the color you get when you mix red and blue
3. What color a firetruck is
4. a pie shaped circle that has the colors on it
6. the color of grass

Across:

2. the color of the sky
5. the colors you get when mixing Primary Colors
7. the colors used to make other colors
8. the color you get when you mix red and yellow
9. the color of the sun

UNIT 4

Lines

Lesson 4.1 Types of Lines

In this lesson, we will look at different types of lines you can use when drawing. A lot of times we may only think we just use straight and curved lines to draw pictures but, there are many types of line work we can do to make our pictures look and feel different.

Let's start out by looking at a few basic lines that we can trace and draw on our own. Here we see straight and jagged lines. Trace the line and move on to the next page.

Straight Line

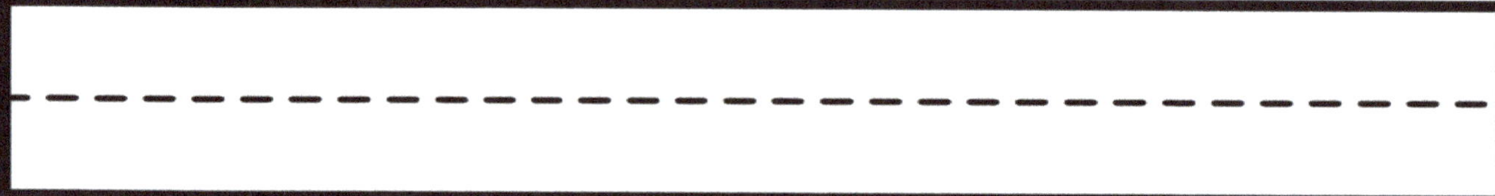

Short Jagged Line

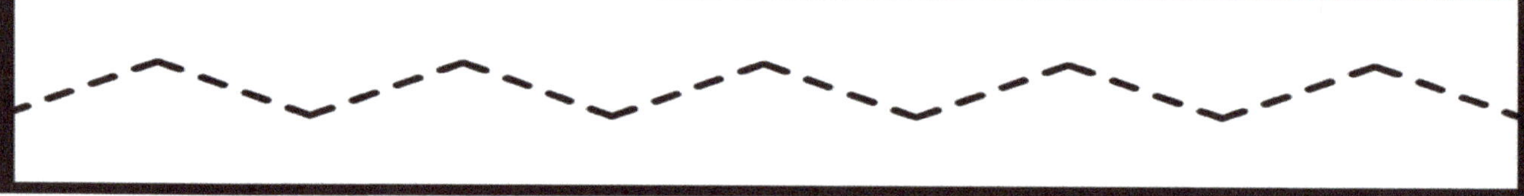

Tall Jagged Line

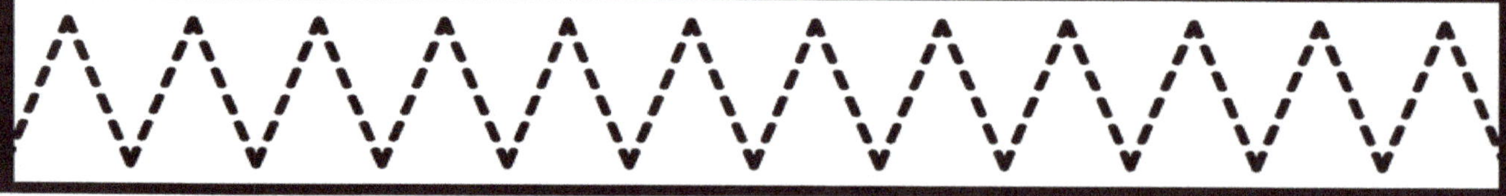

In this lesson, you will need pencils, pencil sharpener, eraser, markers, and colored pencils. Look for the icon next to each project to determine what to use

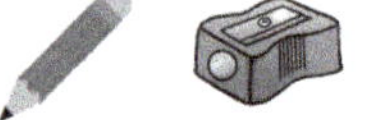
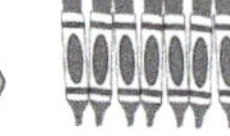
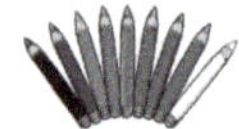

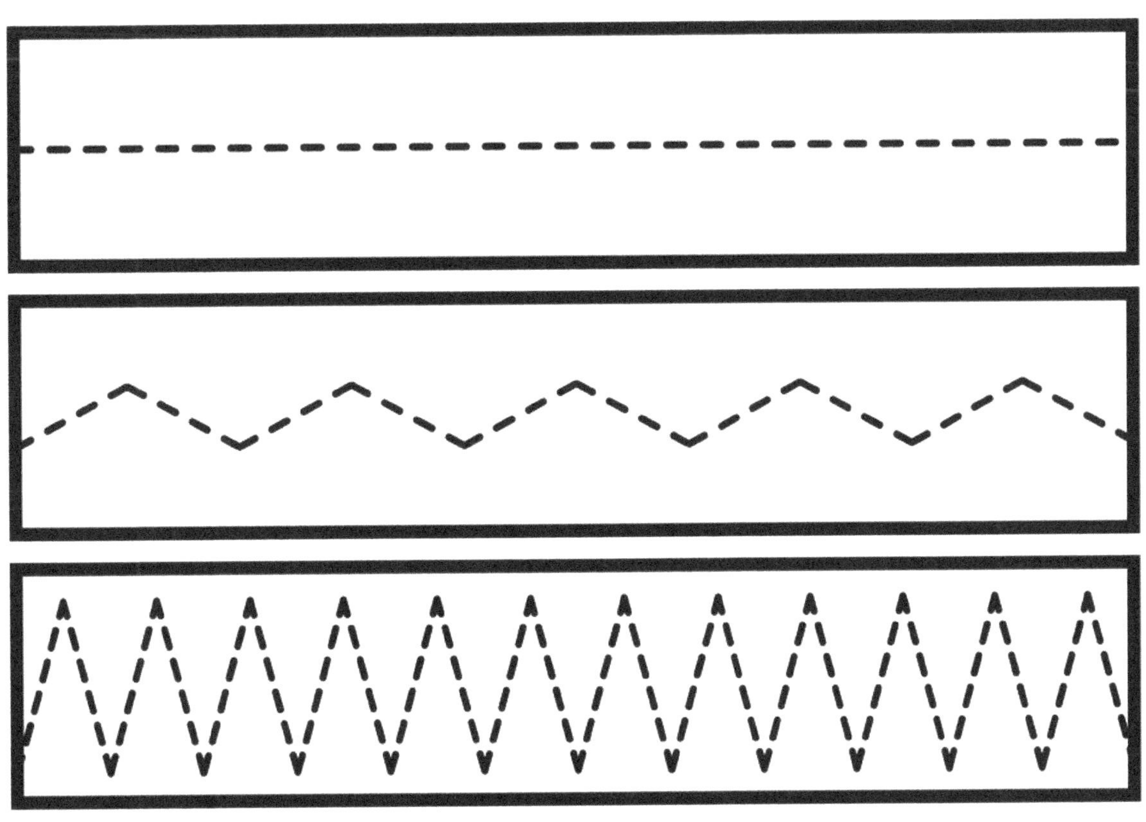

What do you see with these lines? Maybe you see different scenes outside. The straight line could be a flat, grassy field. The short, jagged lines could be mountains in the distance. The tall, jagged lines could be a bunch of trees in a forest. Think of these lines when drawing and what they could be.

Practice these same lines in the spaces below

Let's take a look at some more lines we can practice.

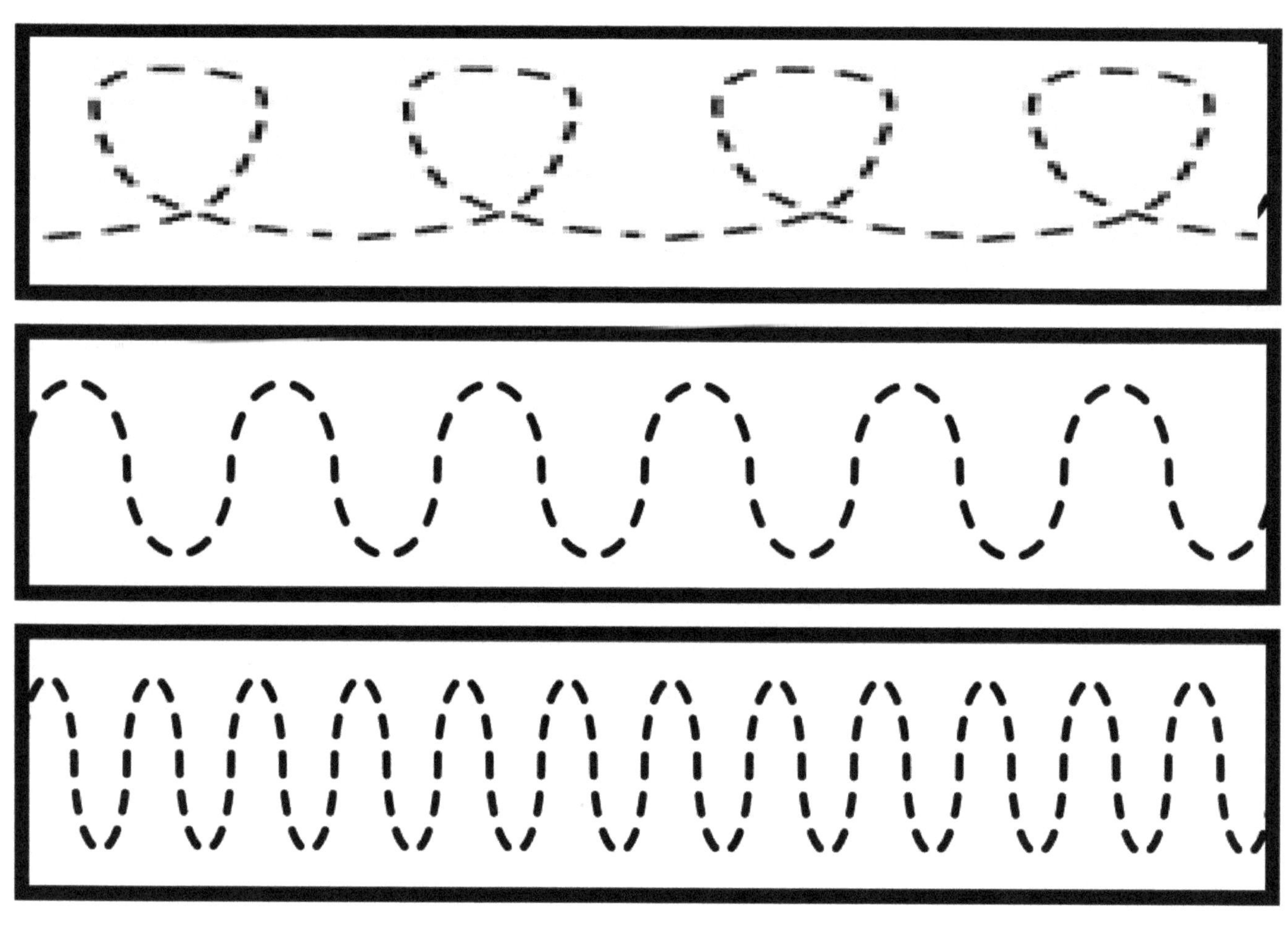

Practice these same lines in the spaces below

Exercise 3

Using your markers, follow the dotted lines in the pictures below to show the movement of the object

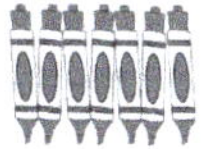

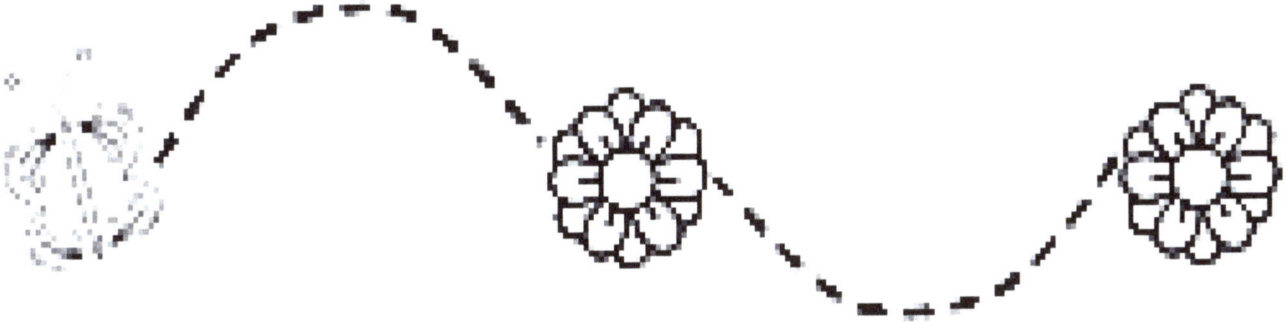

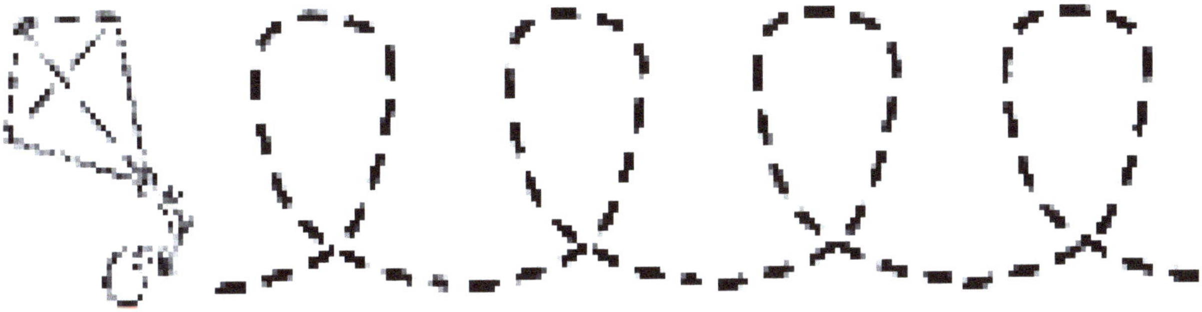

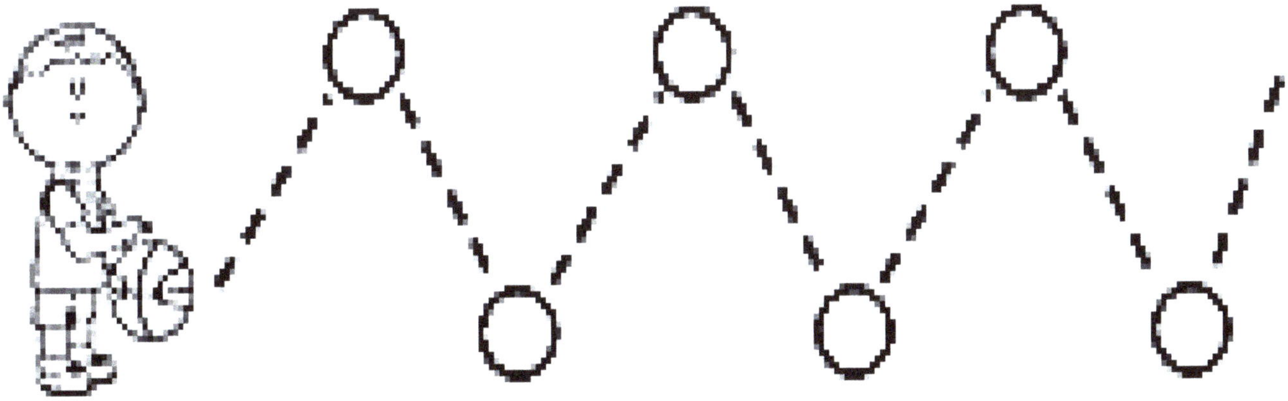

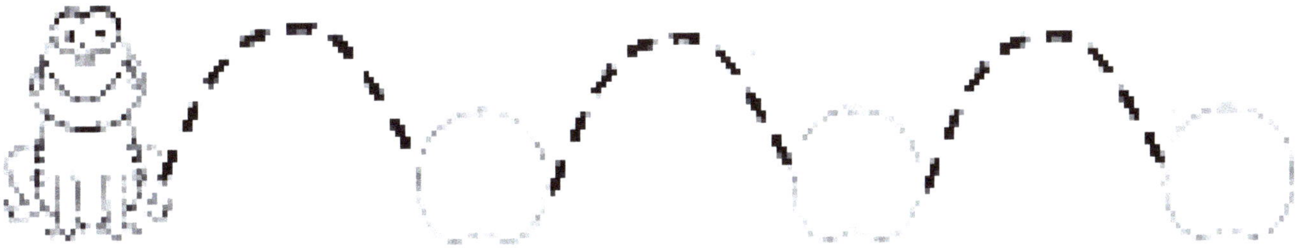

Exercise 2

Continue the line that was started below. Try to match it through the whole way.

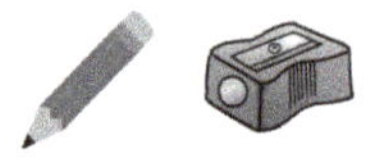

Let's Practice Lines!

1. Straight

2. Wavy

3. Dotted

4. Zig Zag

5. Cloud

6. Castle

7. Curly Cues

Exercise 2

Continue the line that was started below. Try to match it through the whole way.

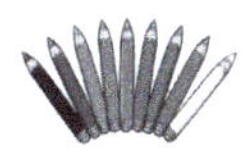

In the space provided, draw the following:

A car driving fast

A Bumblebee flying around

Lightening bolts coming from the sky

A Rabbit jumping through the grass

Lesson 3.1 Using Lines and marks to add to our drawings

In this lesson, we will use lines and marks to make more details in our drawing and make them better. We will use line similar to what we have already learned but, this time, we will make them smaller and more of them

Let's start out by looking at a few basic lines and marks that we will use

Short, straight lines

These are just straight lines, but we change how long they are. These can be **Vertical**, **Horizontal**, or **Diagonal**.

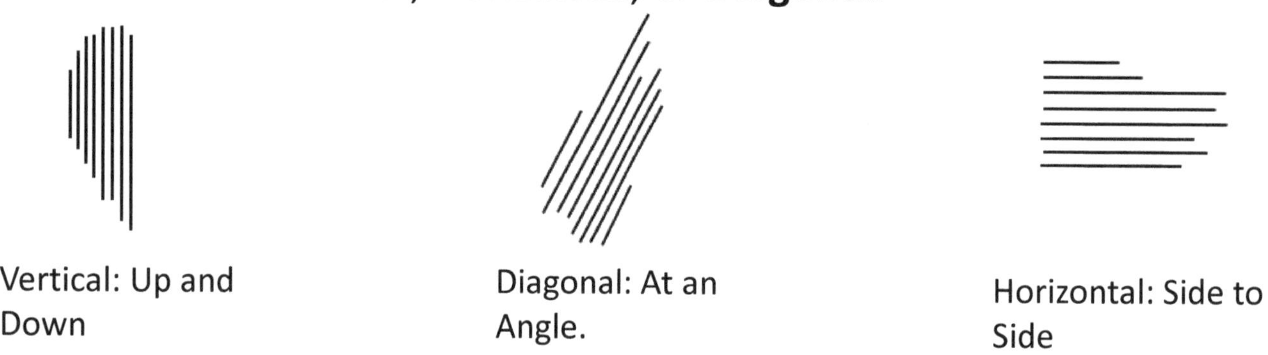

Vertical: Up and Down

Diagonal: At an Angle.

Horizontal: Side to Side

Dots

These are just a bunch of dots together. Do you see how, when you put more and more dots together, the image becomes darker?

Short, curvy lines

These are similar to the short, straight lines but they are even shorter and a little crazier. You can use these lines a lot to create things like hair or fur.

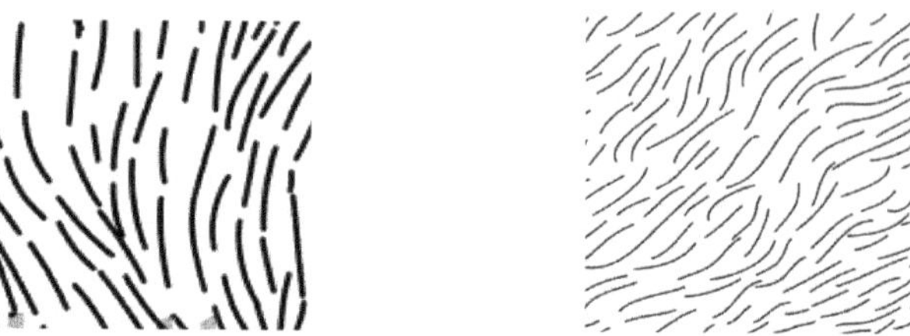

Exercise 3

Use the different lines and marks we just learned to color and finish the drawings below.

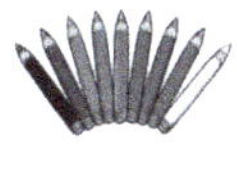

You can make the lines or dots closer together or further apart to create a different looks.

Use Long Lines

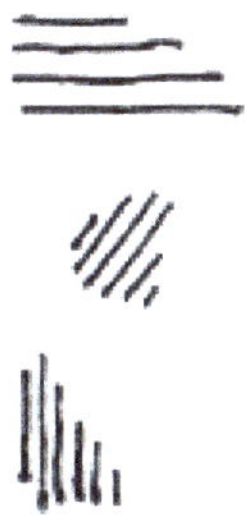

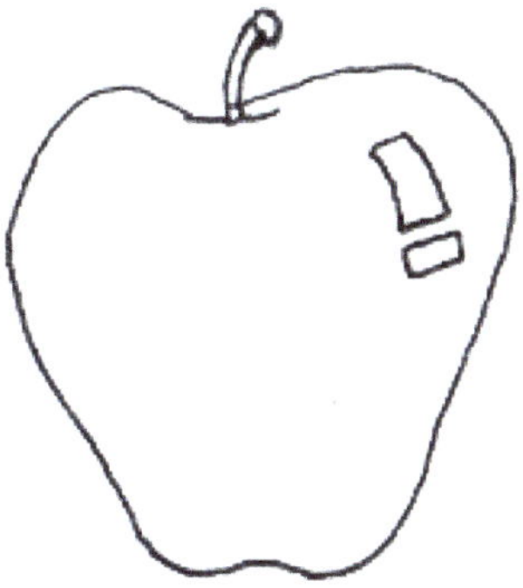

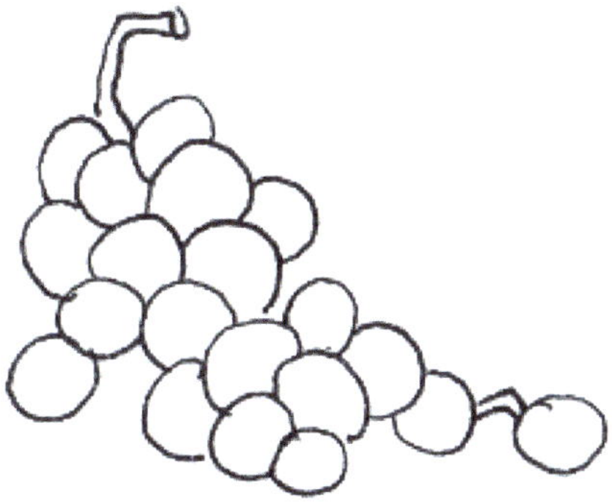

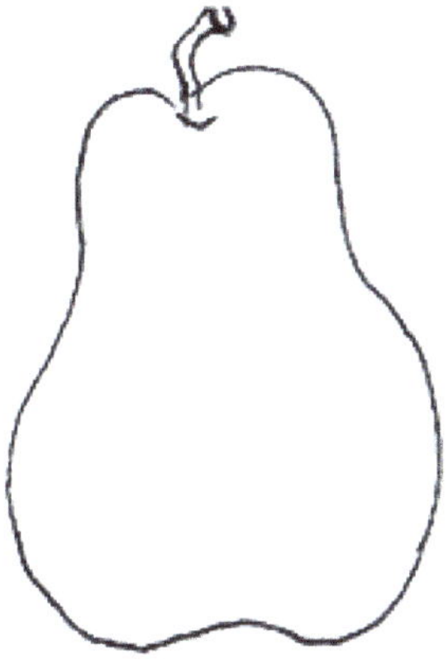

Use Short Lines

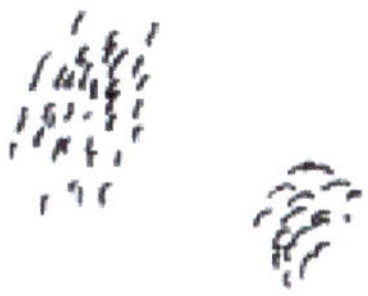

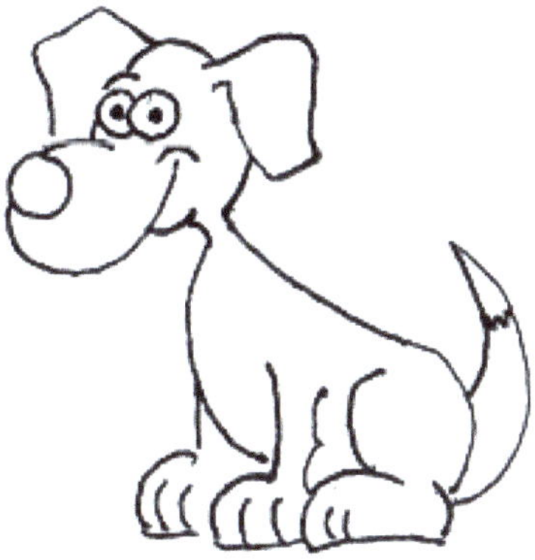

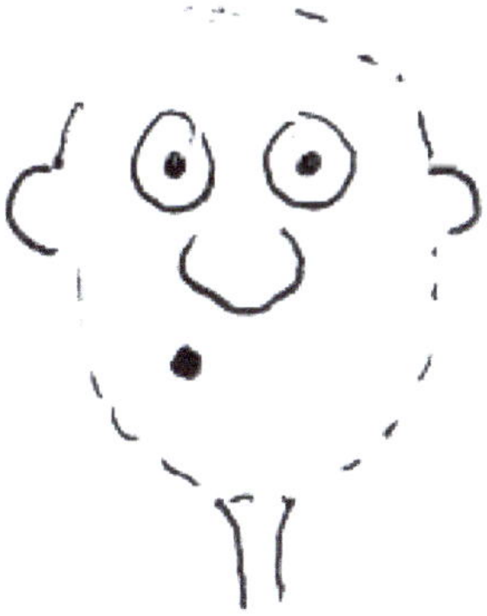

Use Dots

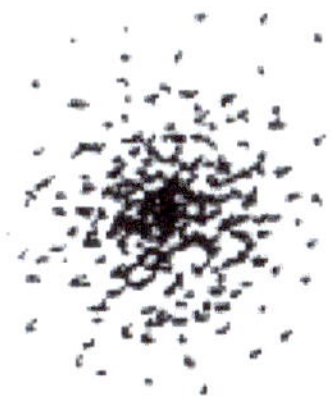

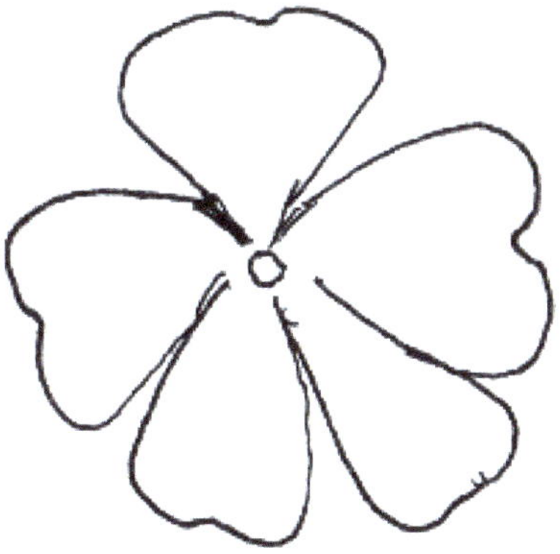

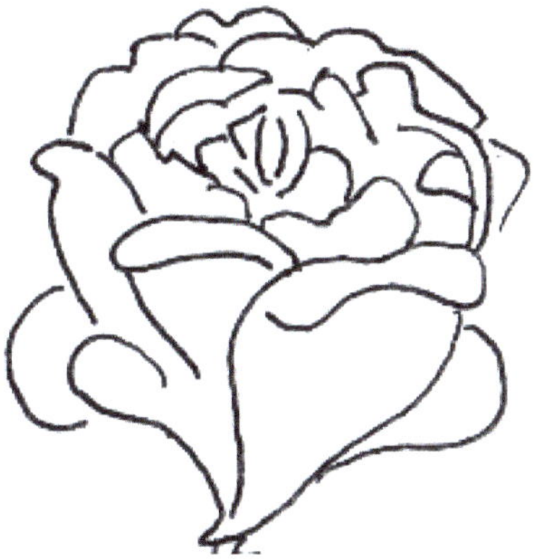

Exercise 4

Using the different lines we learned to redraw our house. 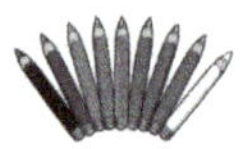

Now let's try to draw the house we did but this time, we will add different types of lines to show more detail. For example, use jagged lines to show grass, used curly lines to show leaves on a bush, and use upside down curved line to show the roof of the house.

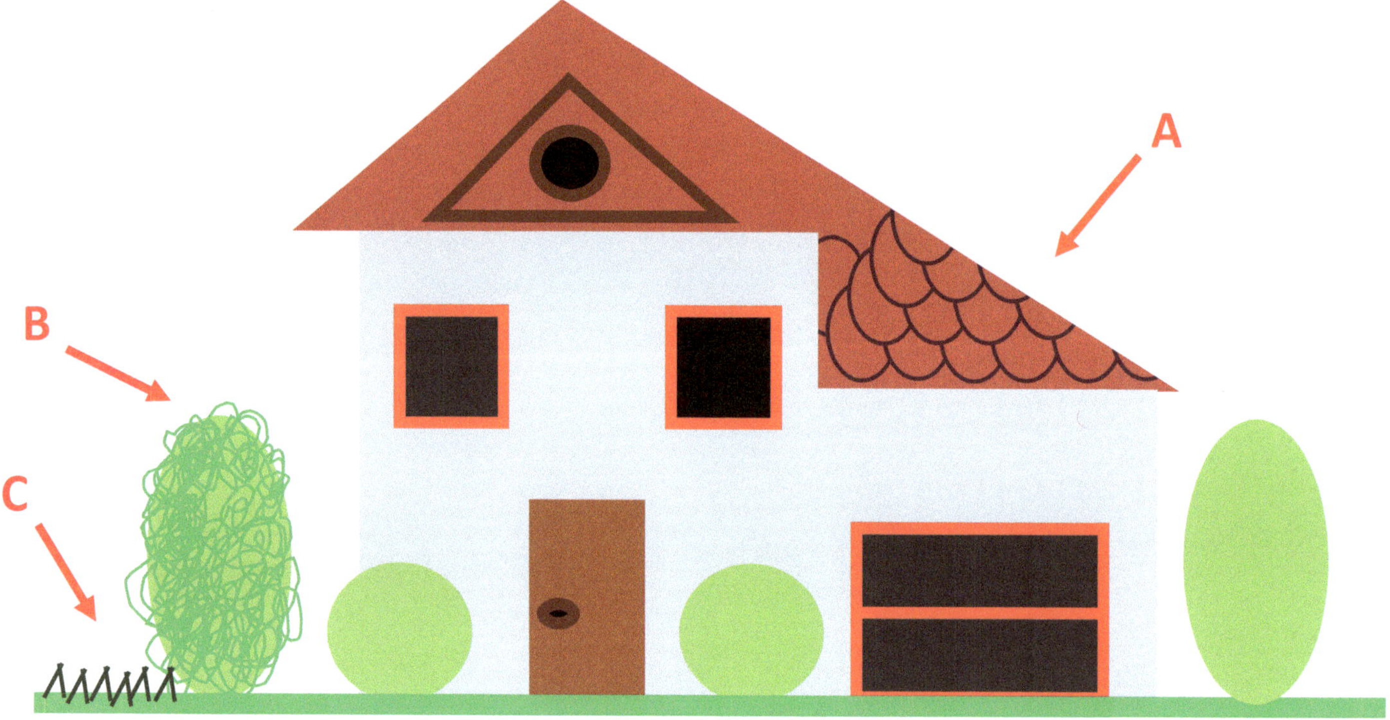

Start out by doing the following:

A. Add upside down curvy lines to show the shingles on the roof
B. Use curly lines to show the leaves and shape of the bushes
C. Use jagged lines to show grass

Are there any other lines that you can add to your drawing to make it more realistic? If your house had a chimney, how would you draw the smoke coming out of it? If you had a sun, how would you show light coming from the sun? There are all sorts of lines you can use but be careful not to do too much or your drawing may start to look too busy.

Use the space provided on the next page to draw your house again.

Redraw your house in the space provided using different lines to show details

Remember to sign your name to your work

Art History Lesson Four

Each lesson we will go over some Art History that follow what we have learned in each lesson. During this lesson, we learned about lines and how they are used in different ways.

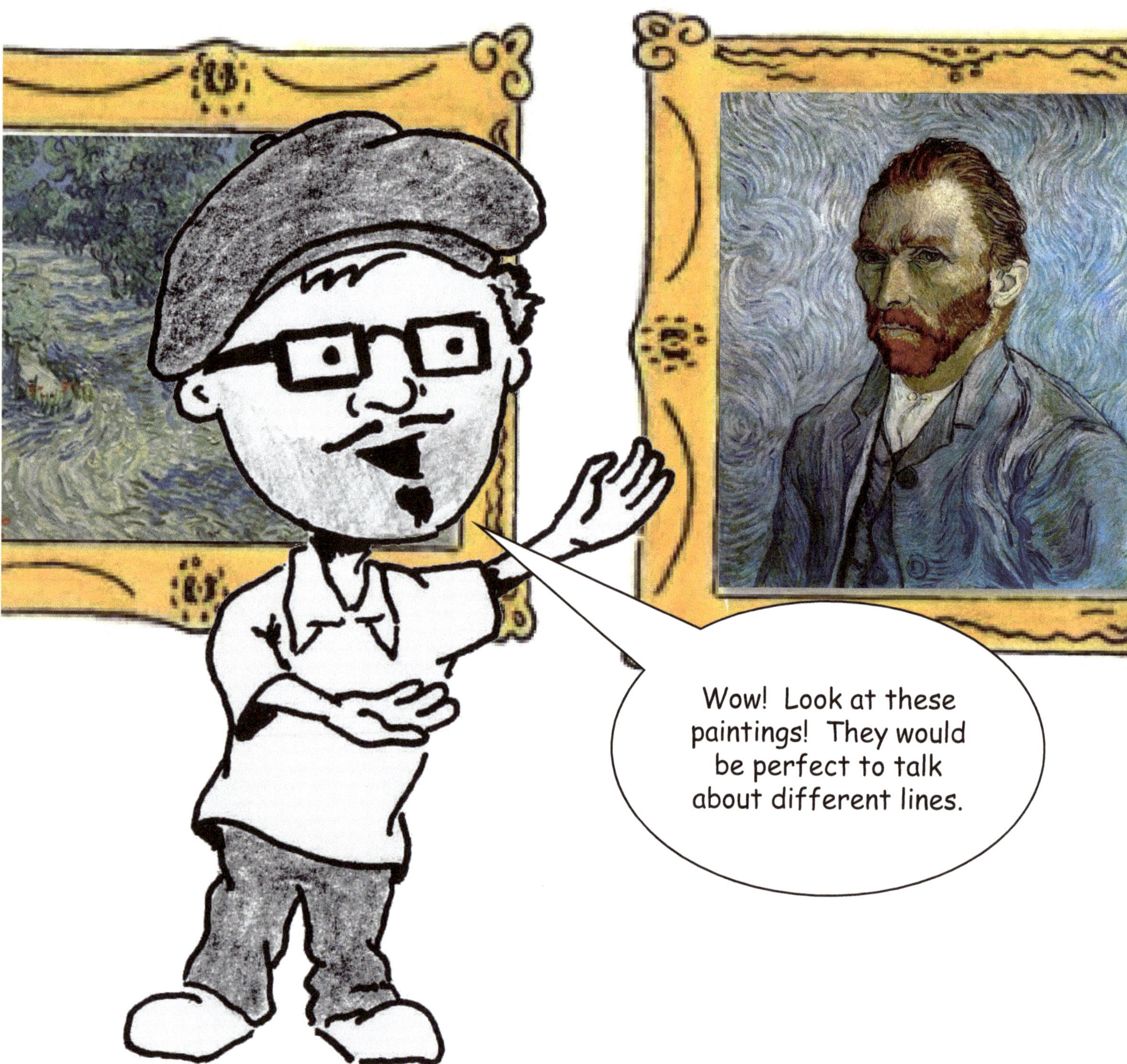

Vincent Van Gogh

Vincent Van Gogh was a Dutch painter in the later 1800's. He used a lot of different lines to create his art and used those lines to almost make paintings move. Here are a couple examples of his paintings. Notice all the different lines he uses and how they move around the painting.

Here he used wiggly lines for the trees and leaves and then short, thick lines for the ground. The lines on the ground almost lead you into the background.

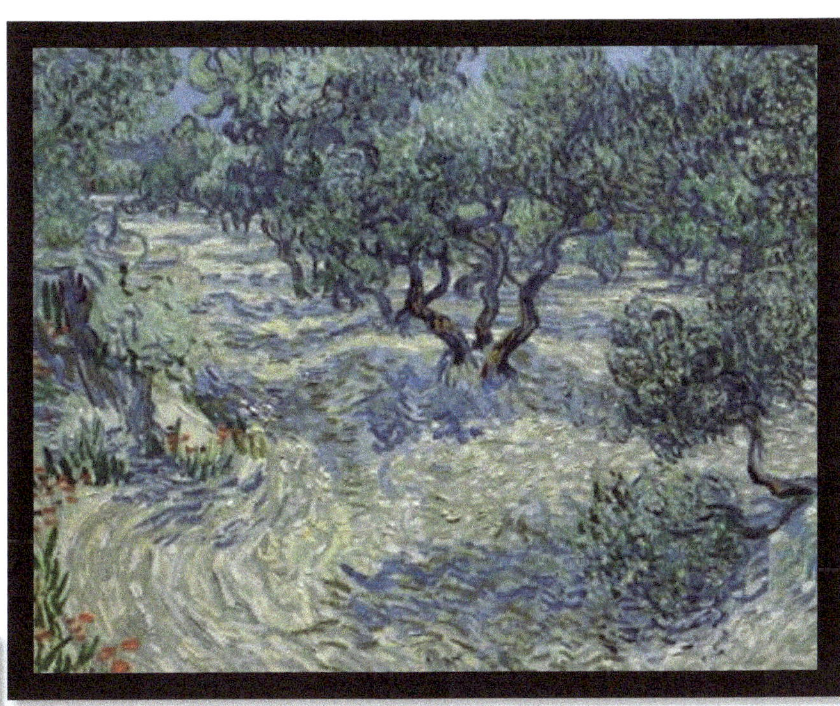

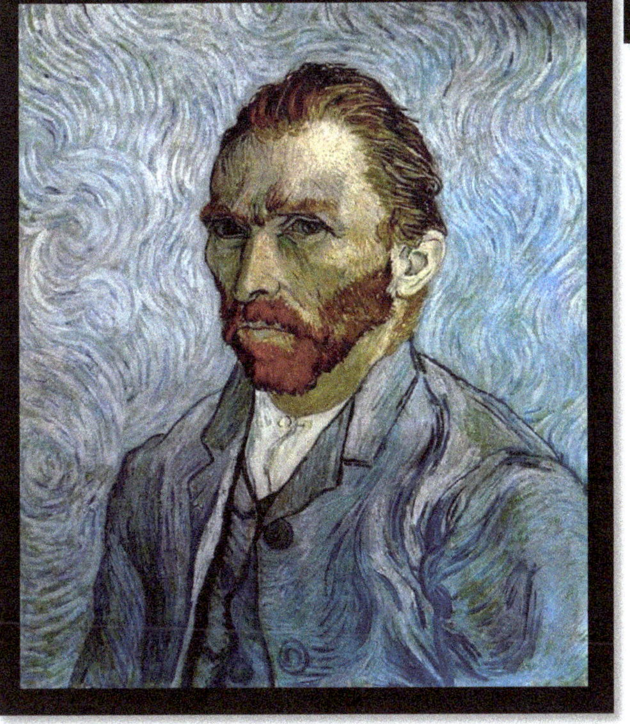

Do you see all the lines in the background and how they kind of match his jacket? He used long lines for those but short, little lines for the face.

Art History Project

Here is another painting by Vincent Van Gogh. It is his most famous painting title "Starry Night". Again, do you see how he uses different types of lines to create a swirling sky, wavy bushes, and square buildings? Does it make your eye move along the painting? What do you think of this painting? Do you like it? Do the colors of the stars seem bright against the blue background?

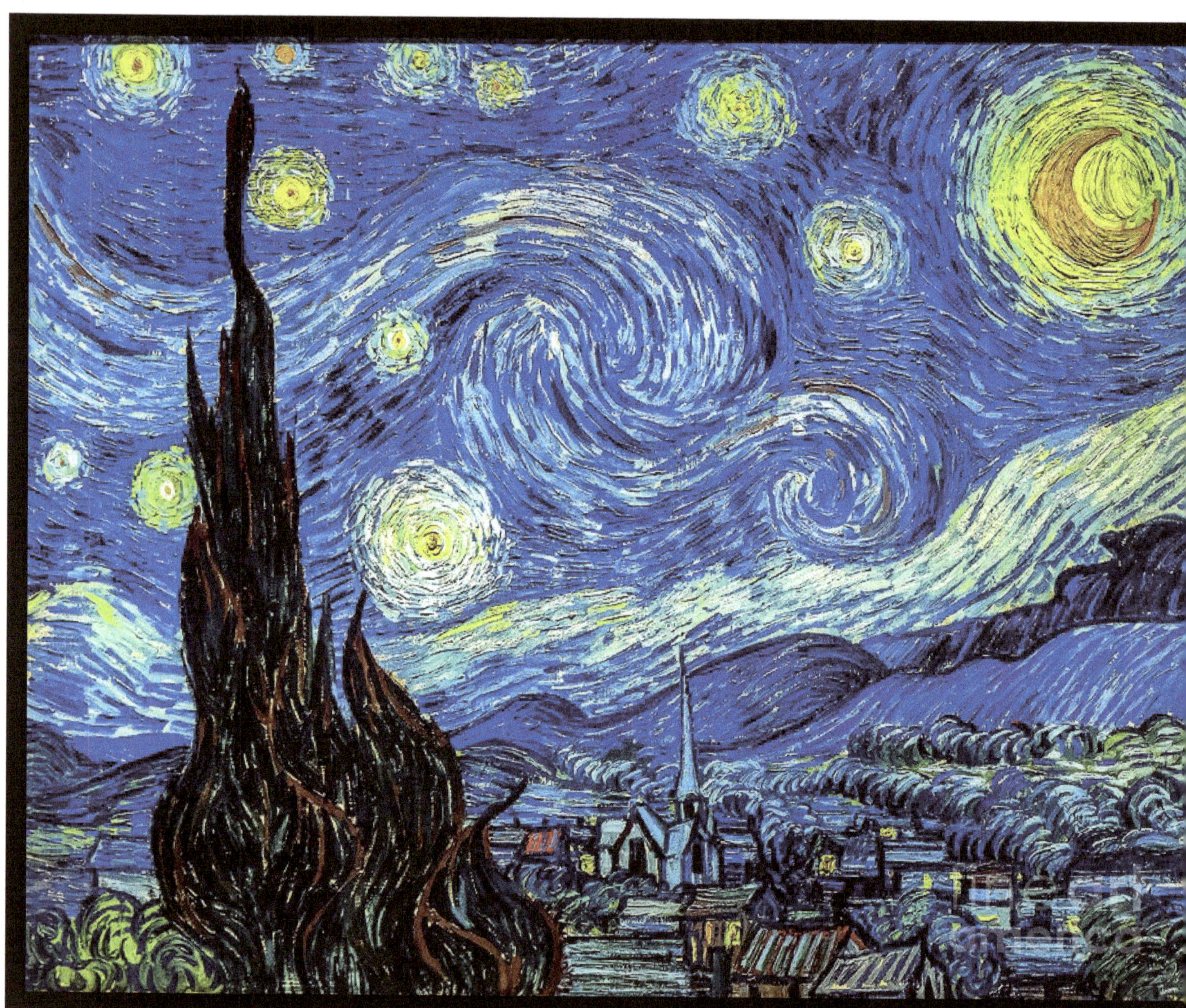

On the next two pages are coloring pages of this painting. The first one just color in with markers. The second picture, draw the lines in with markers.

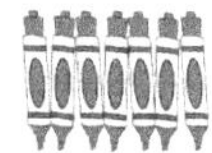

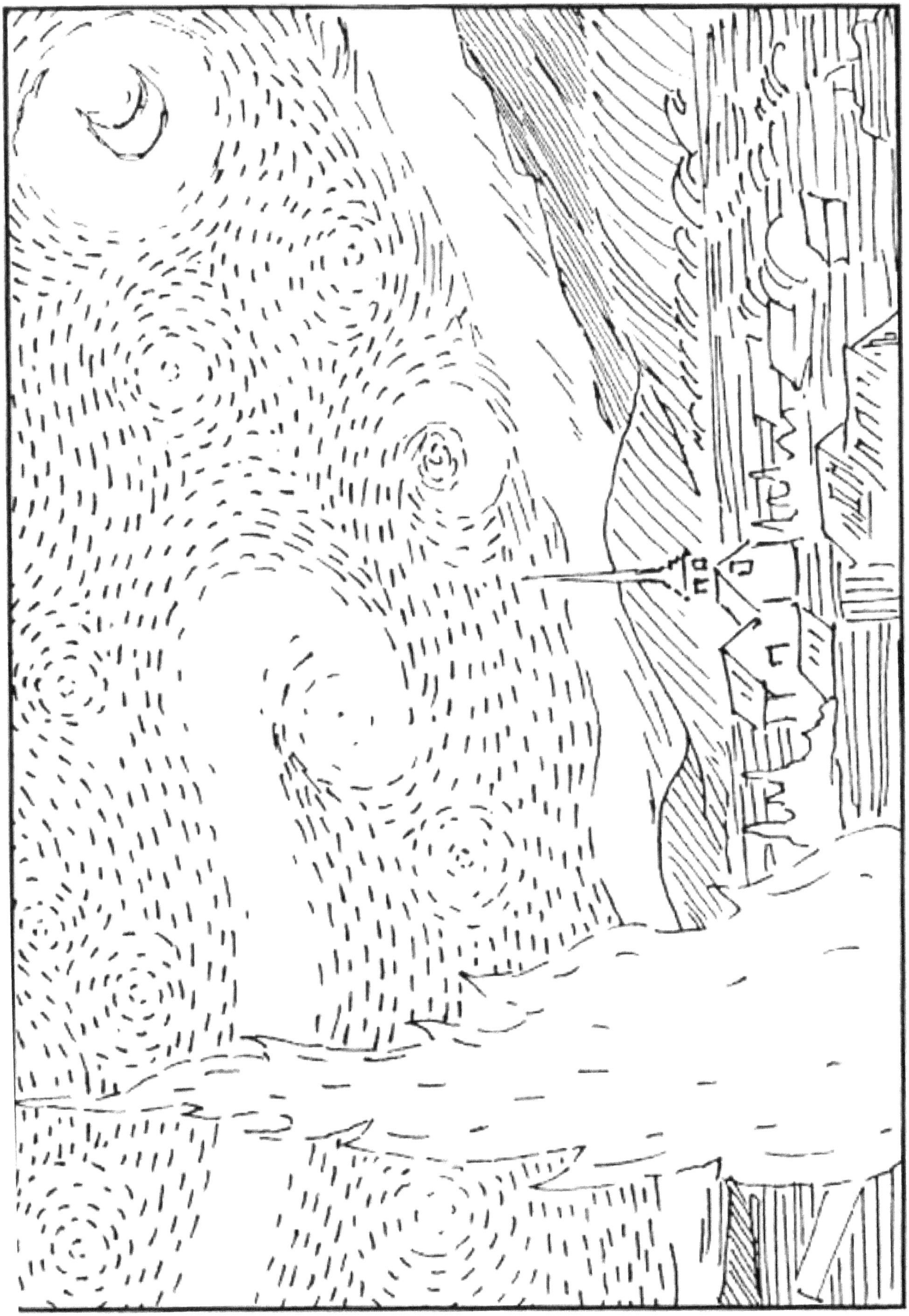

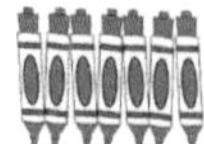

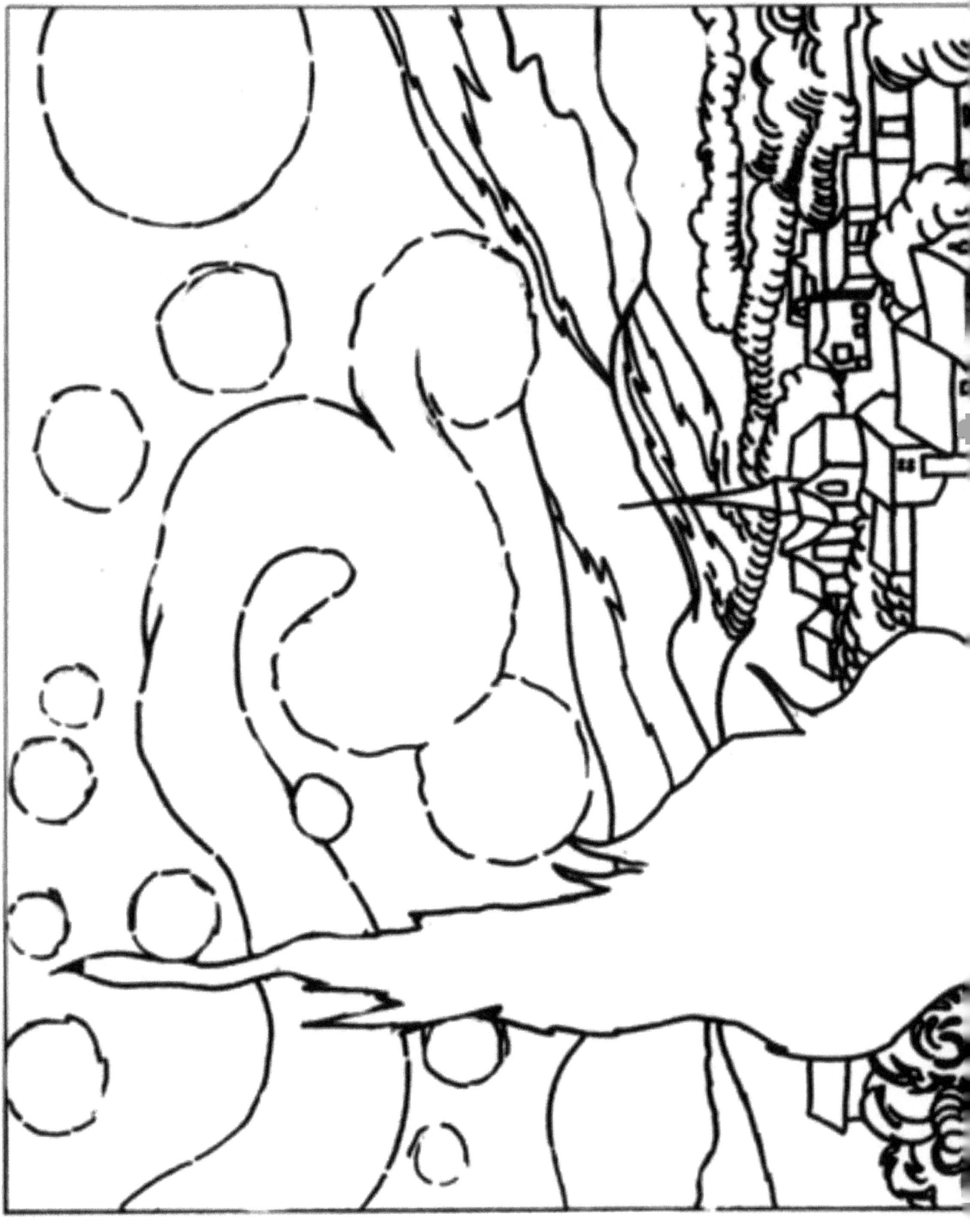

Chapter Fun

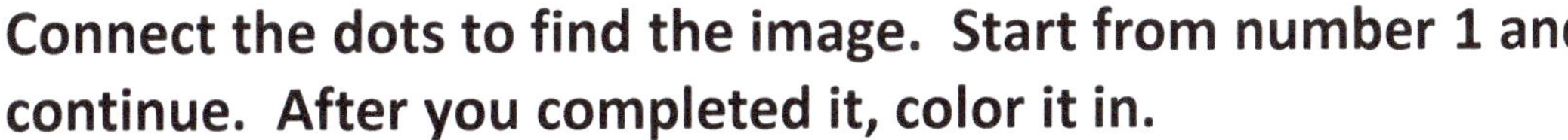
Connect the dots to find the image. Start from number 1 and continue. After you completed it, color it in.

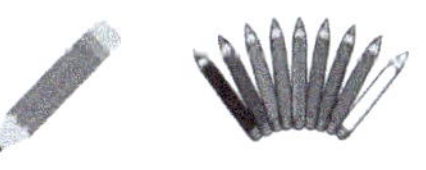

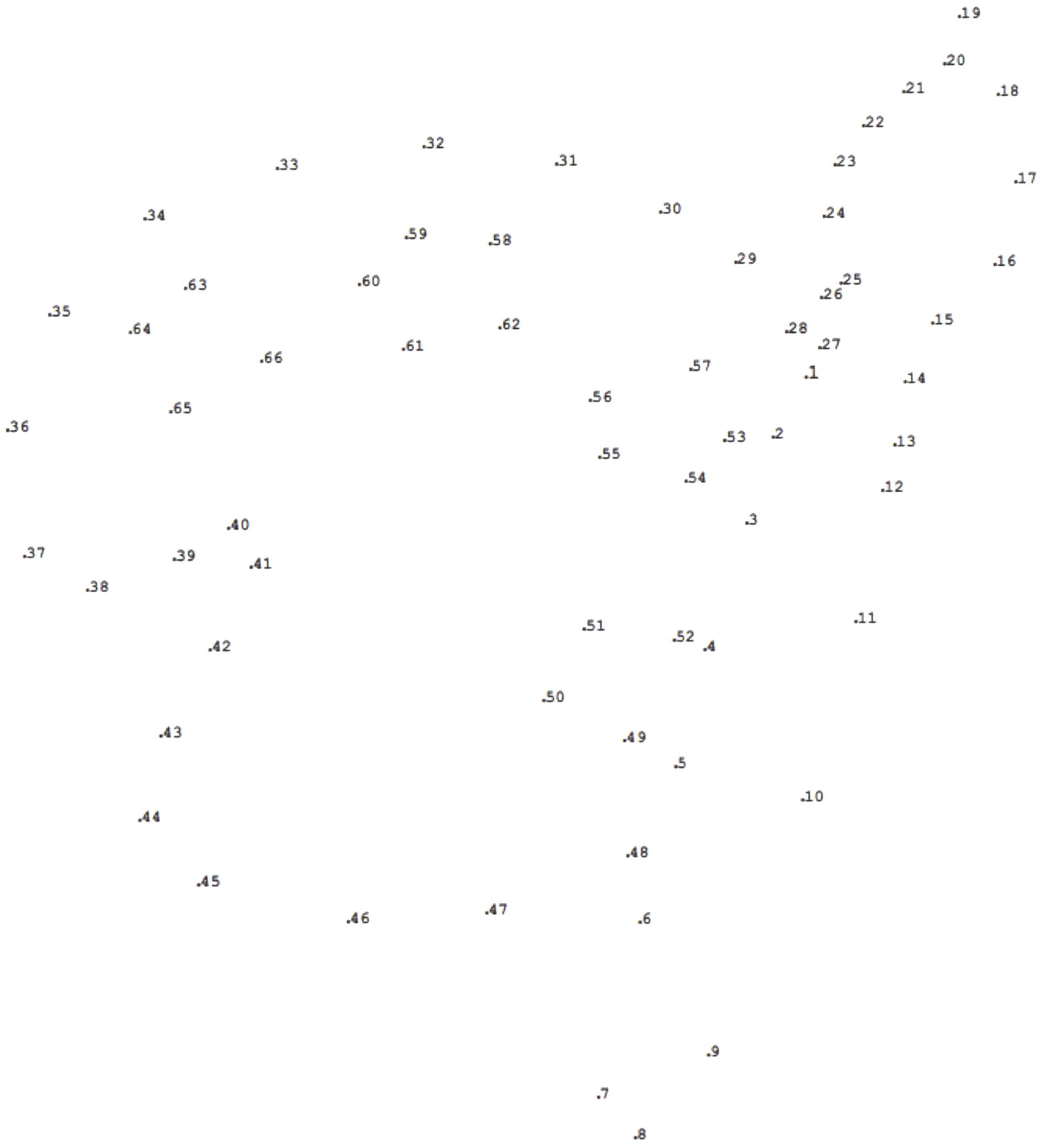

UNIT 5 Patterns

Lesson 4.1 How to Draw Patterns

In this lesson, we will begin working on patterns. A pattern is a series of lines, dots, or colors that repeat over and over again. When we add patterns to our artwork, it can really make them noticeable. Whether it is in nature, buildings, or even our clothes, we see patterns all around us. Think of a zebra's stripes, a leopard's spots, or even your bed sheets. Those are patterns!

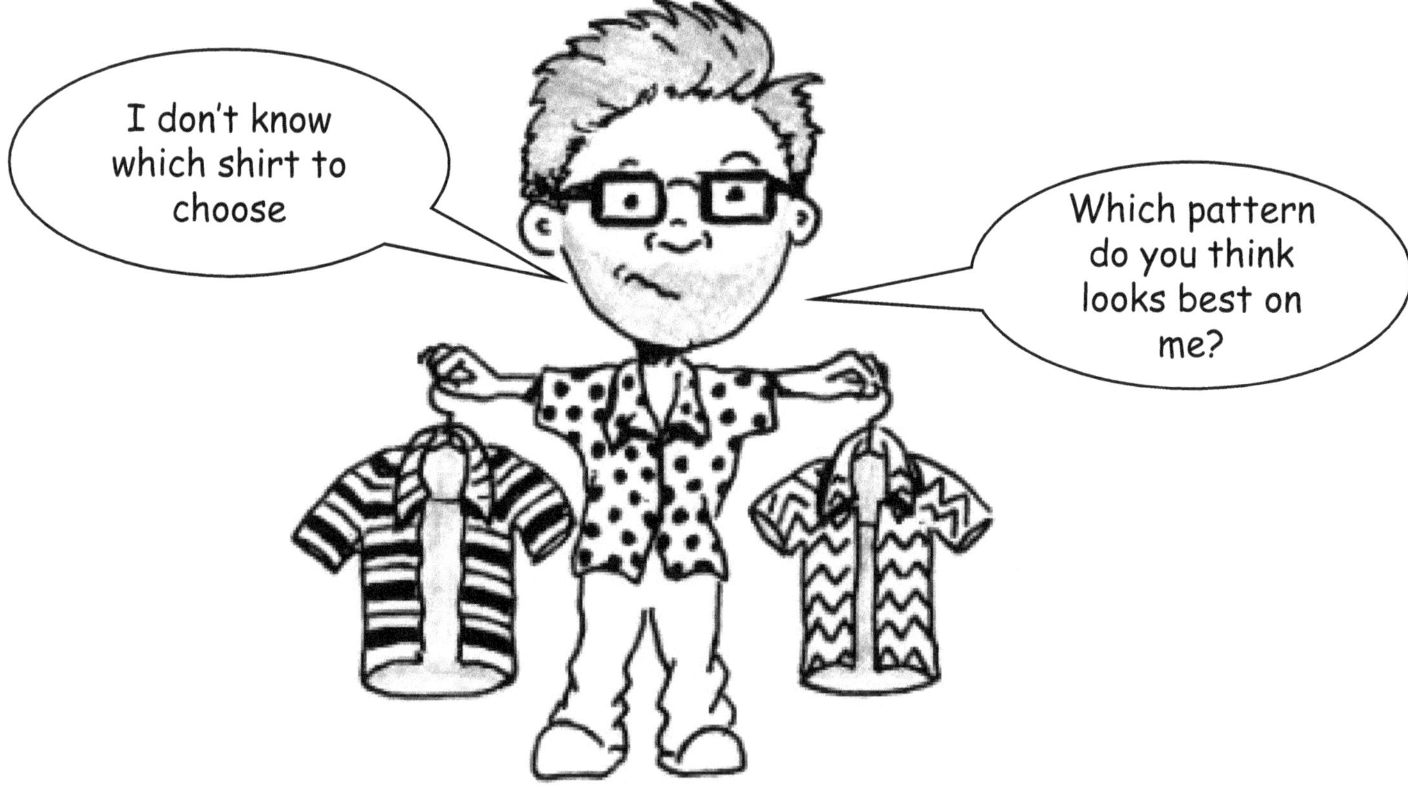

In this lesson, you will need pencils, pencil sharpener, eraser, markers, and colored pencils. Look for the icon next to each project to determine what to use

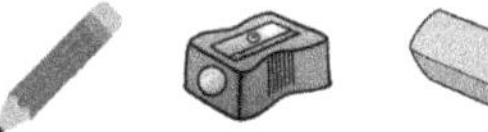
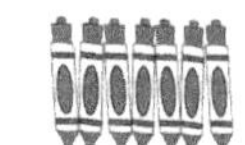
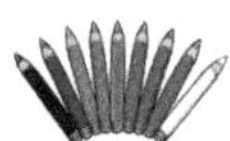

Exercise 1

Follow the lines below. Start by tracing then continue on your own. 

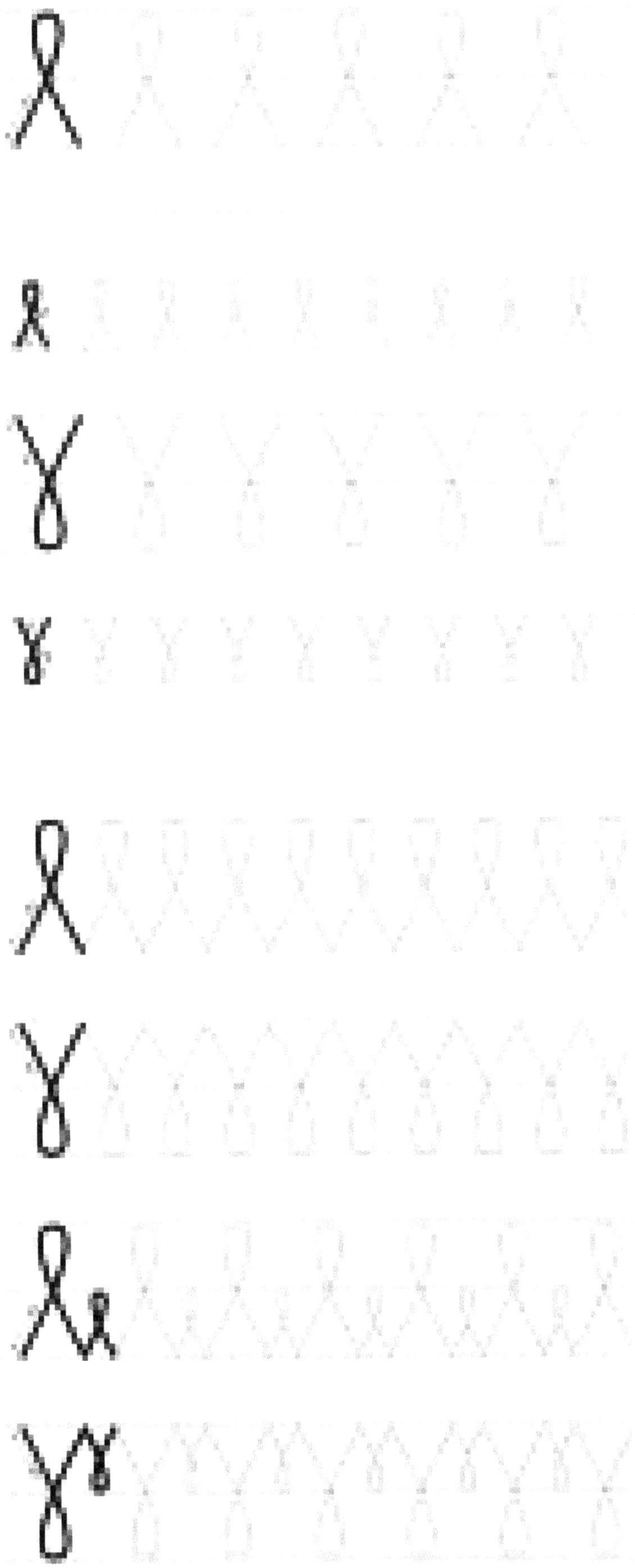

Exercise 2

Follow the lines below. Start by tracing then continue on your own. 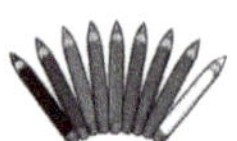

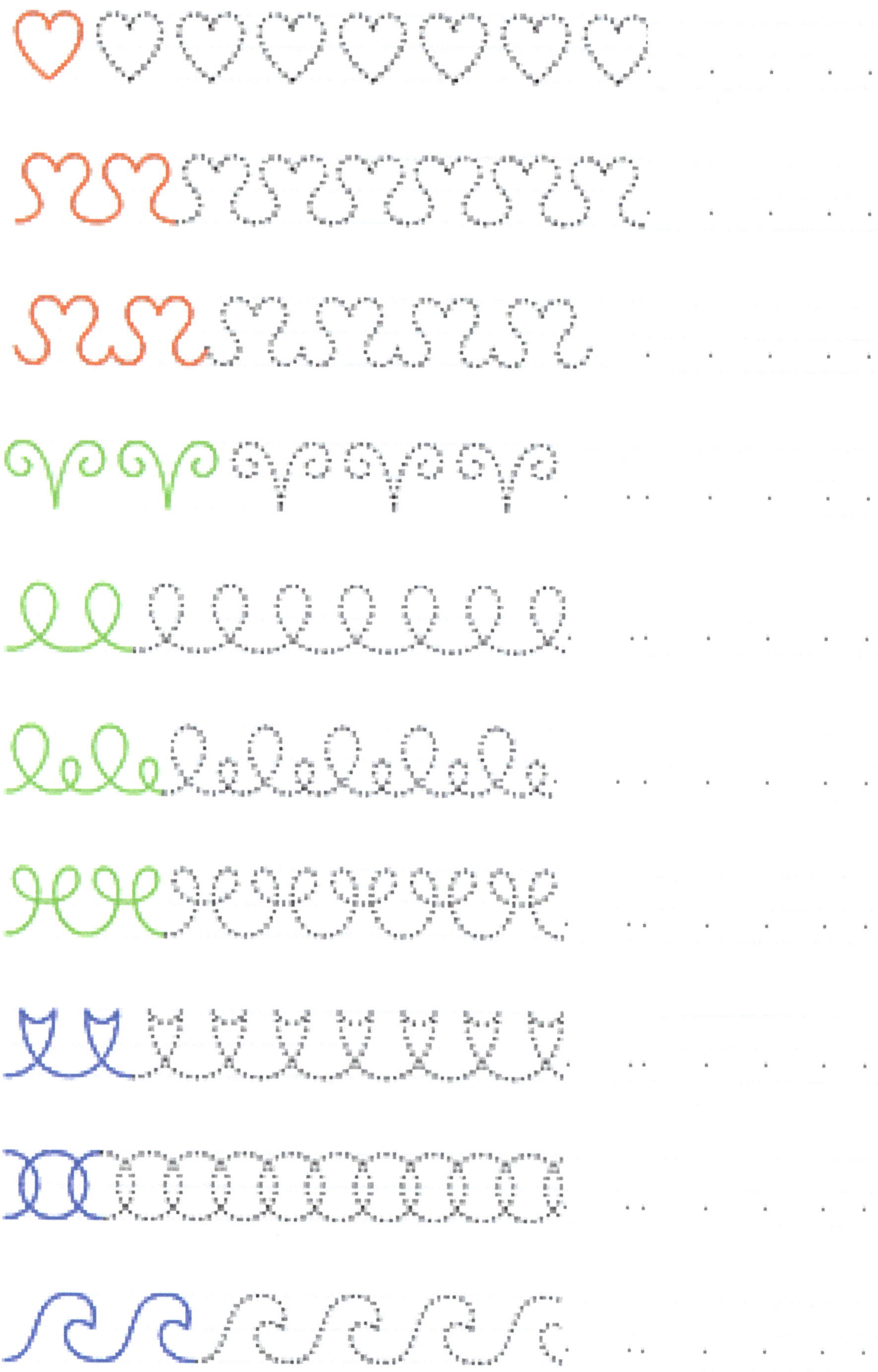

Project 1

Begin practicing patterns

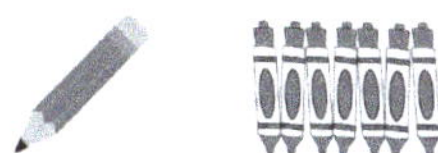

Now that we have practiced creating a pattern of lines, we will use that to help draw similar lines over and over again to create a pattern. By practicing this, it will help improve your drawing skills later on.

In the box below, you see a series of jagged lines over and over again. In the empty box, try to draw the same lines. Try your best to draw the lines straight and to get the space between each line the same. If you don't, don't worry, the more you practice drawing, the easier it will be.

First, draw it with your pencil and then go over it with a black marker. Use the very tip of the marker so as not to make too thick of a line

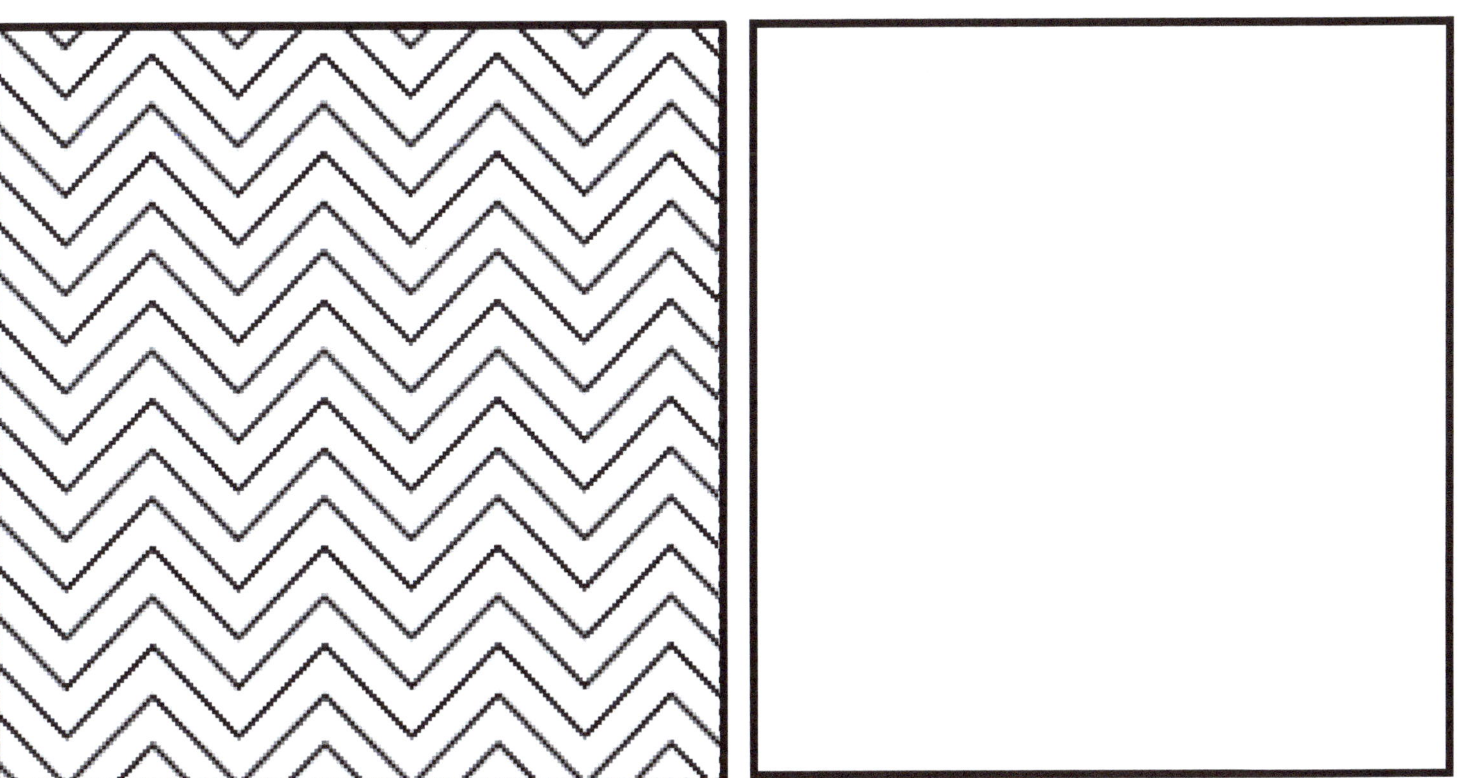

On the next page, we will do this again but add something to make the design more interesting.

For the next part of this project, I want you to do the same thing as you did before. Make a bunch of jagged lines in the empty box. Again, use a pencil to draw out the lines and then outline them with the tip of your black marker

Now, go over all of the lines that are **going up** with your marker again, but this time make the mark a lot thicker. Try to follow the example below.

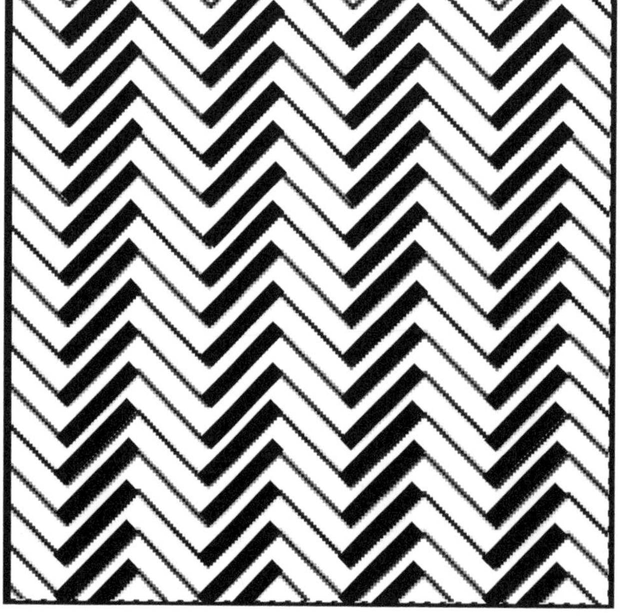

Do you think the design is more interesting now? In your sketchbook, you can try similar things with different lines. Be creative and see what you come up with.

Exercise 3

Drawing Patterns. Use examples on the next page to make your own patterns

Use examples on the next page

PATTERN EXAMPLES

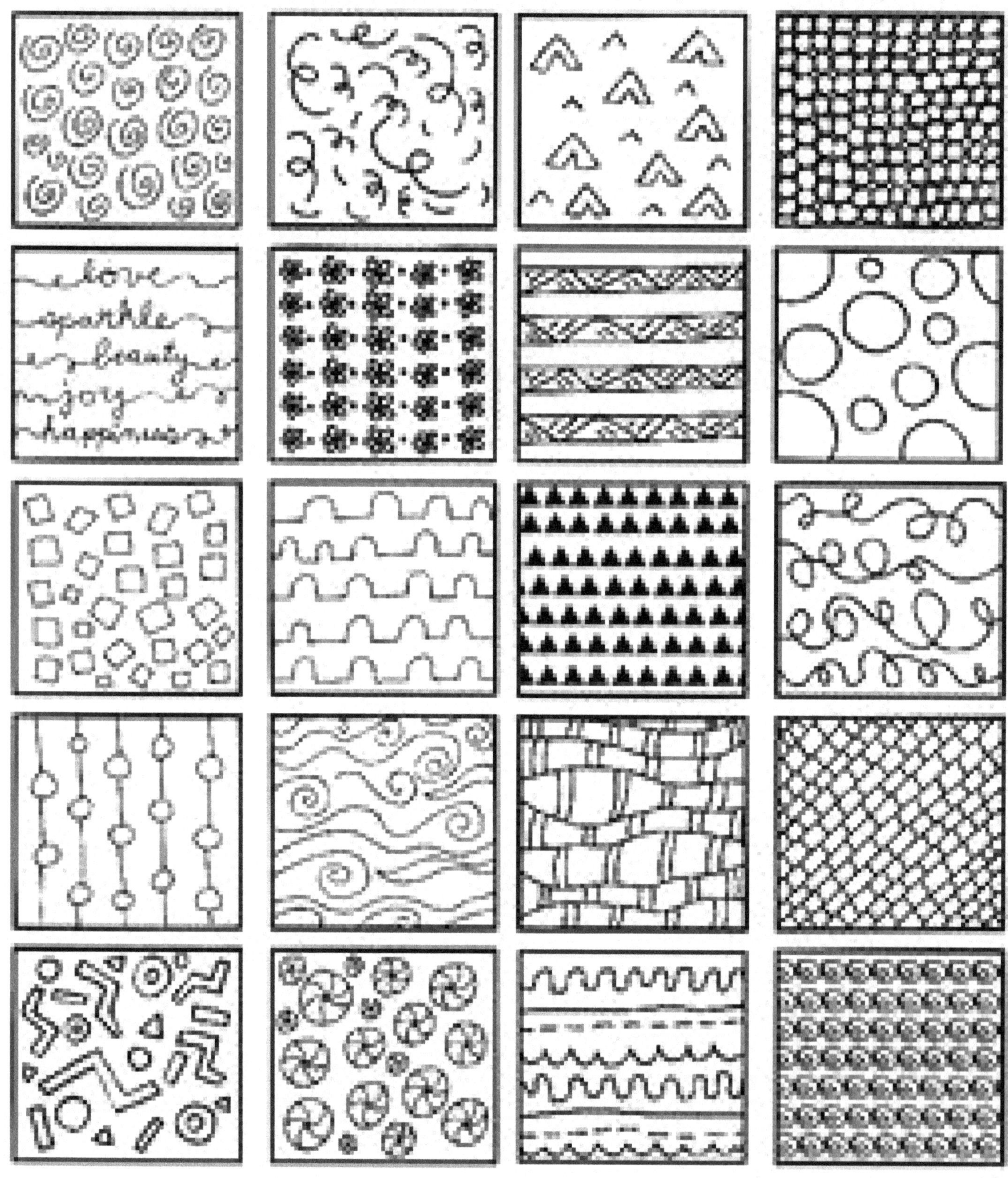

Project 1

Drawing patterns in butterflies 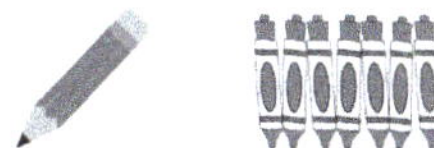

Nature has some of the most beautiful patterns. Look at some of these butterflies and the patterns on their wings.

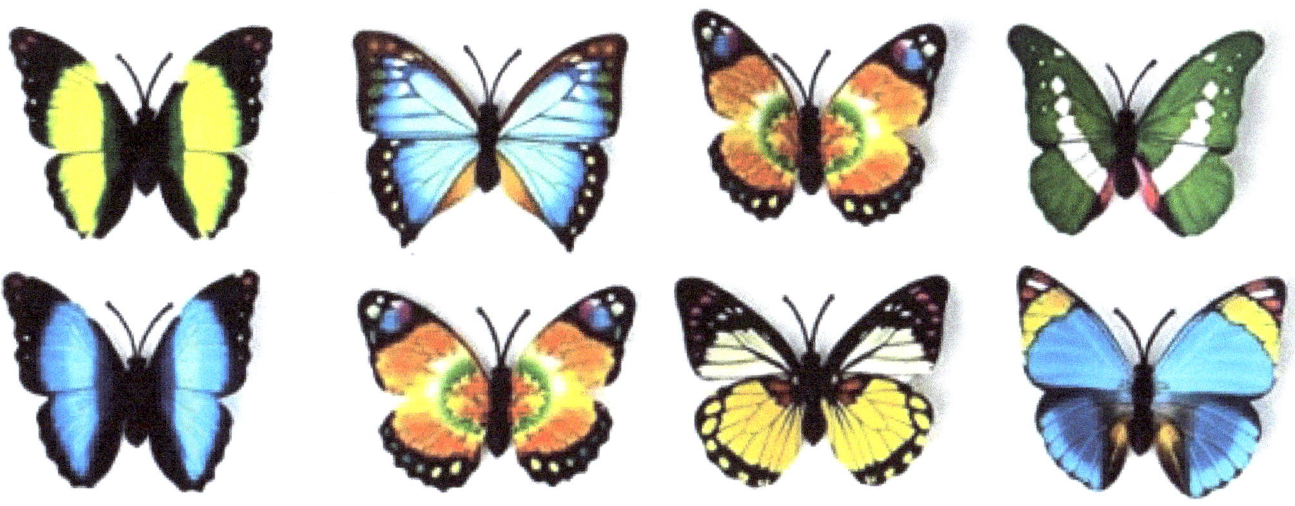

Color your own butterfly. Start drawing with your pencil and then color it with markers

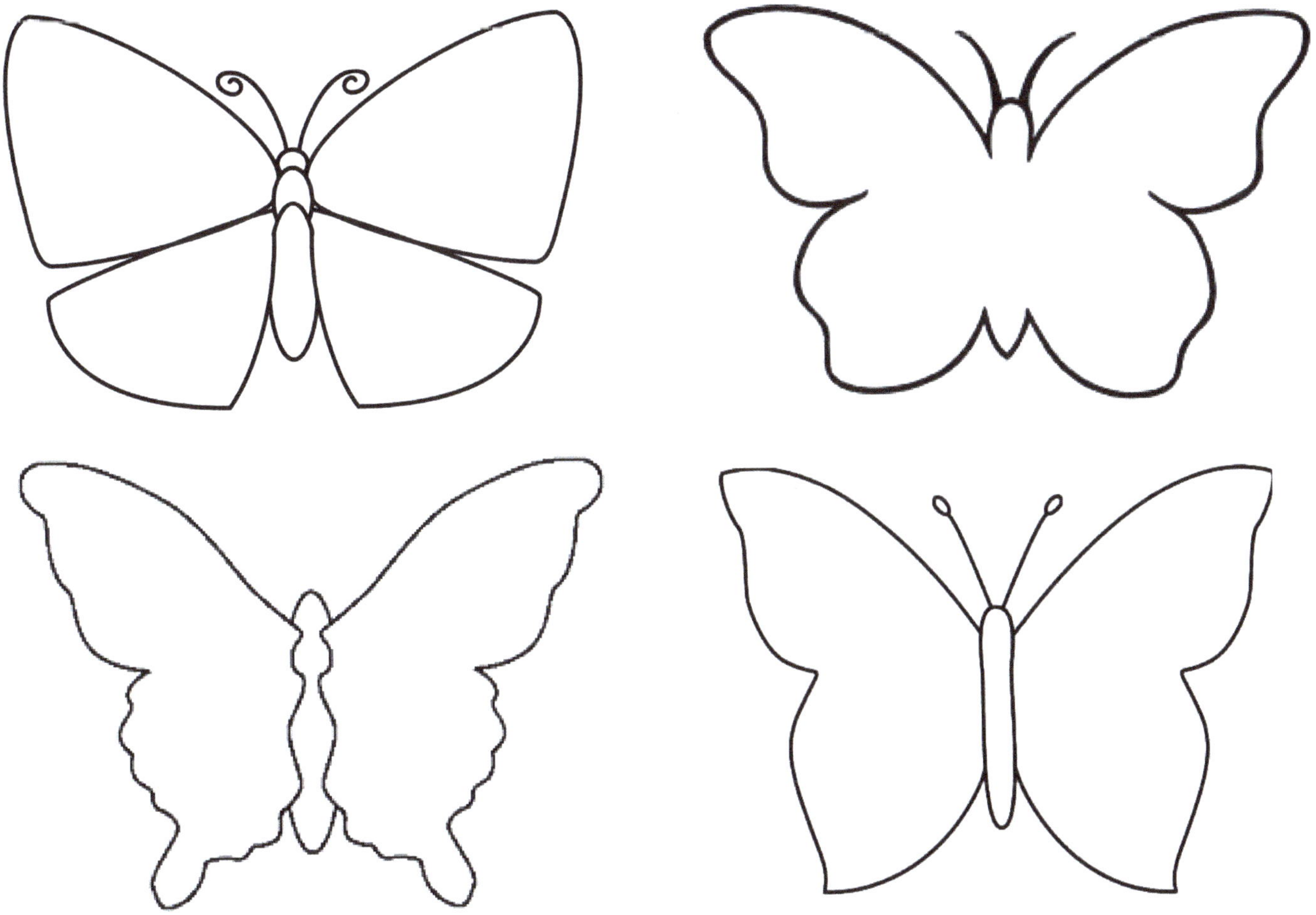

Project 3

Making patterns on your hand 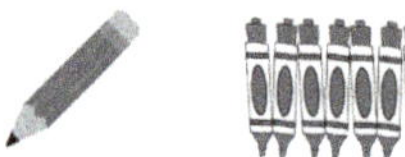

We will make a design with patterns using an outline of our hand.

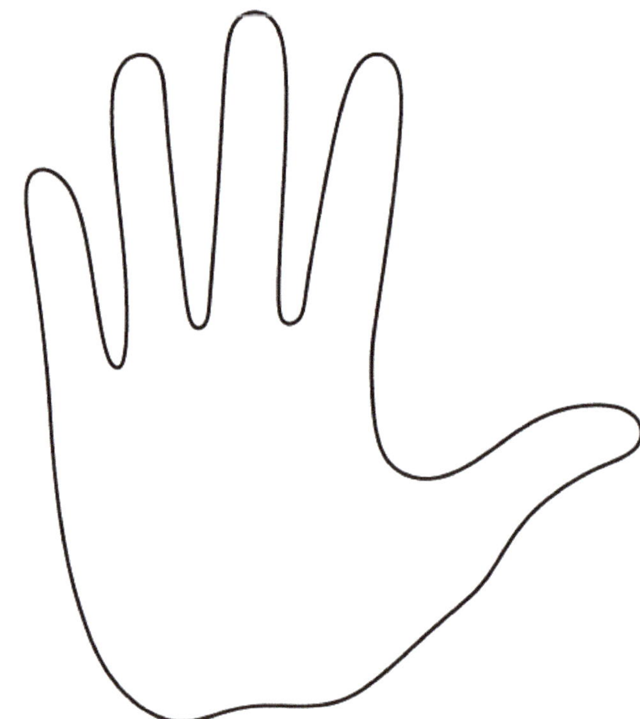

Step 1: On the next page, draw and outline of your hand with a pencil

Step 2: Draw straight lines in different directions across the outline of your hand like in the picture

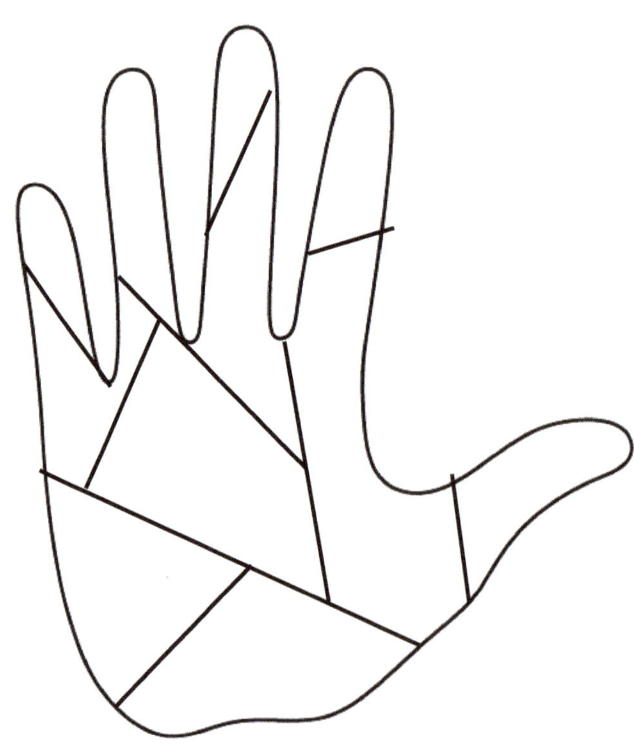

Step 3: In each section that you created, draw a different pattern. You can use the examples from the previous page. You can also use different colors.

Project 1

Making patterns on your hand

You can trace your hand here.

Remember to sign your name to your work

Art History Lesson Five

Each lesson we will go over some Art History that follow what we have learned in each lesson. During this lesson, we learned about patterns and how to create them.

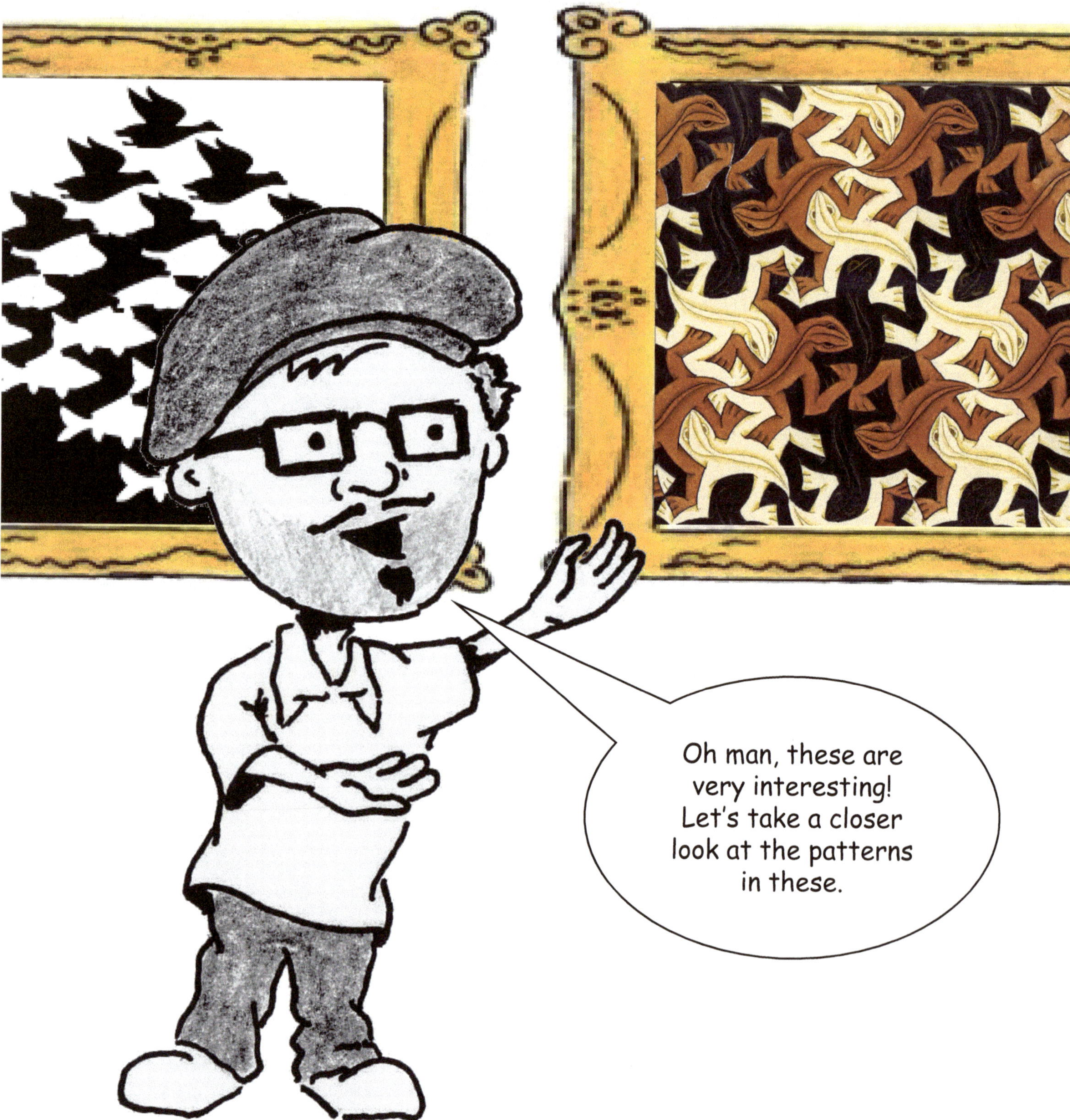

M.C. Escher

These drawings are by M.C. Escher, a Dutch artist in the early and mid 1900's. He did a lot of designs that involved mathematics and patterns. Here are two of his works. The top one is titled "Lizards: and the bottom one is titled "Sky and Water". Do you see the patterns he used to create these?

How many lizards do you see? Can you count them all? Do you see how they all fit in together?

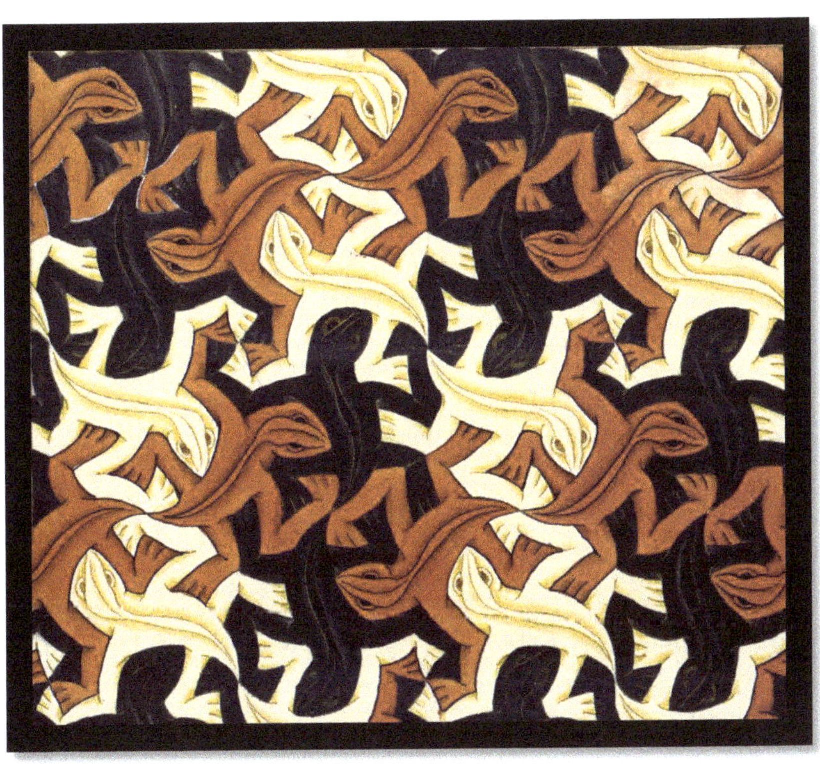

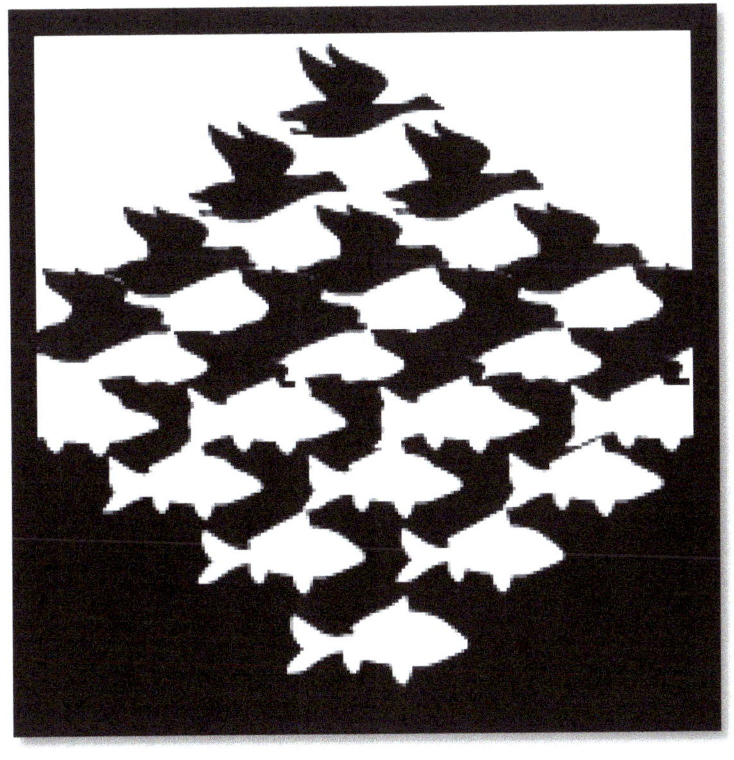

Can you see how the white outline of the fish at the bottom slowly blend together at the top to make the sky? Then how the black outline of the geese at the top blend together to make the water?

Art History Project

We are going to make our own M.C. Escher type drawing. Below is the design you will use but it is also at the end of the book which you will cut out there.

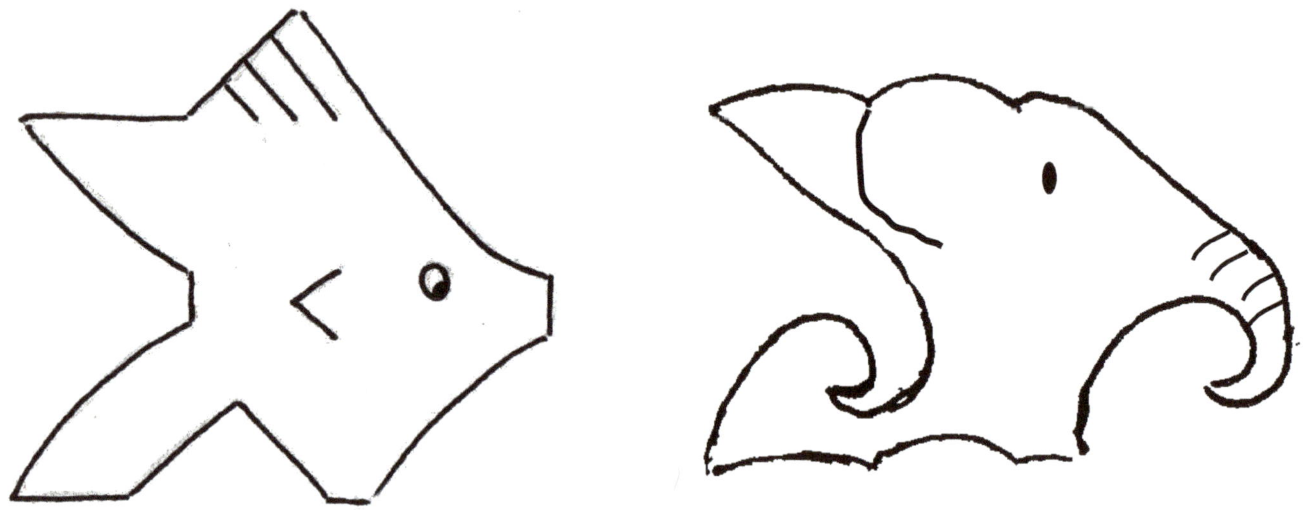

Do not cut these images out. Cut out the images at the back of the book on page 153

Once you cut it out, trace the image on a cereal box and cut it out again. If you need an adult to help, please ask.

When you have the cardboard cutout. You will put it on a piece of paper and trace it one more time.

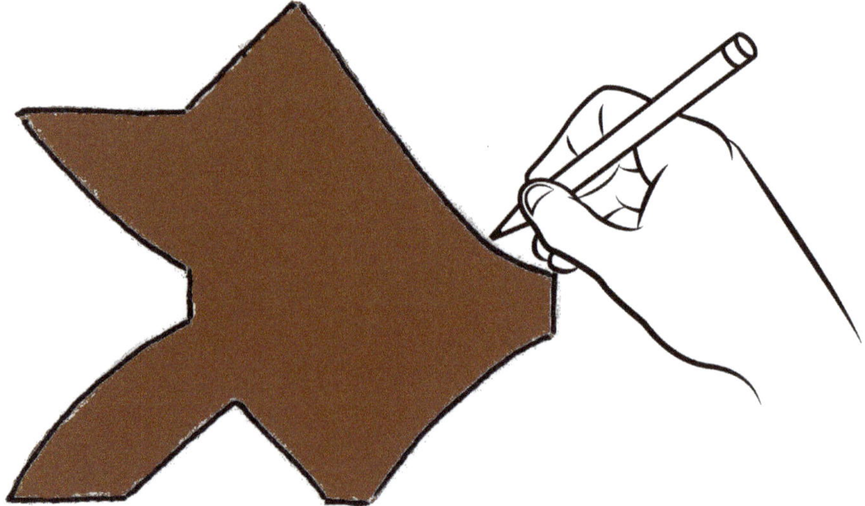

Once you finished tracing it, move the cardboard piece over so it lines up with your first drawing and trace it again.

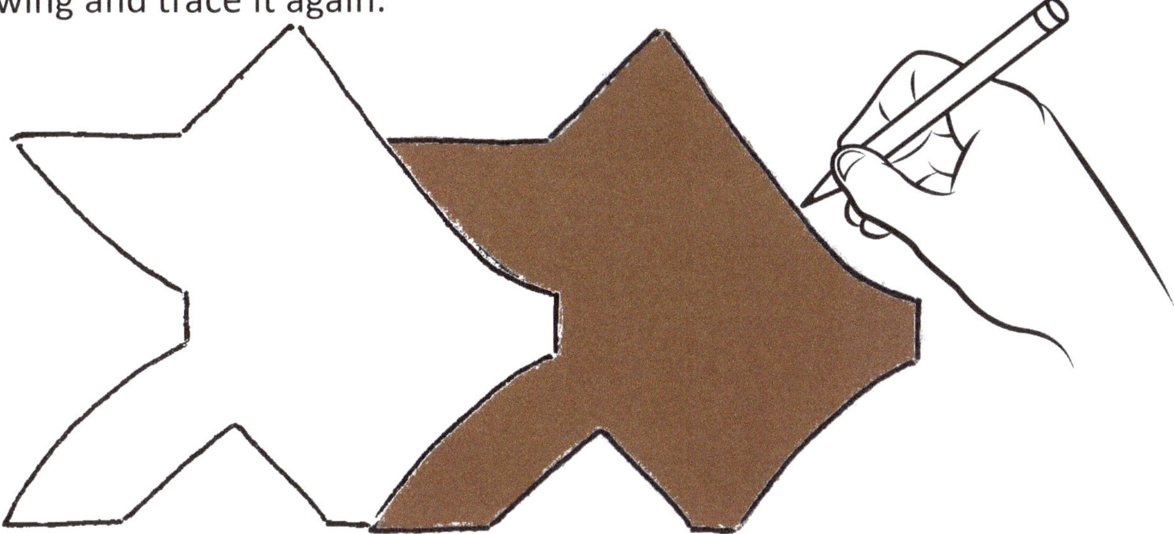

Keep tracing this until you fill up your whole paper. It should start to look something like this.

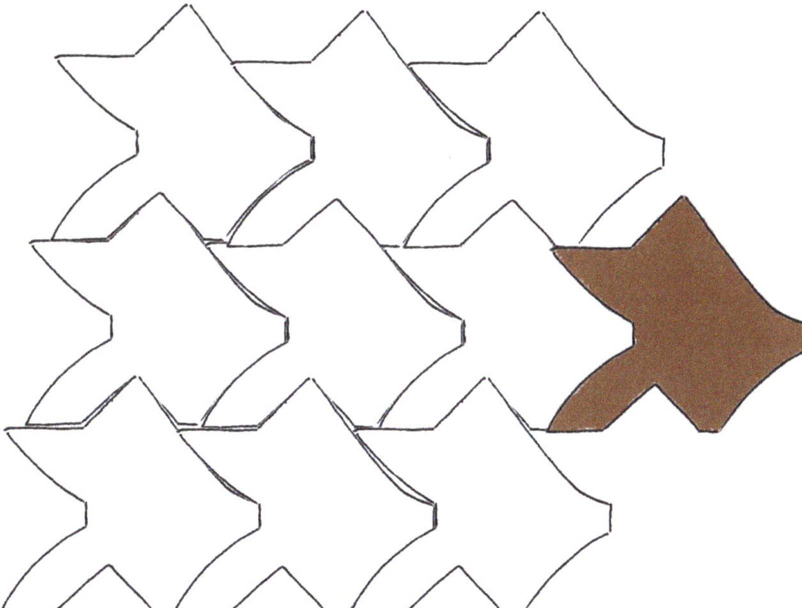

Once you filled up your whole paper with these. Draw an eye and fins on everyone like this.

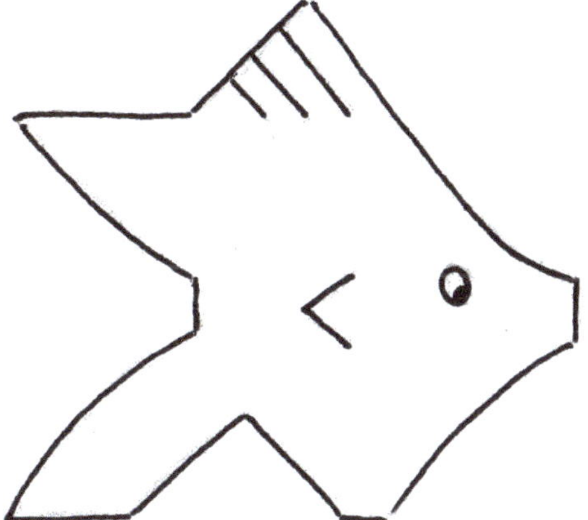

You can then color the fish in different colors to make it look similar to this.

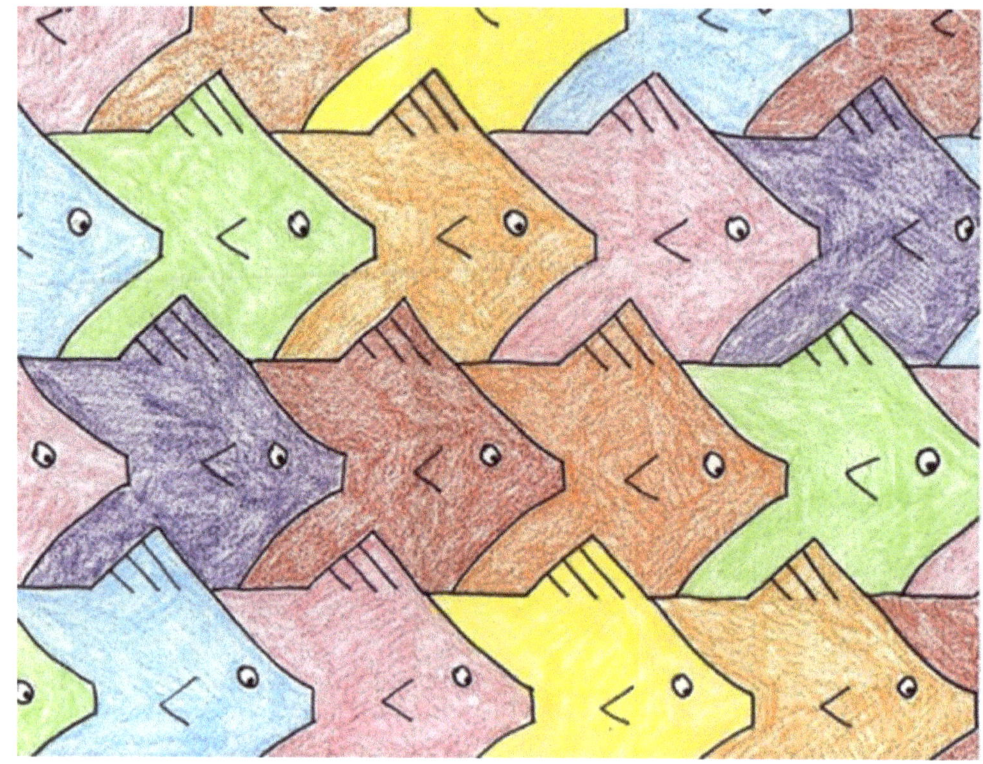

Now, you can do the same thing with the elephant (This is a little harder). Once you cut out the drawing, trace the image on a cereal box and cut it out again. If you need an adult to help, please ask.

When you have the cardboard cutout. You will put it on a piece of paper and trace it one more time.

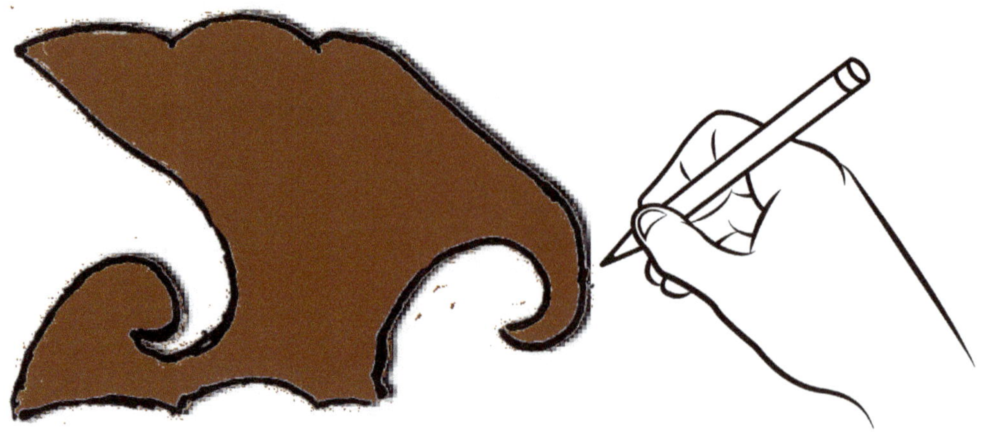

Once you finished tracing it, move the cardboard piece over so it lines up with your first drawing and trace it again.

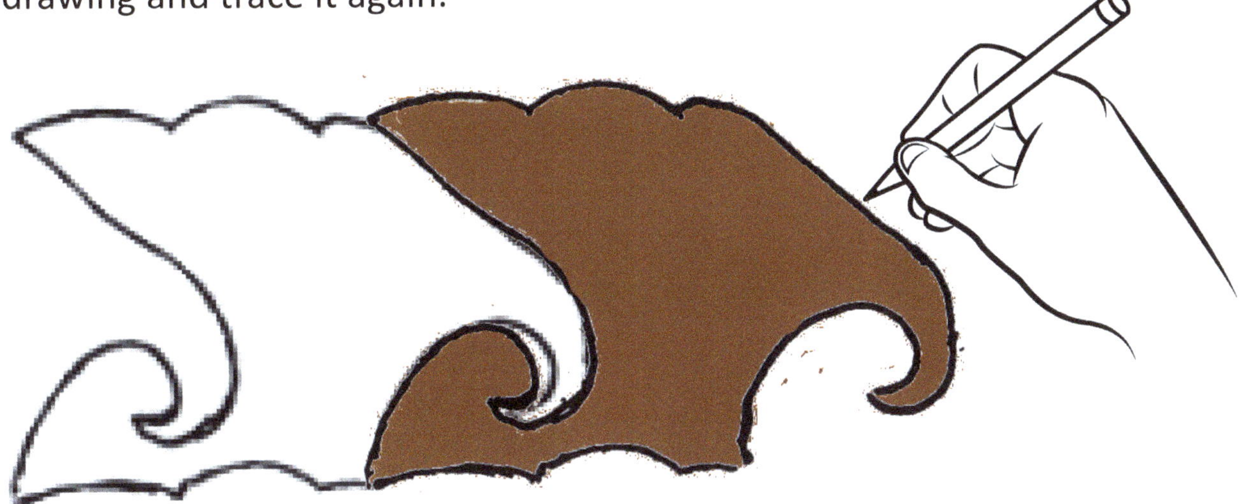

Keep tracing this until you fill up your whole paper. It should start to look something like this.

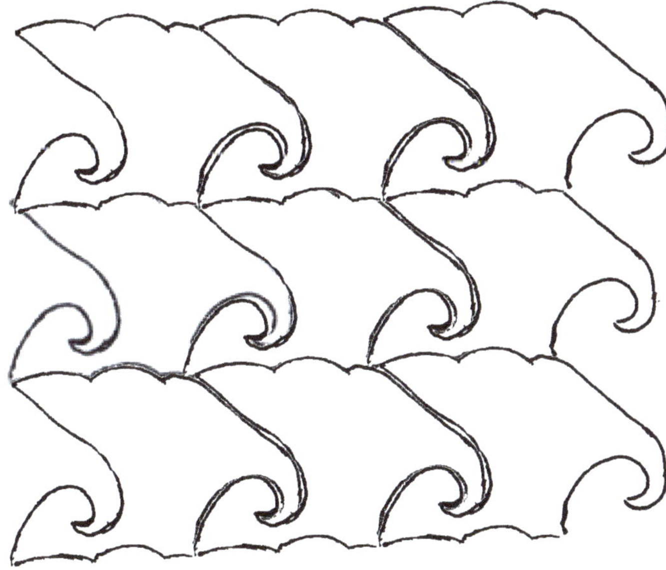

Once you filled up your whole paper with these. Draw an ear, an eye, and lines on the trunk for every one like this.

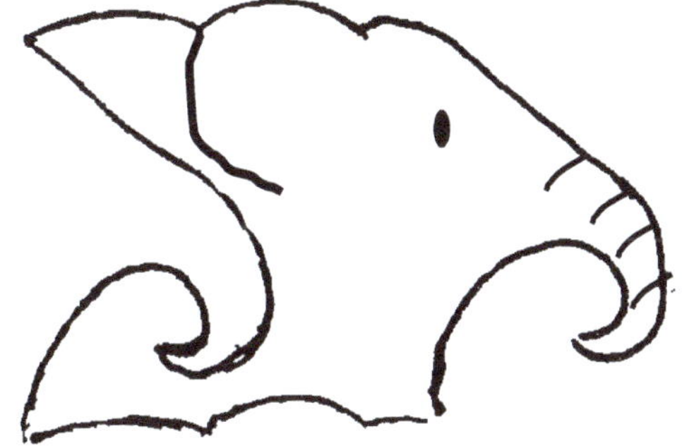

You can then color the elephants in different colors as we did with the fish

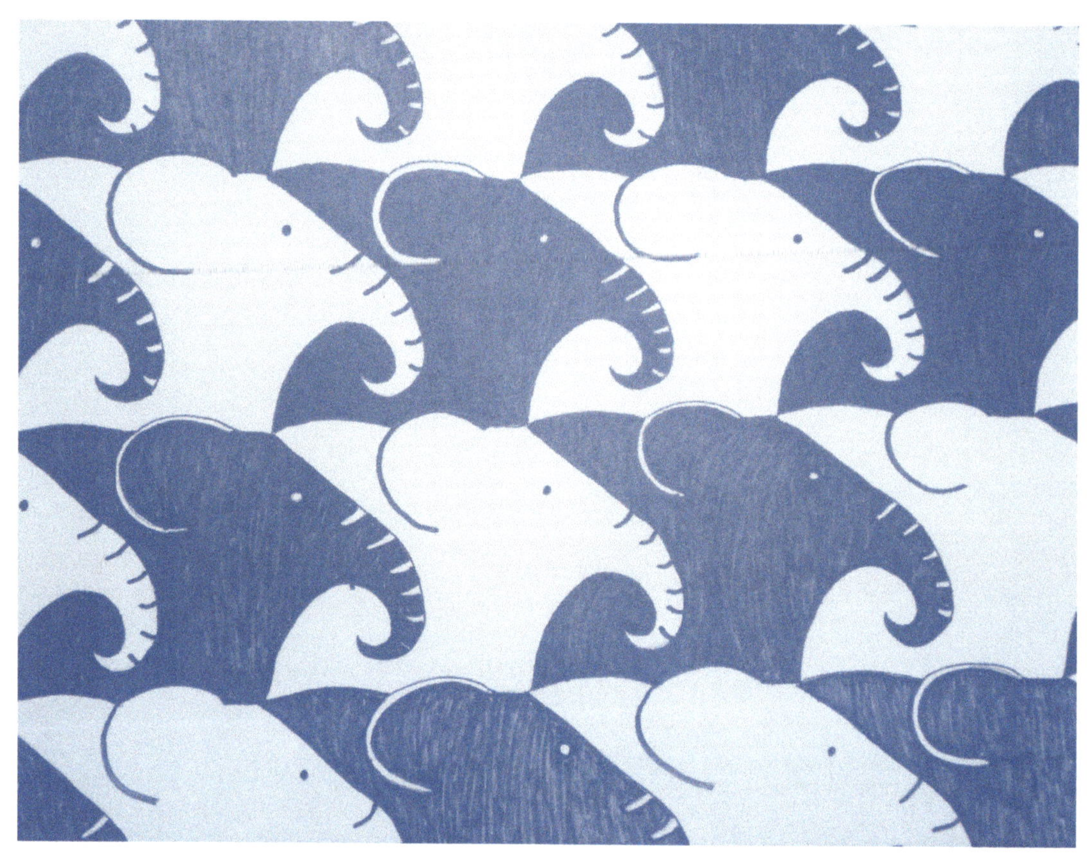

You have now made your own M.C. Escher design!!

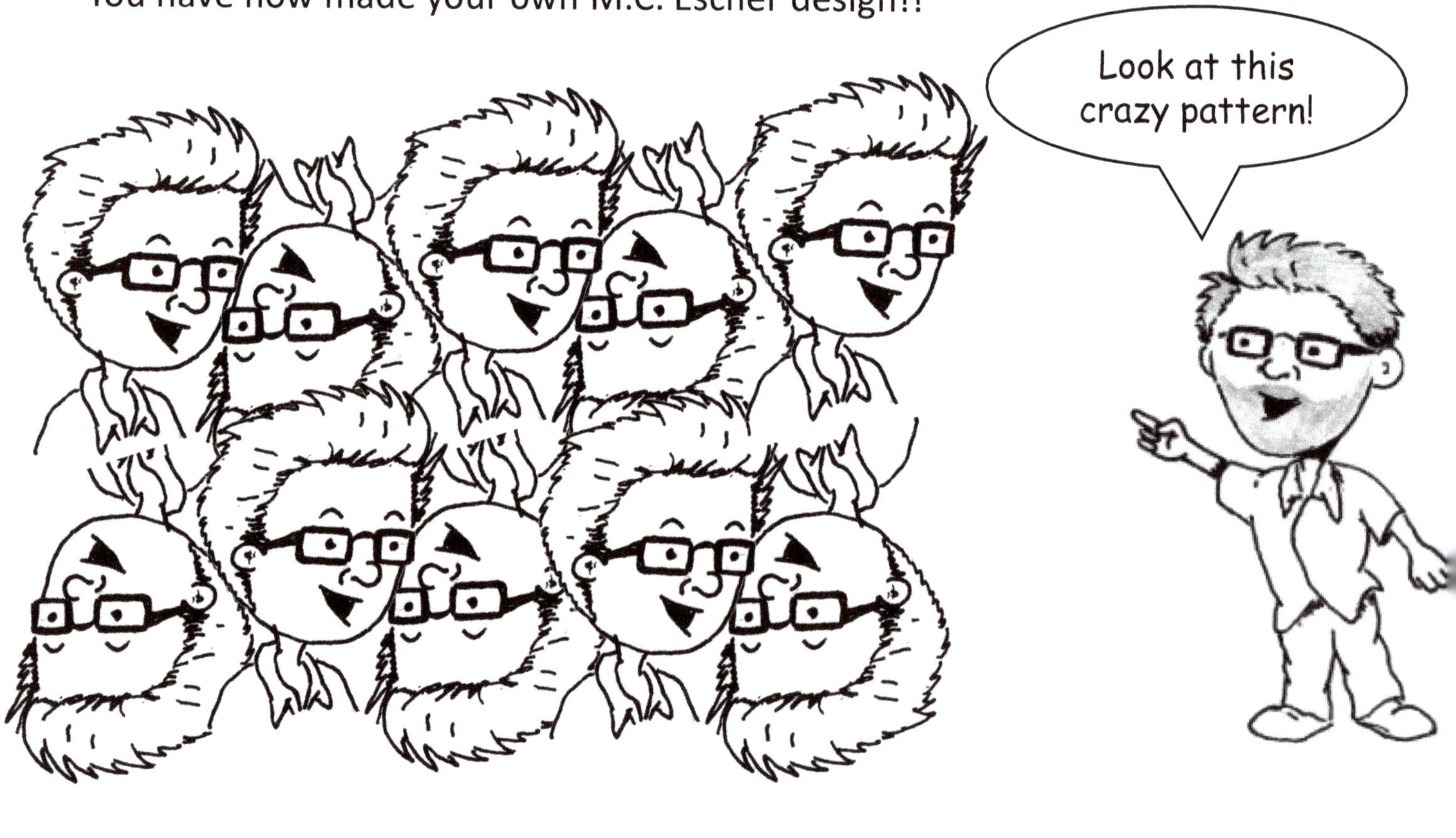

Look at this crazy pattern!

Chapter Fun

The art frames broke apart! Match the broken picture frames with the correct pattern

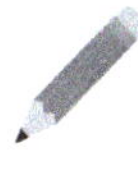

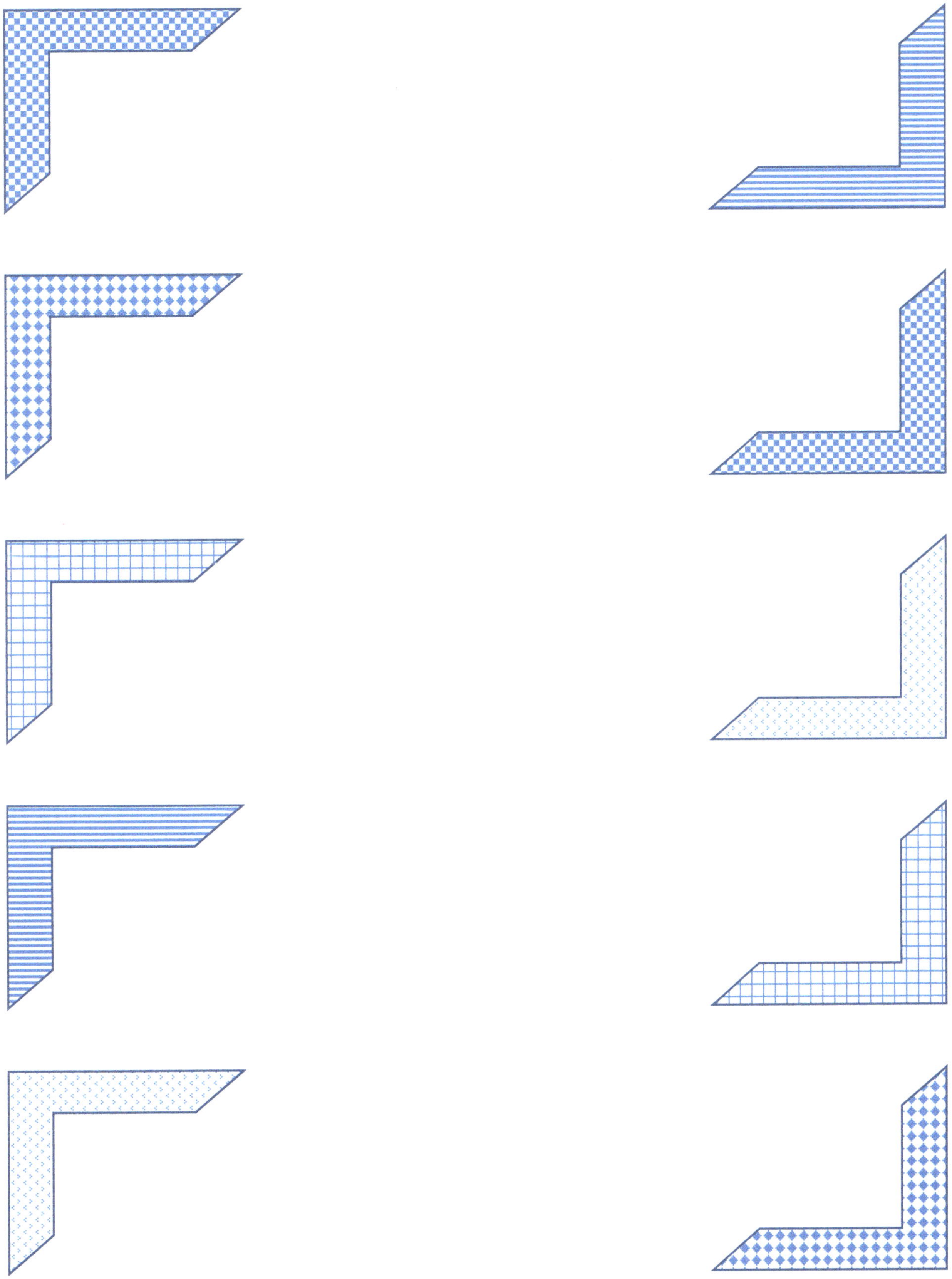

UNIT 6

Faces

Lesson 4.1 Drawing Faces

In this lesson, we will be learning how to draw faces. Faces can be difficult, but we will take small steps to learn how to draw everything. We will practice first with cartoon like drawings

We will go over some tips before we start.

1. Don't press too hard when drawing. If you draw softly, it will be easier to erase later.
2. Try not to draw one continuous line. It can be very difficult to draw something correct on the first try. It is easier to make short soft lines to draw.
3. Always make sure your pencil is sharpened but not too sharp. The sharper your pencil is, the darker your line will be.

In this lesson, you will need pencils, pencil sharpener, eraser, and colored pencils. Look for the icon next to each project to determine what to use

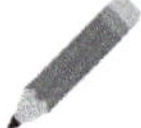 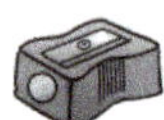 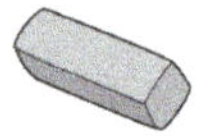 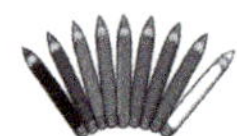

Exercise 1

Drawing Your Face. 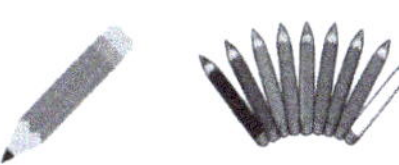

Let's start by having you draw your face. Do you remember in the last lesson how we used different lines and we used those lines to make the drawing of our house more details. Try to remember to use different types of lines when you draw the face as well.

In the space provided, use your pencil or colored pencils to draw a picture of just your face

Remember to sign your name to your work

Does your picture look something like one of the pictures below? We will work on how to improve your drawings.

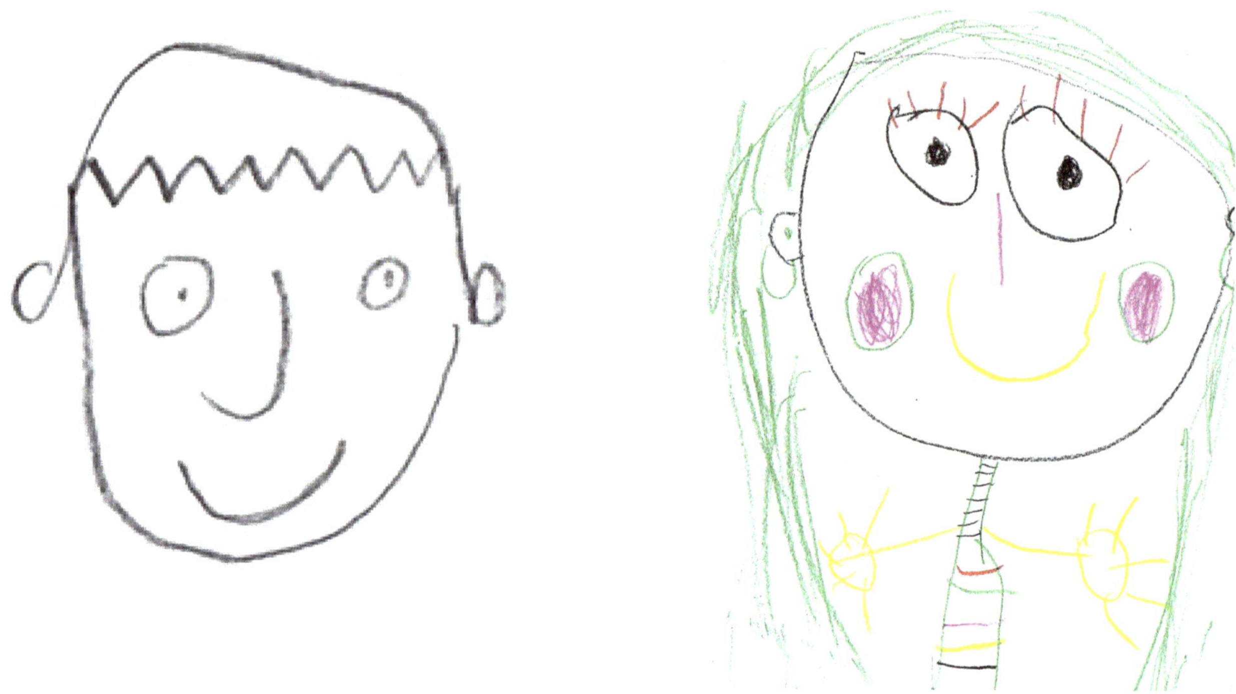

Let's start by looking at different ways we can make eyes. Again, we will begin with drawing eyes that are not super realistic just to practice. Which eyes look sad? Which ones look angry, scared, surprised? When drawing eyes, you can make the person show certain emotions

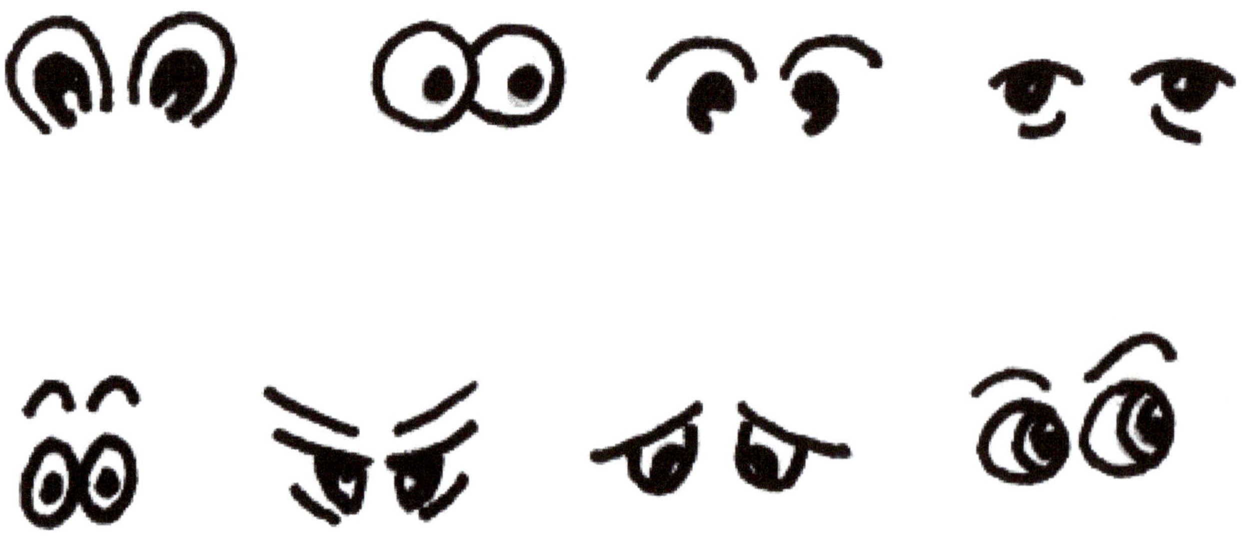

Exercise 2

Practice Drawing Eyes.

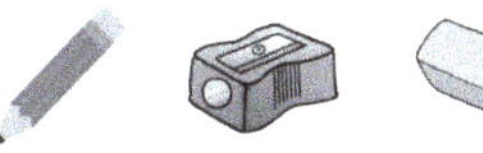

In the spaces provided, use your pencil to practice drawing eyes similar to what was on the previous page

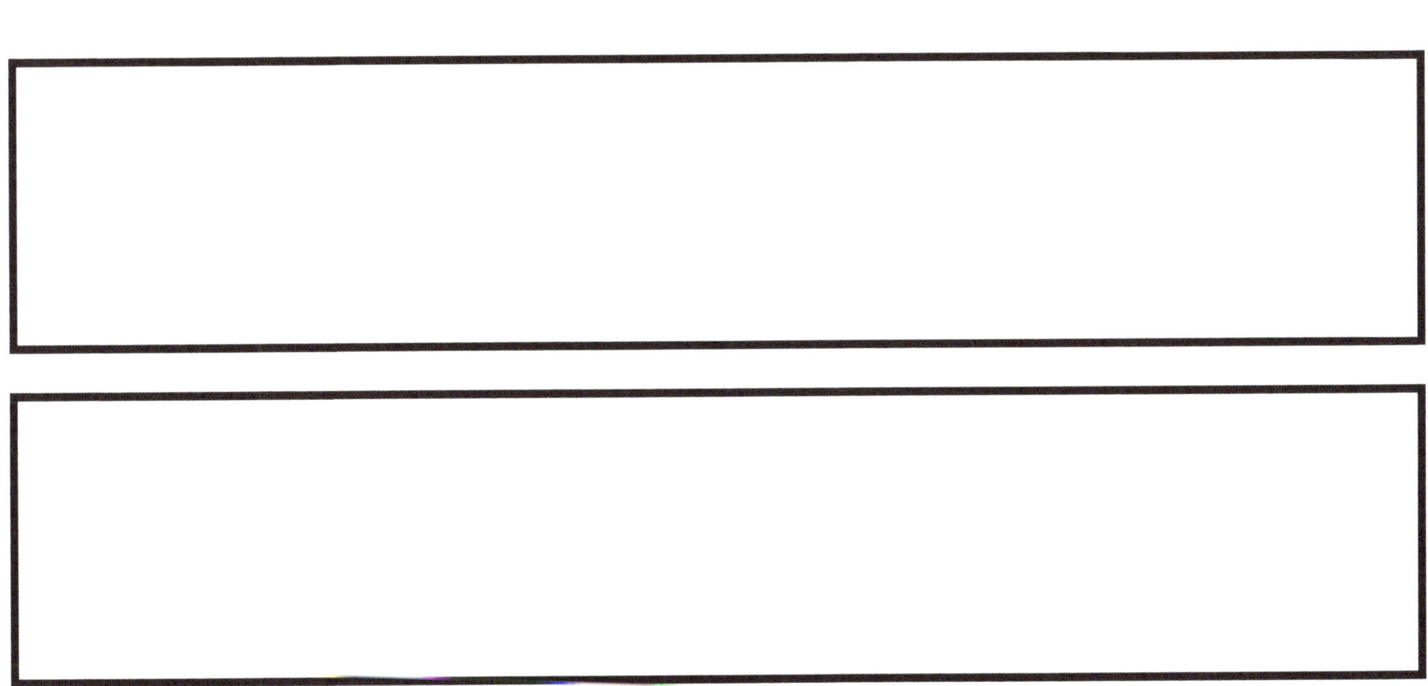

Great! Now let's look at a couple noses.

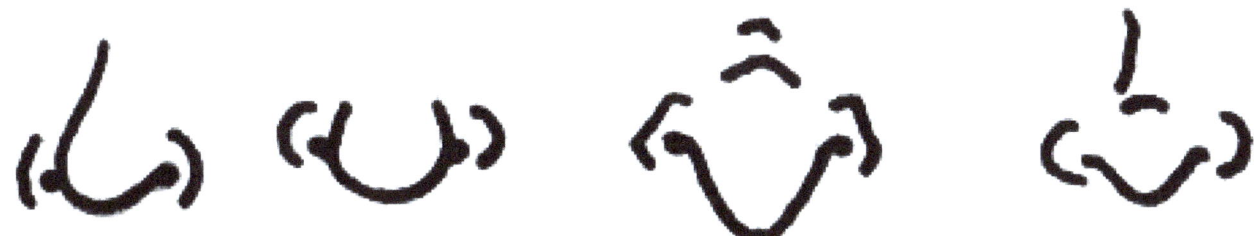

When drawing a nose, the easiest way is to draw the bottom part first, then draw a small arc on each side, draw a small rounded arc on top and finally, draw twoovals for nostrils at the end of each side of the bottom part

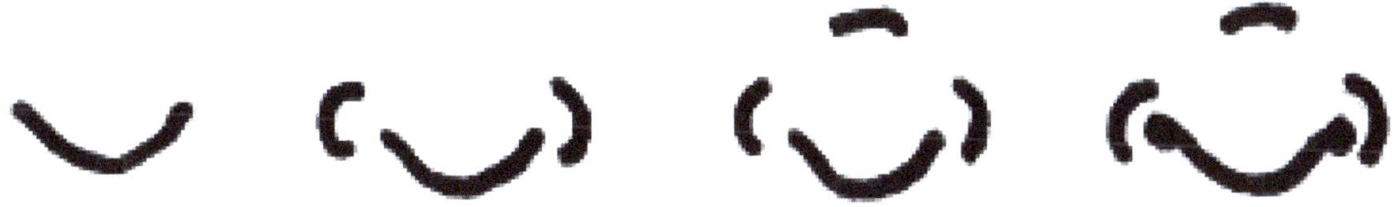

Exercise 3

Practice Drawing Noses. 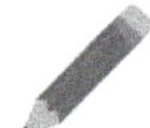 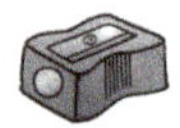 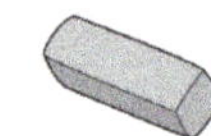

In the spaces provided, use your pencil to practice drawing noses similar to what was on the previous page

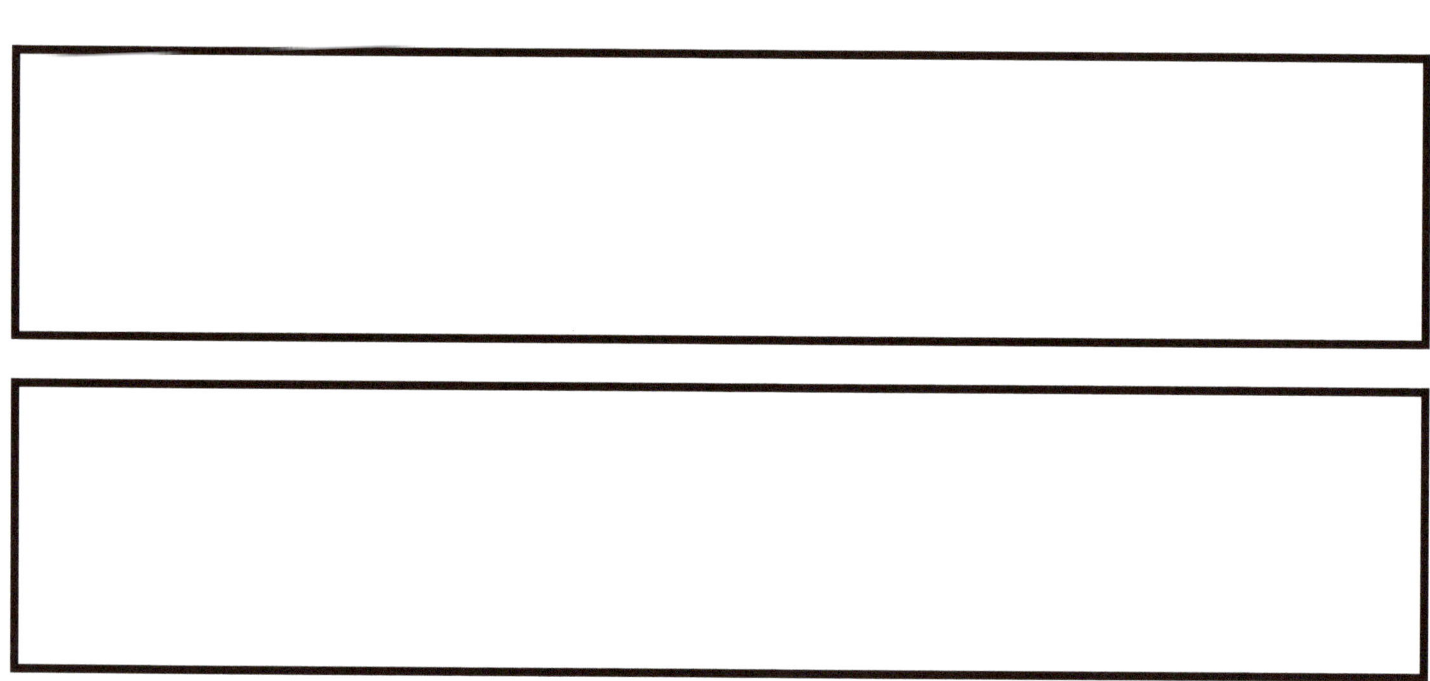

Great! Now let's look at a couple mouths.

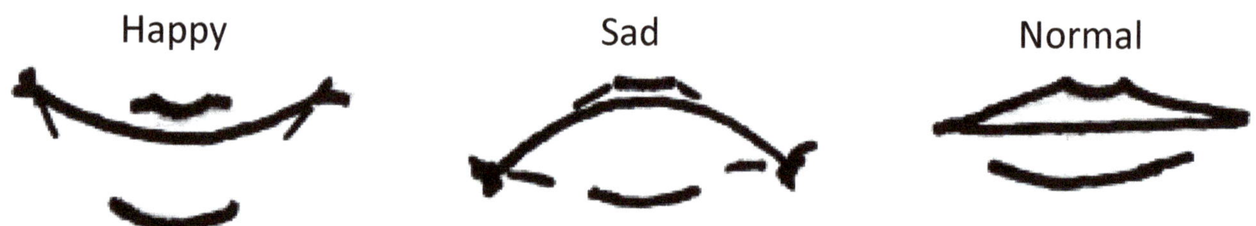

Instead of drawing one line for the mouth, do you see how we drew the line for the middle of the mouth where the lips meet? Then we added a small curve underneath to show the bottom lip and a small line, like a stretched out, upside down W for the top lip. We didn't have to draw the whole lip, just enough to show it's there.

Exercise 4

Practice Drawing a Mouth. 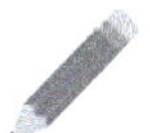 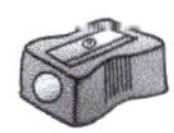 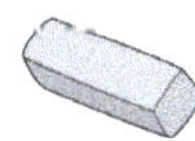

In the spaces provided, use your pencil to practice drawing mouths similar to what was on the previous page

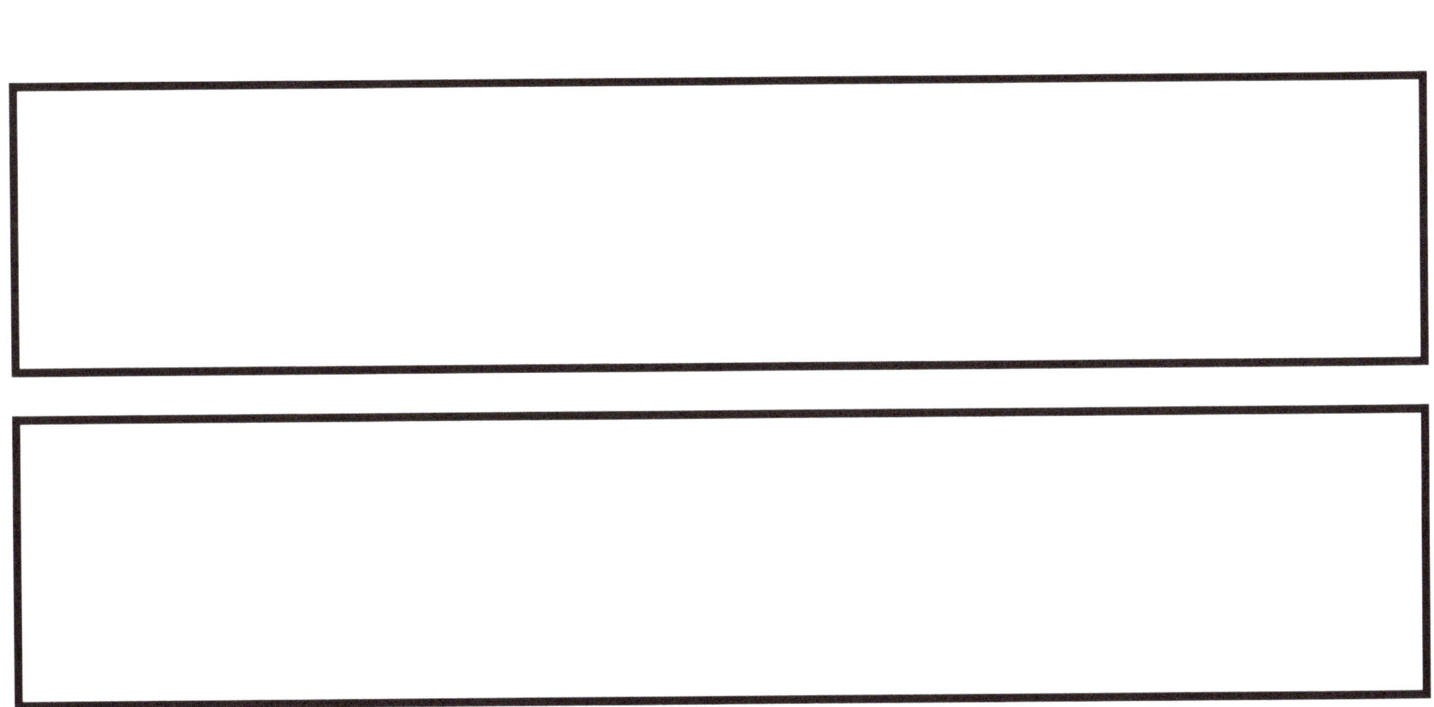

Great! Try to combine what we learned to finish off the face of these people below

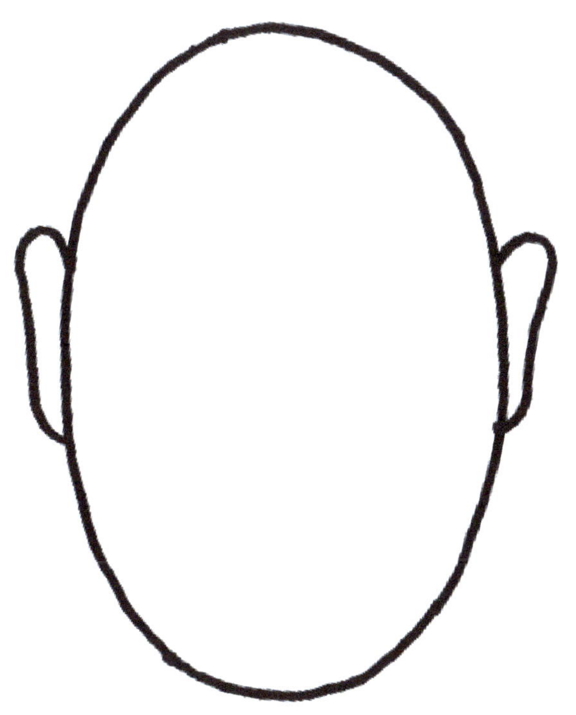

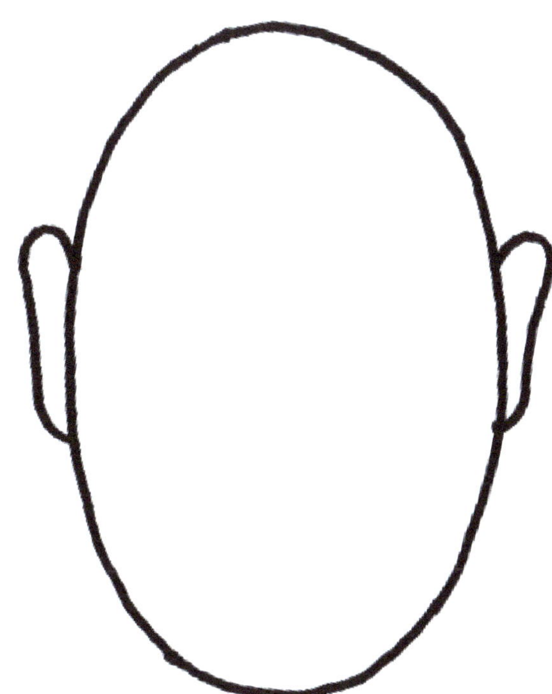

Now we are going to learn how to draw hair. When drawing hair, do not try to draw every piece of hair on a person's head. Think of hair as a whole object and not individual pieces of hair.

Do not try to draw every strand of hair. Also, the hair doesn't sit right on top of the head. It grows all around the head.

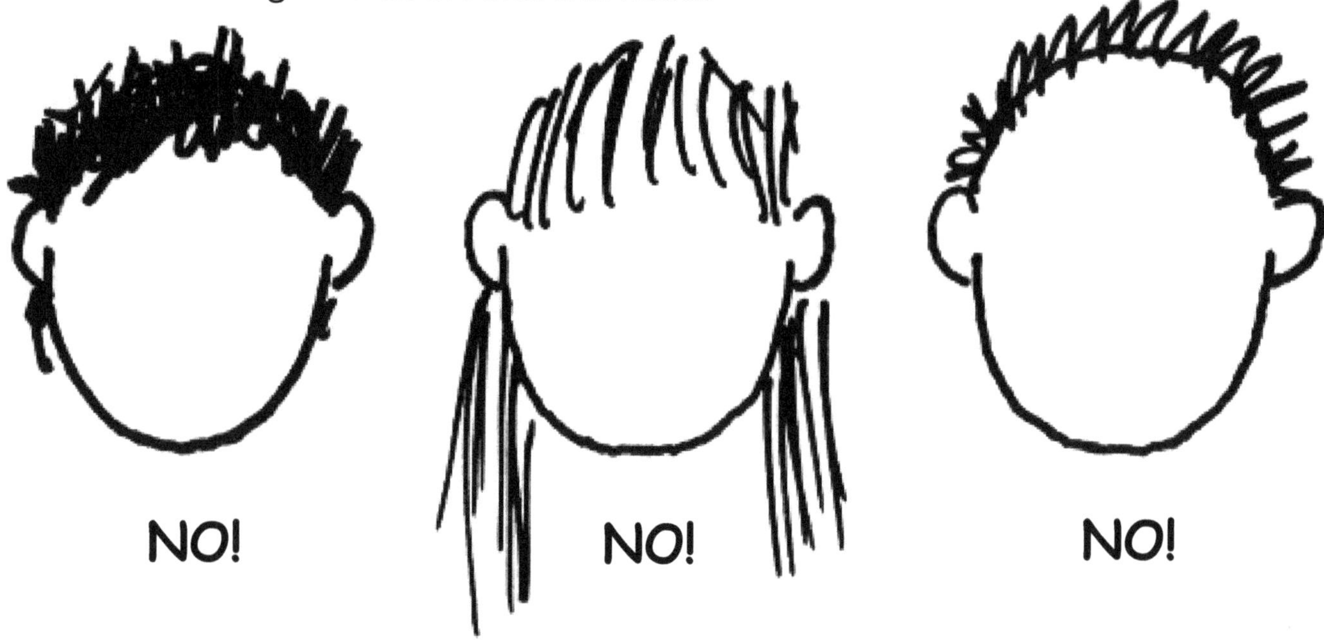

Think of the hair as a one object, almost like a hat that goes over the top of your head. Do you see in the images below how I just outlined the hair and then drew a few lines to show which way the hair is going? You can see if it is straight hair or wavy hair by these lines.

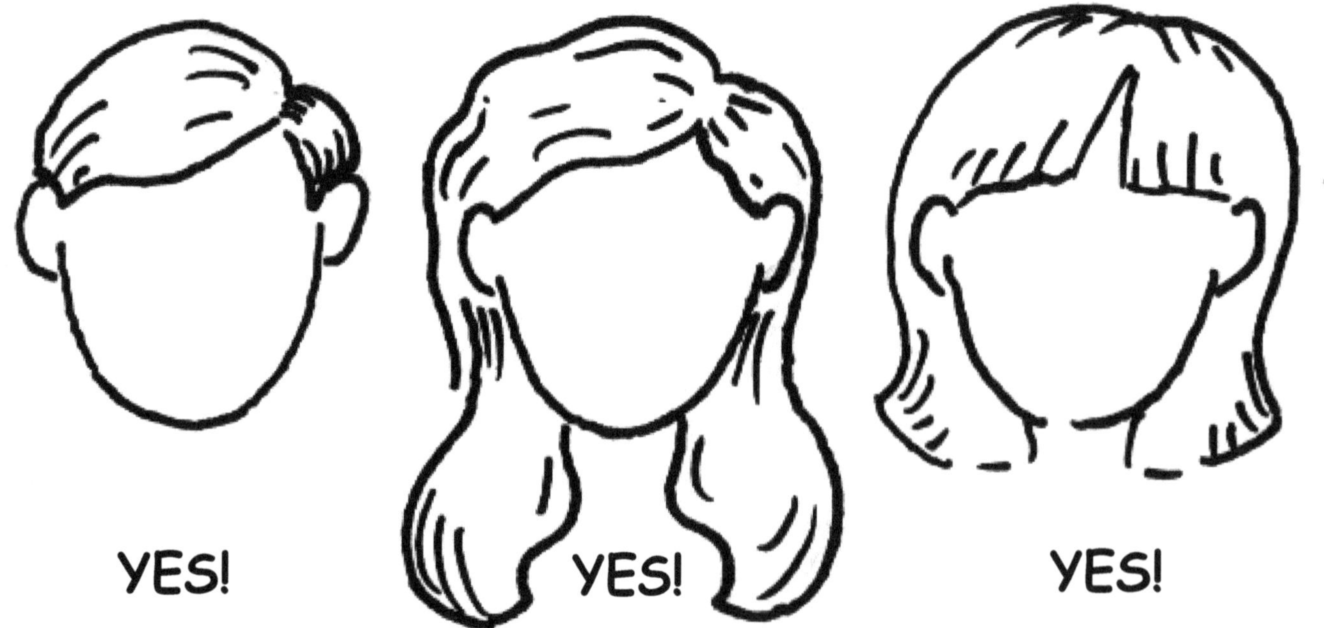

Project 1

With your pencil, finish drawing these faces by the description given for each person.

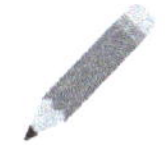 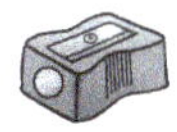 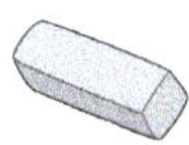

More faces can be found on pages 154-156

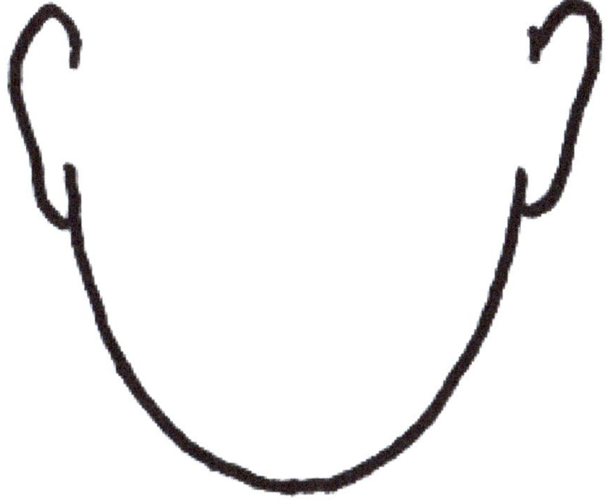

Draw this person sad and with long hair

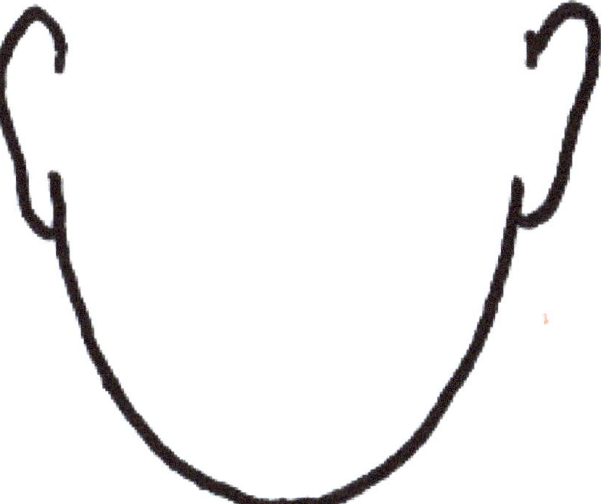

Draw this person happy and with short hair

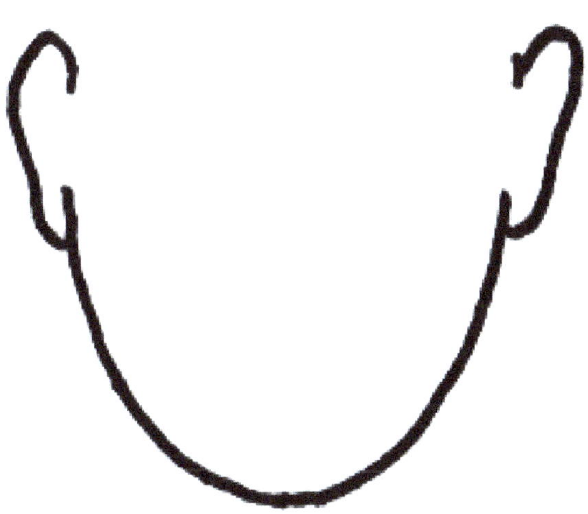

Draw this person angry with medium length hair

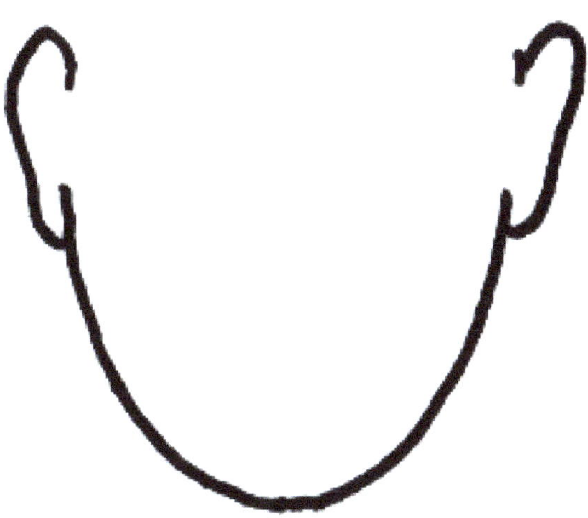

Draw this person normal with no hair

Lesson 6.2 Drawing Faces From the Side

So far, we learned how to draw eyes, nose, mouth, and hair from the front. But what if the person is turned? How would we draw someone's face from the side? In this short lesson, we will practice drawing the side of the face. This can be difficult so don't get frustrated if it doesn't turn out correctly right away. That's why we practice.

Here are a few common mistakes when drawing the side of the face.

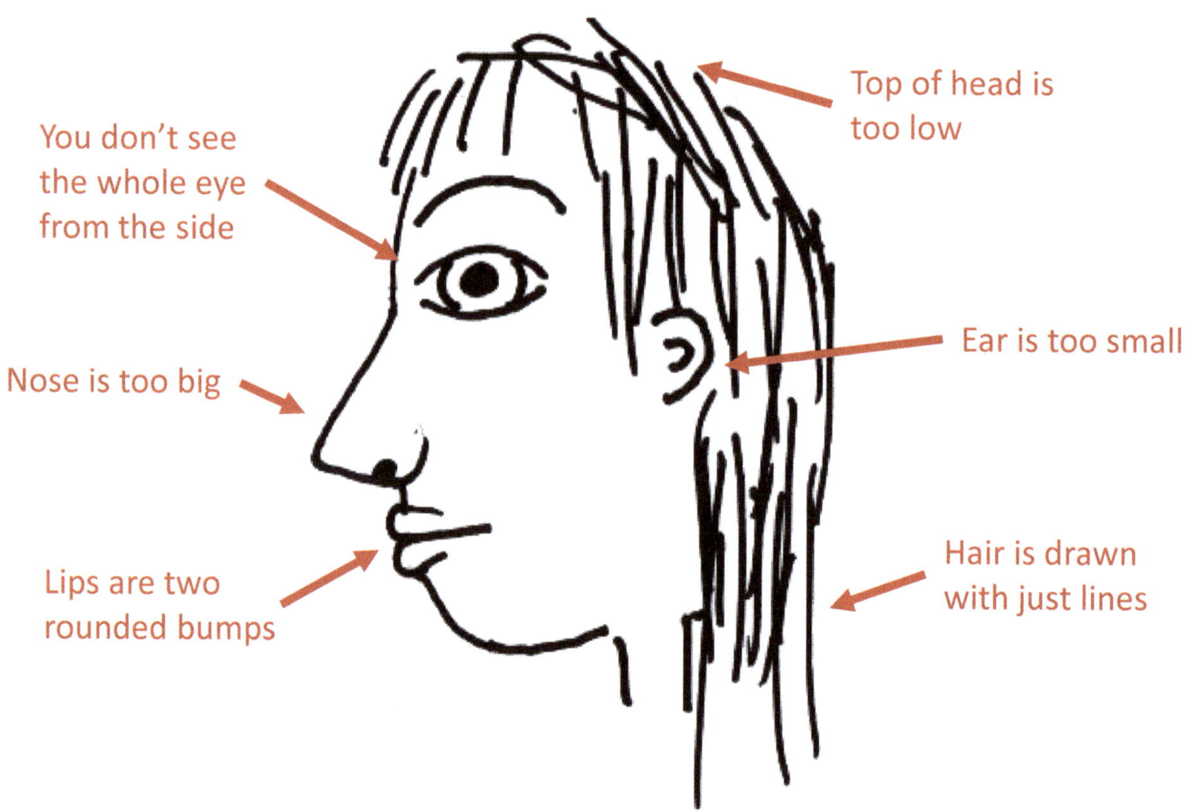

Let's learn how to fix some of these problems on the next page

Exercise 4

Practice drawing parts of the face. 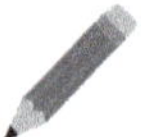

When drawing the eyes from the side, we will not see the whole eye. Look at the image below and then try drawing it a couple times in the space provided

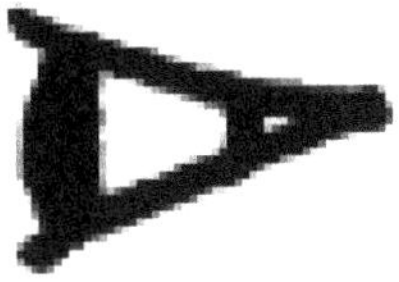

When drawing the nose, don't make it too big. Also, the upper lip attaches to the bottom of the nose at a slight curve. Look at the image below and then try drawing it a couple times in the space provided

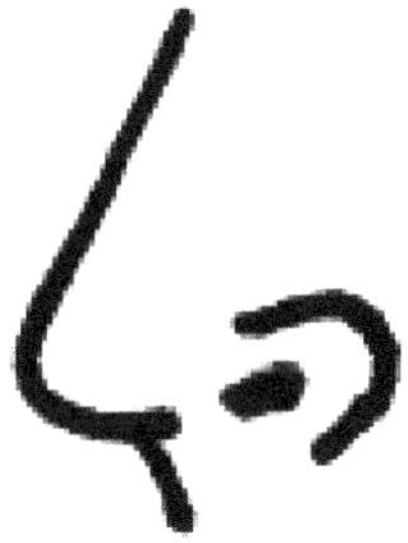

When drawing the mouth and chin, the upper lip is at an angle and the lower lip is rounded. Do you see how the chin curves in from the lip and then out for the chin? Look at the image below and then try drawing it a couple times in the space provided

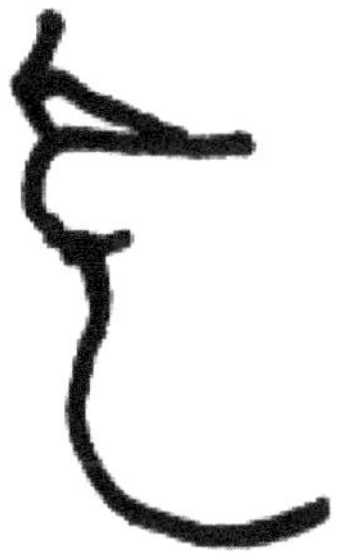

Exercise 5

Practice Drawing the Face from the Side. 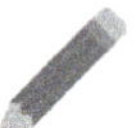 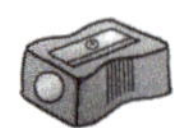 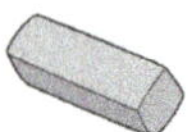

Look at the image below. Does it look better than the first image we saw? We will add hair to the person later but, for now, we are just looking at the eyes, nose, mouth and chin.

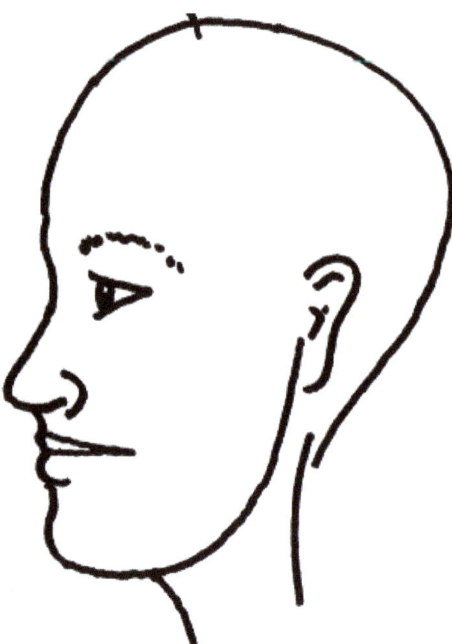

Use what you practices to try and finish the faces below. Don't draw too big or else you won't be able to fit everything in

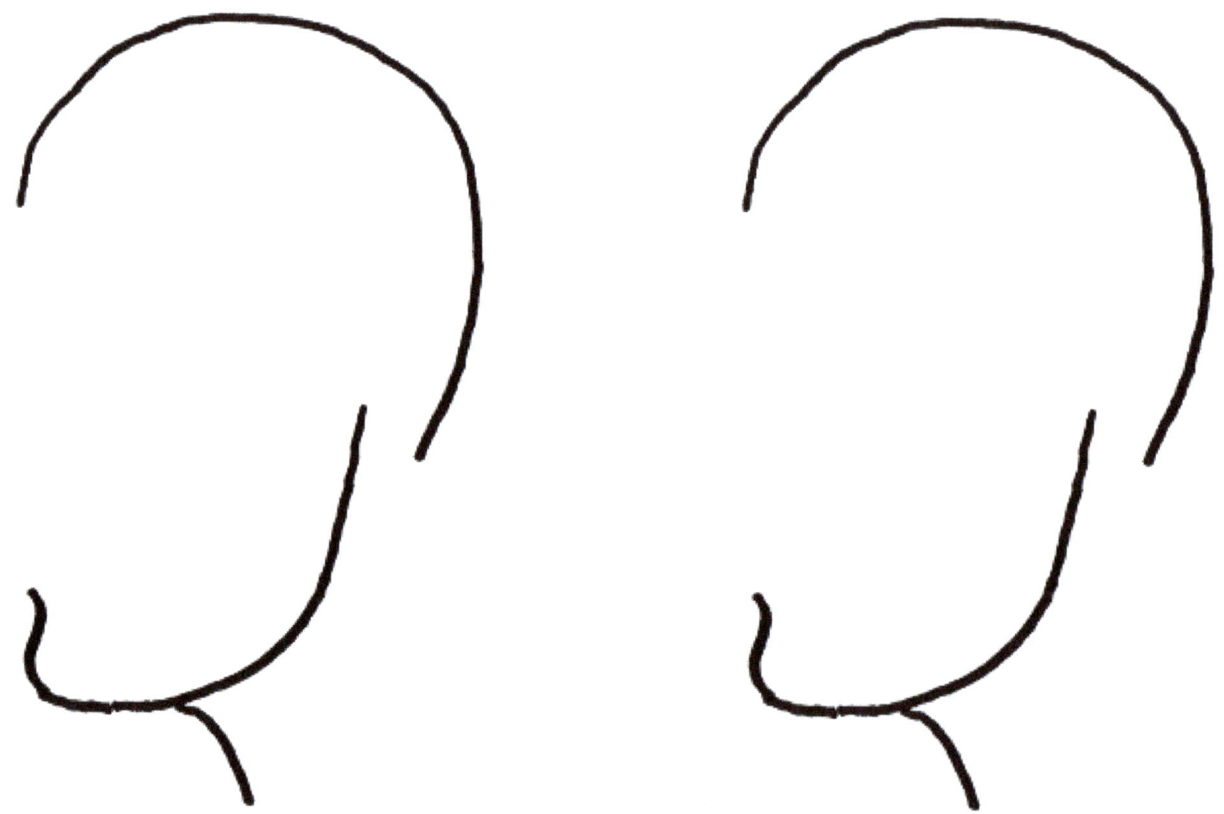

Now let's draw some hair on these people. Used what you learned from the previous exercises with hair to draw different types of hair on the people's heads. We will practice this more in later books.

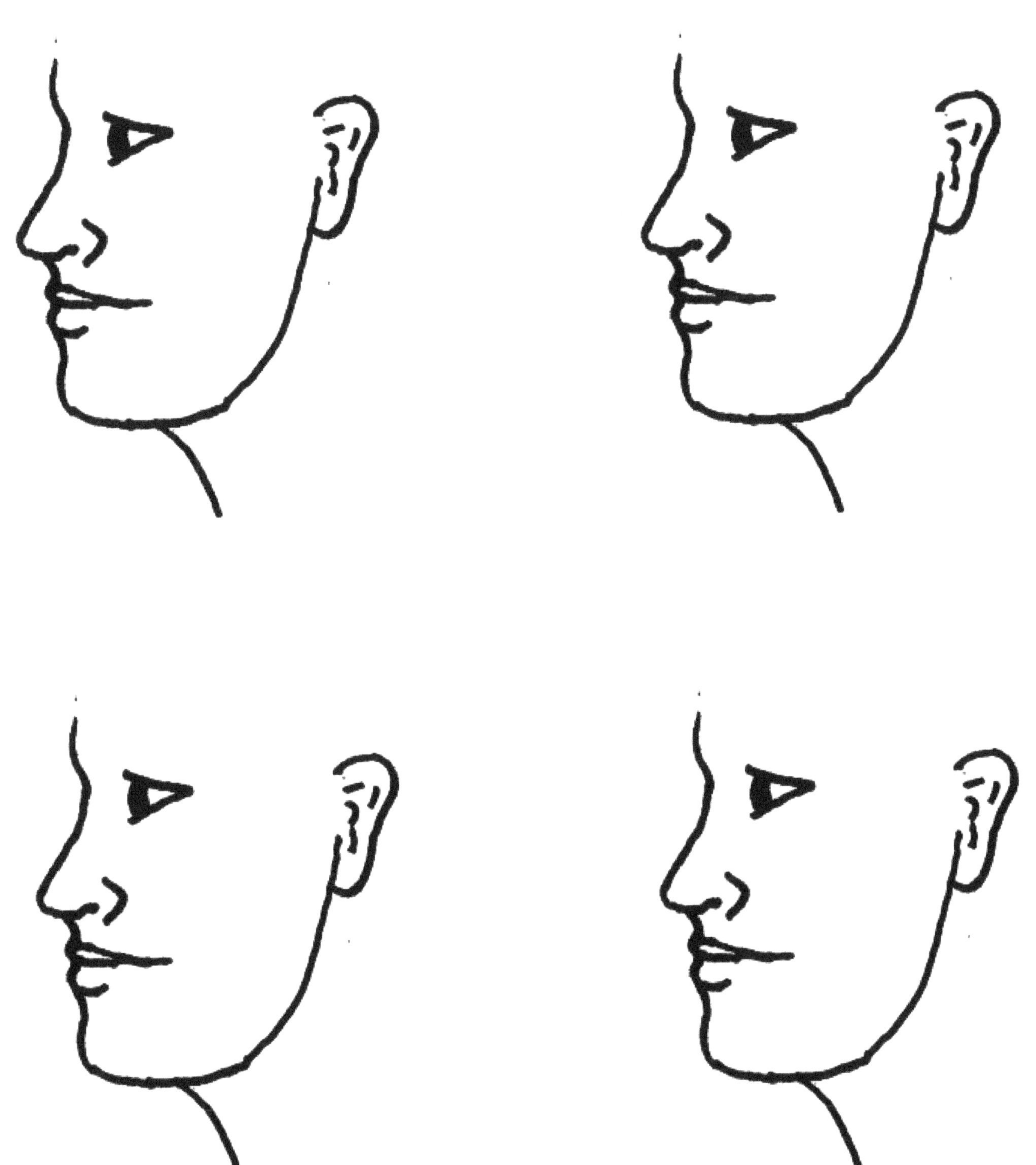

Project 2

Draw your Face from the Front

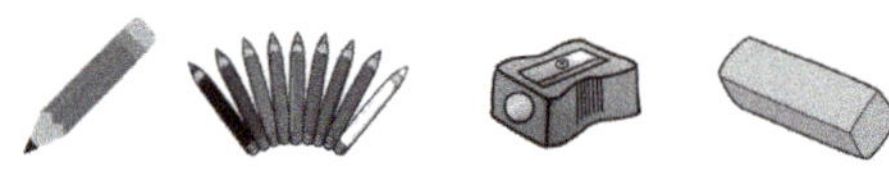

Take what you learned in this lesson and draw you face again from the front. If you need to go back and look at the exercise to see how to draw everything, do it. The best way is to look at how to do it and practice. When you are done, compare with your first drawing.

Remember to sign your name to your work

Project 2

Draw your Face from the Side

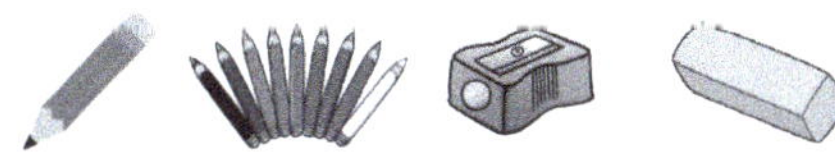

Take what you learned in this lesson and draw you face from the side. If you need to go back and look at the exercise to see how to draw everything, do it. The best way is to look at how to do it and practice.

Remember to sign your name to your work

Art History Lesson Six

Each lesson we will go over some Art History that follow what we have learned in each lesson. During this lesson, we learned about drawing faces

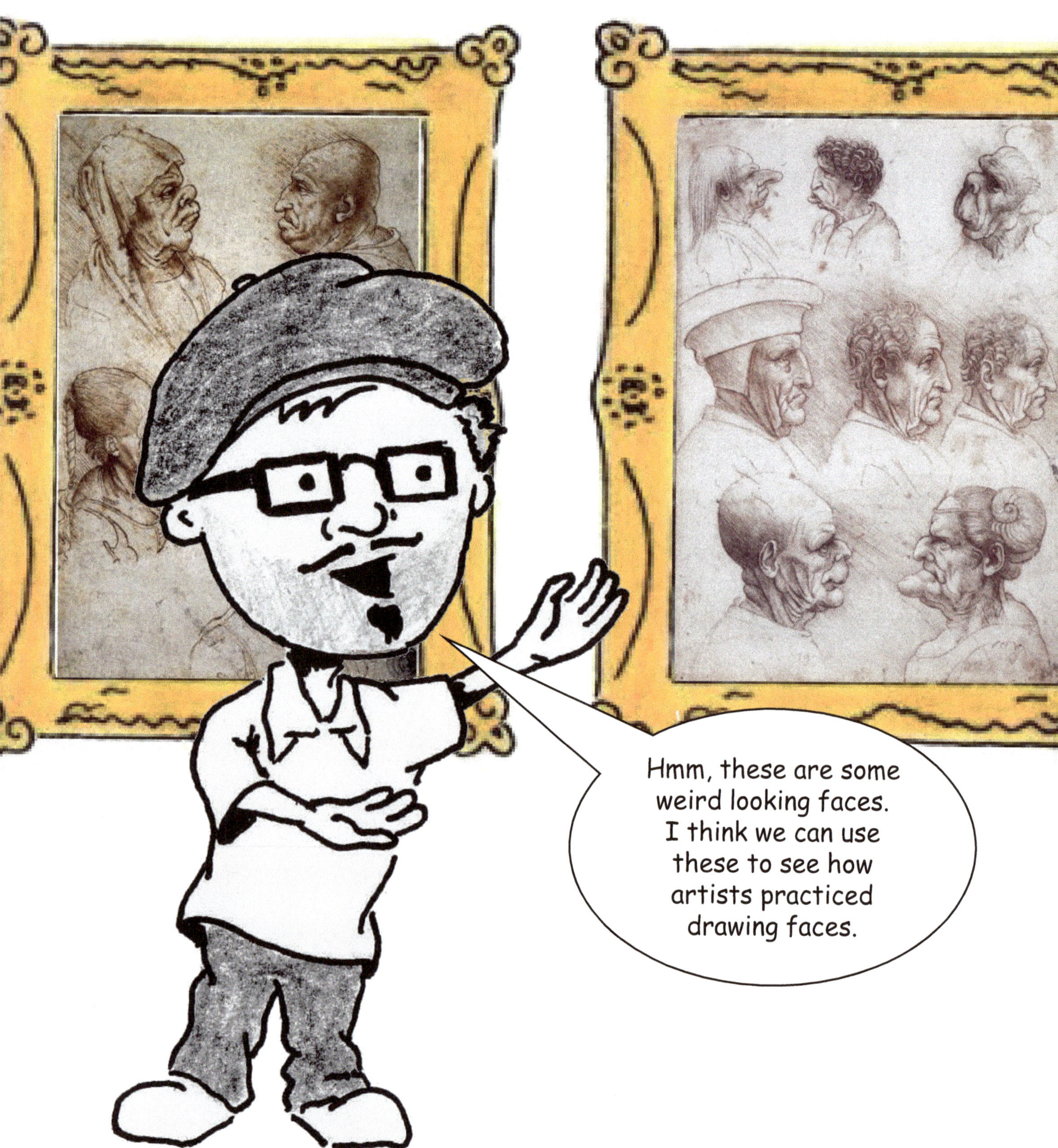

Leonardo da Vinci

Leonardo Da Vinci was an Italian painter in the 1500's. Aside from Painting, he did lots and lots of drawings. He would draw things he saw outside like birds and nature. He would draw new inventions that he thought of and, he would draw a lot of faces. By practicing drawing so much, he became better and better and is known as one of the greatest artists.

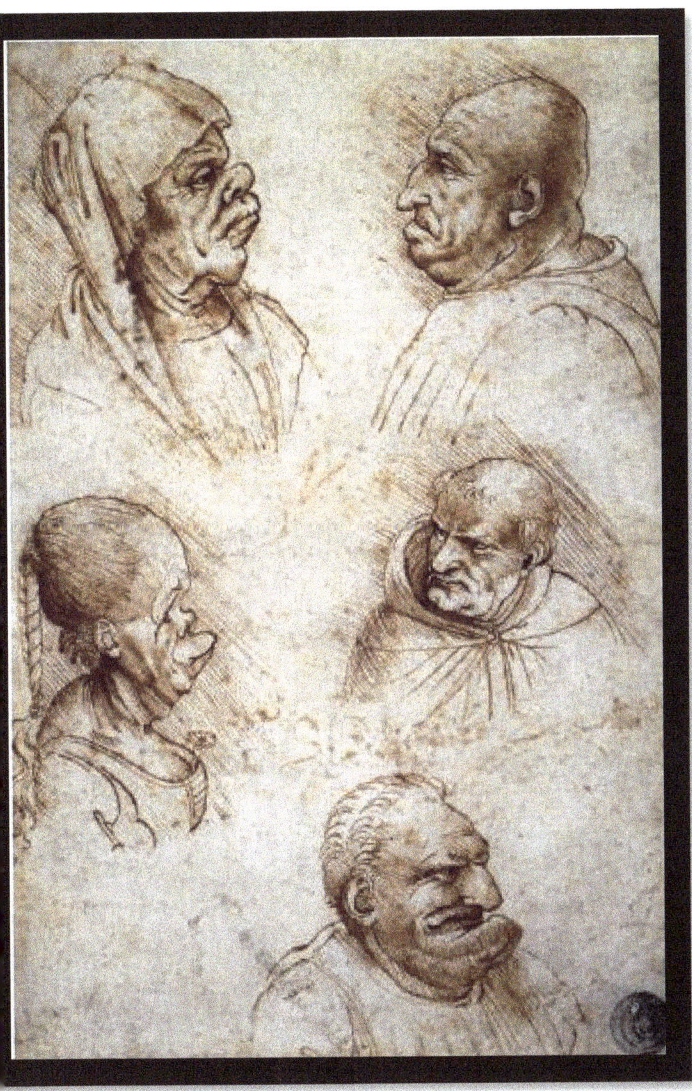

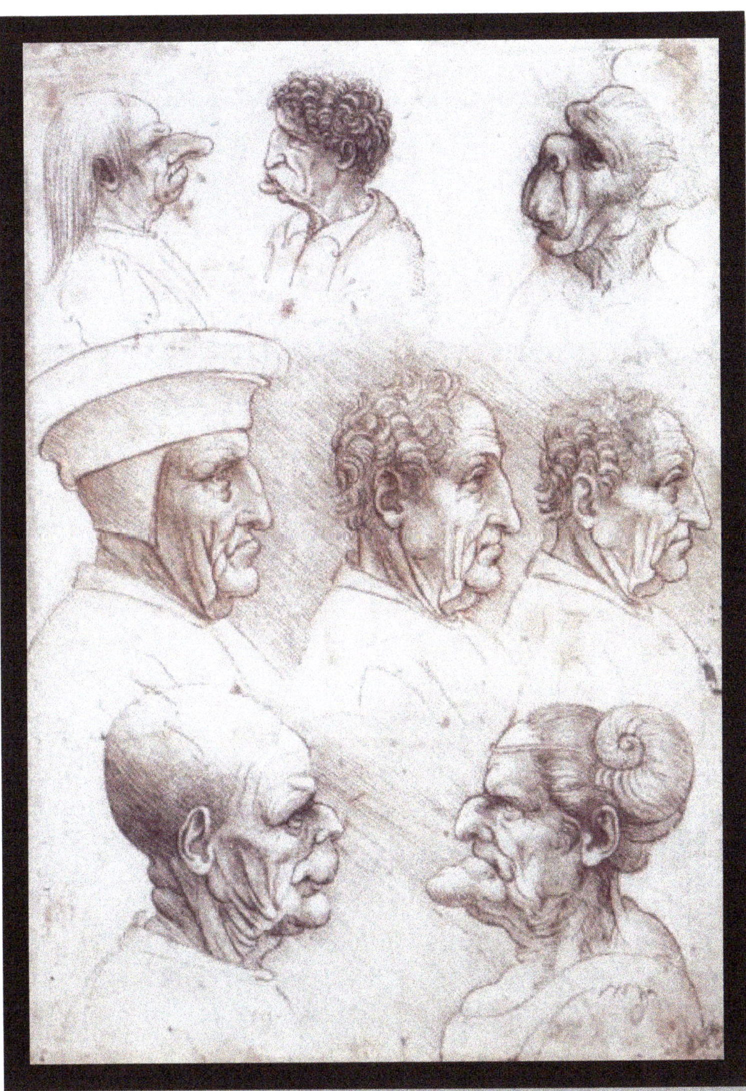

These are some of the drawing Leonardo Da Vinci did. Look how he was drawing weird faces. He was experimenting by drawing different parts of the face bigger. Some have a large nose, some have big chins. What else do you see that looks funny?

Art History Project

Try to draw some funny faces like Leonardo Da Vinci. Maybe make different parts of the face bigger than others. Try different things.

Remember to sign your name to your work

Chapter Fun

Uh oh! Art Joe has lost his face! Put the correct eyes and mouth on him to make him sad, surprised, and angry

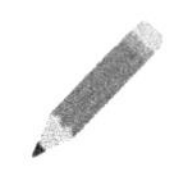

Make Art Joe Sad

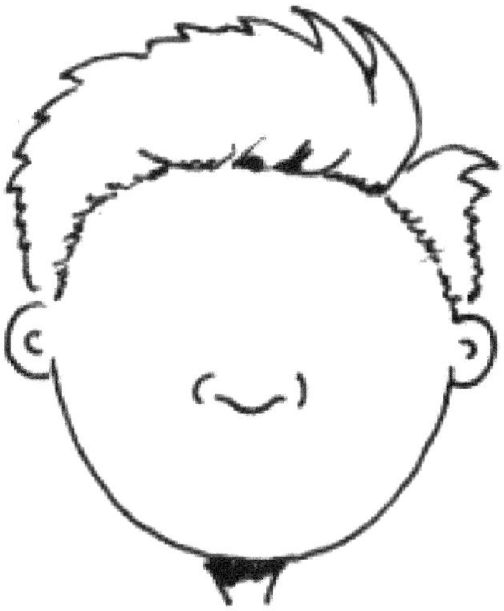

Make Art Joe Surprised

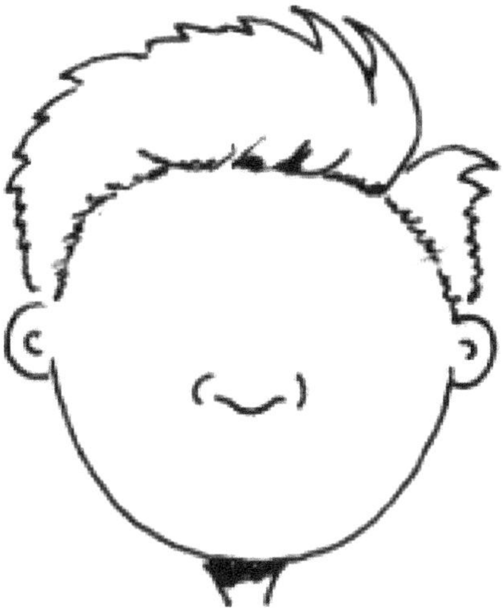

Make Art Joe Angry

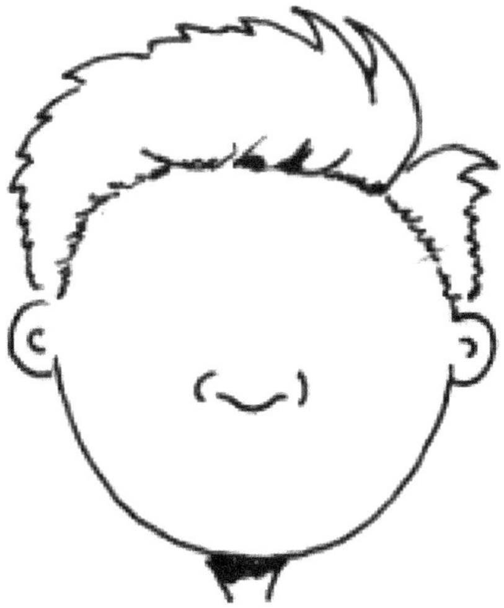

Use these eyes

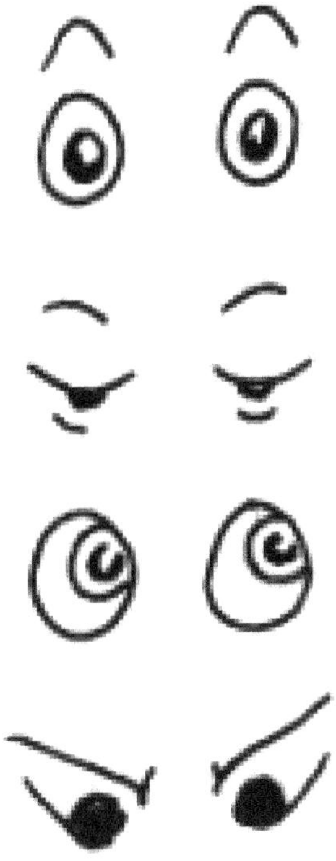

Use these mouths

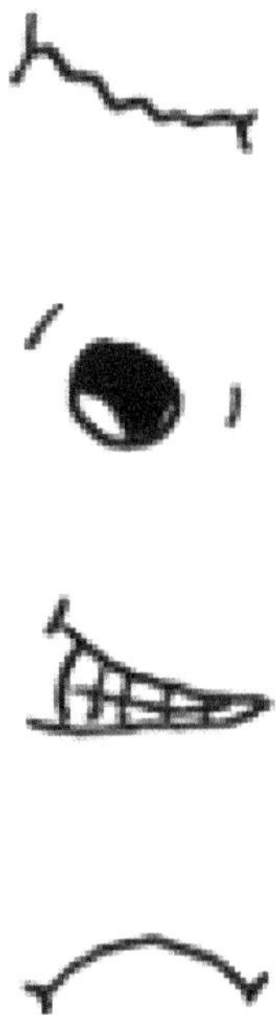

UNIT 7 Perspective

Lesson 7.1 Beginnings of Perspective

Perspective is something you can add to your drawings to make them more realistic. Perspective can make something that is flat look like it is solid. Let's first talk about some terms.

When talking about something that is flat, we use the word **2-Dimensional**. That means it has two directions.

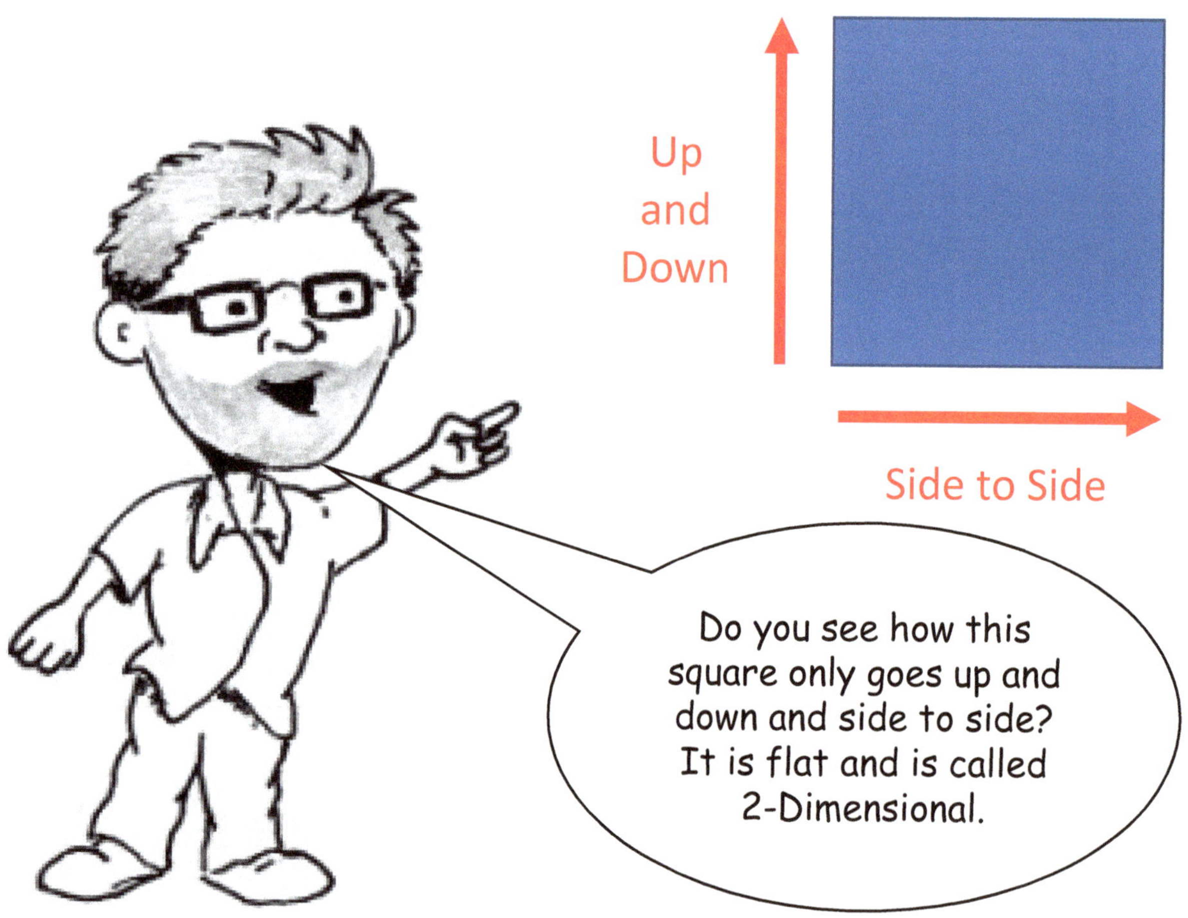

In this lesson, you will need pencils, pencil sharpener, eraser, and colored pencils. Look for the icon next to each project to determine what to use

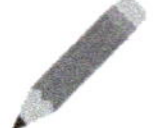 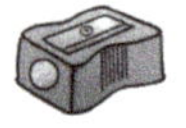 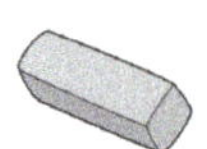 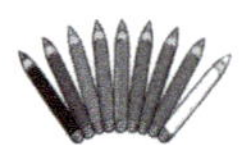

What if we added another side. Then there are now three directions. This is called **3-Dimensional**.

Up and Down

Back to Front

Side to Side

Now that we added another side, it is no longer a square but a cube! This is called 3-Dimensional.

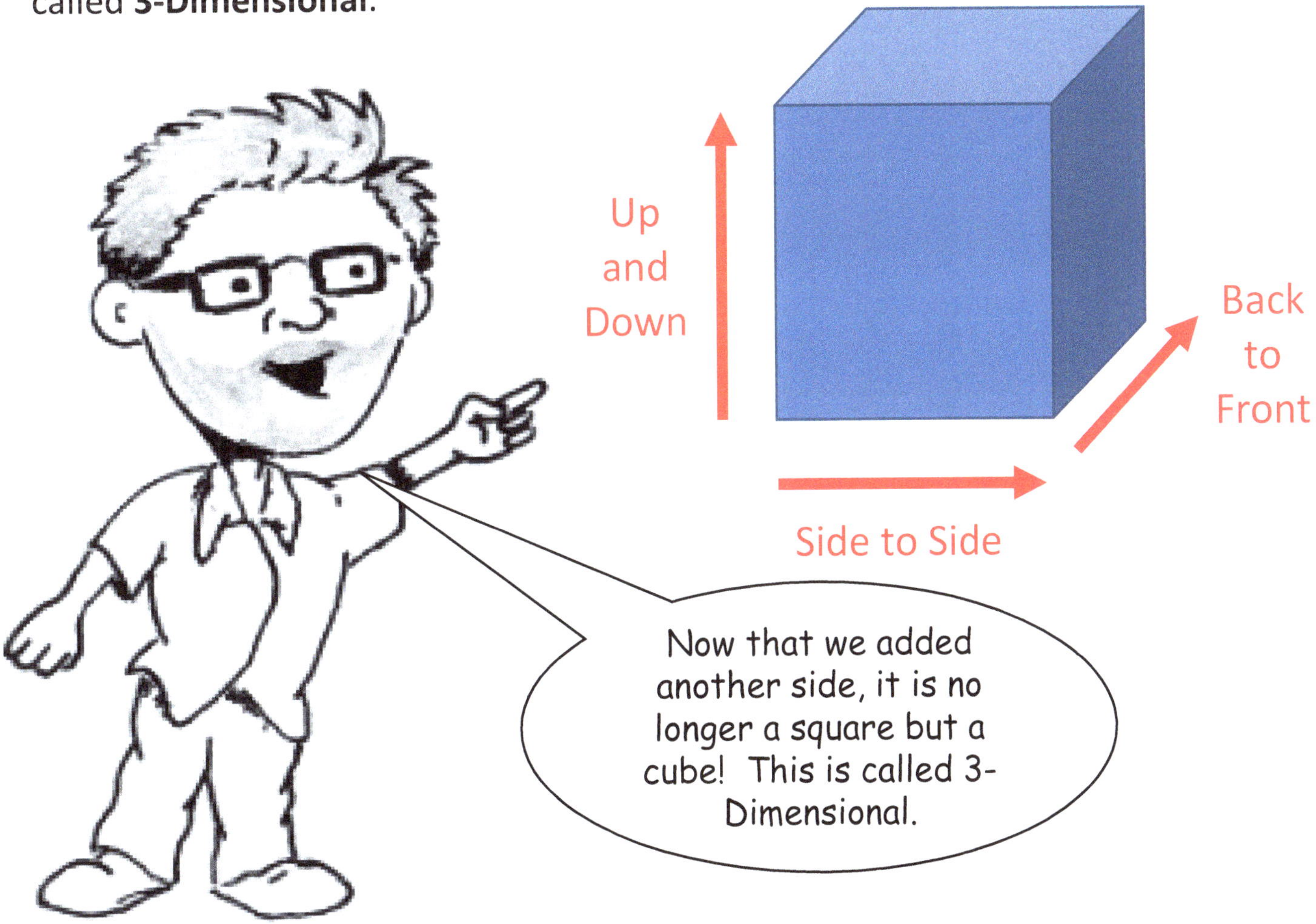

Let's practice drawing 3-Dimensional shapes first.

1. Draw a square
2. Draw another square behind it
3. Now, connect the corners together
4. You can erase the inside lines if you would like

1

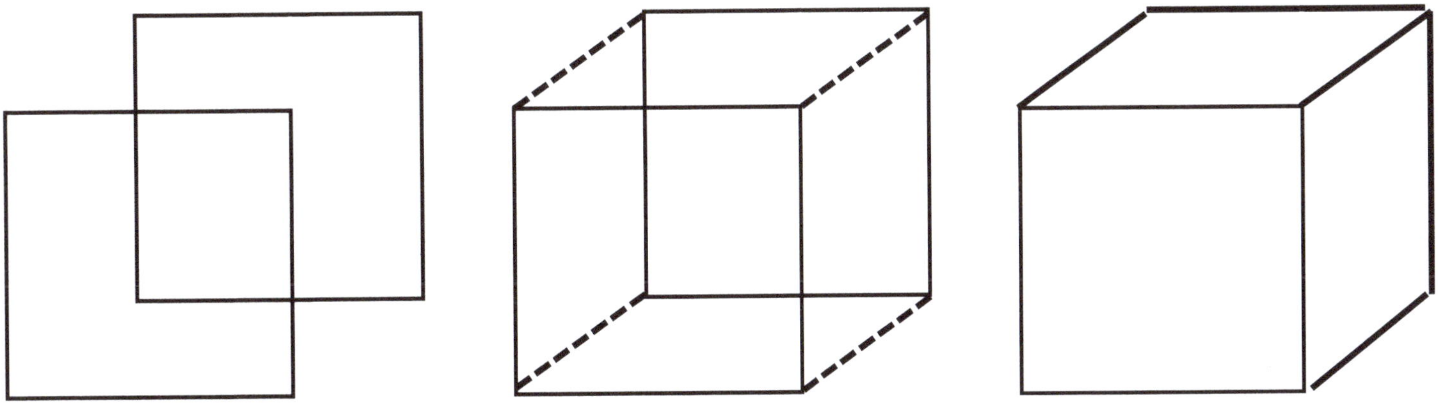

2

3

4

Exercise 1

Practice drawing 3-Dimensional Shapes

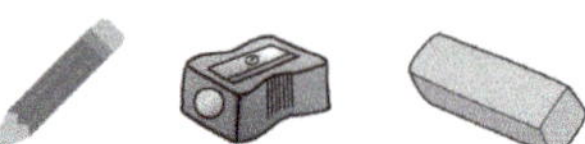

Let's try with other shapes now!

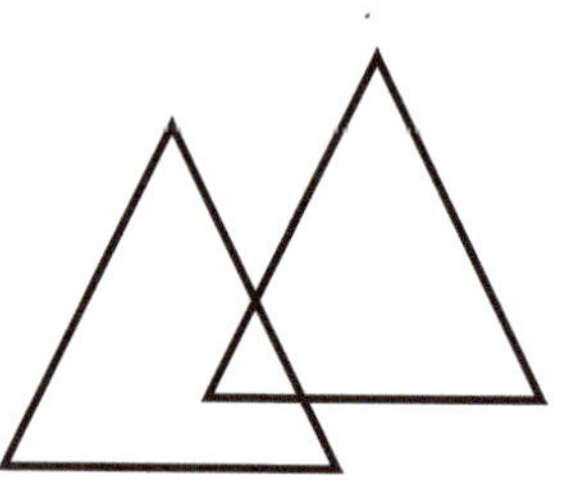

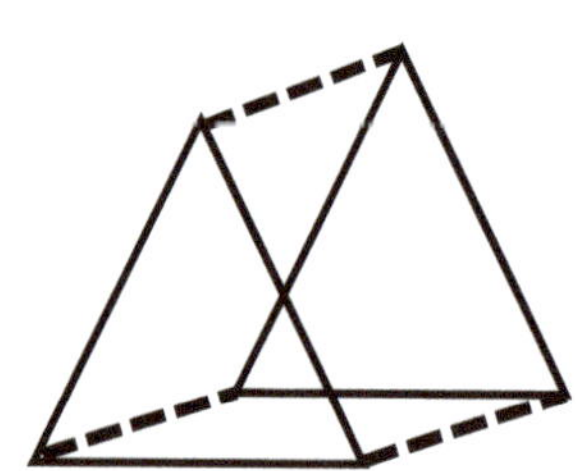

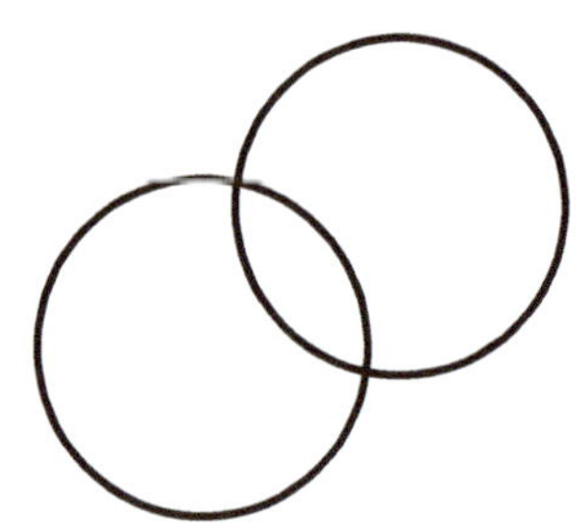

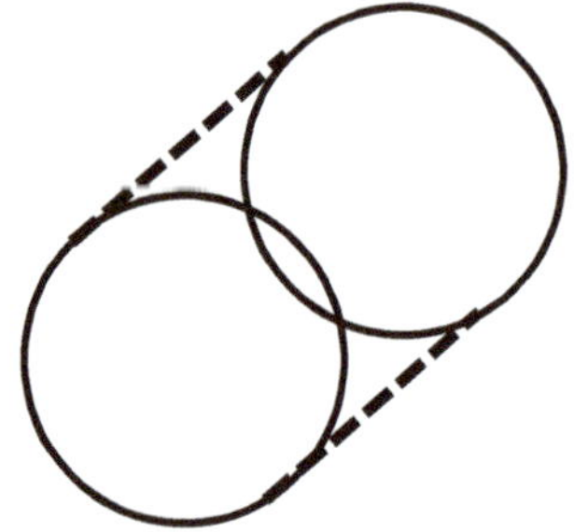

In the space provided, try drawing these shapes.

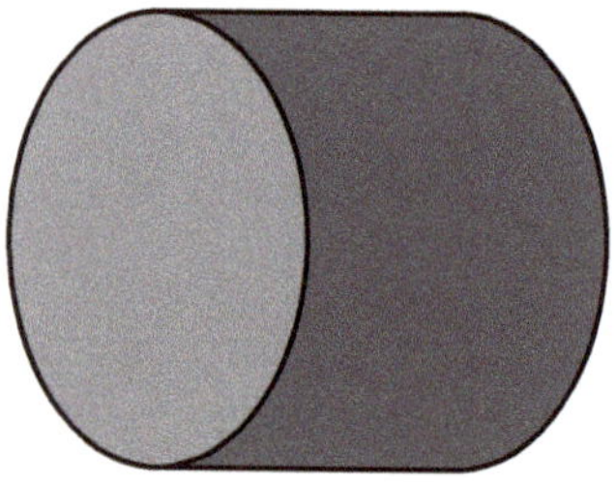

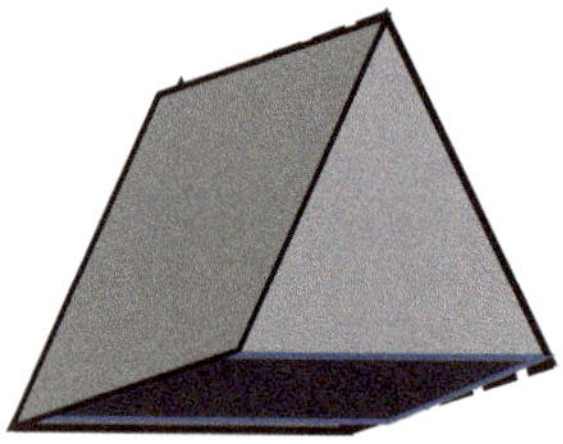

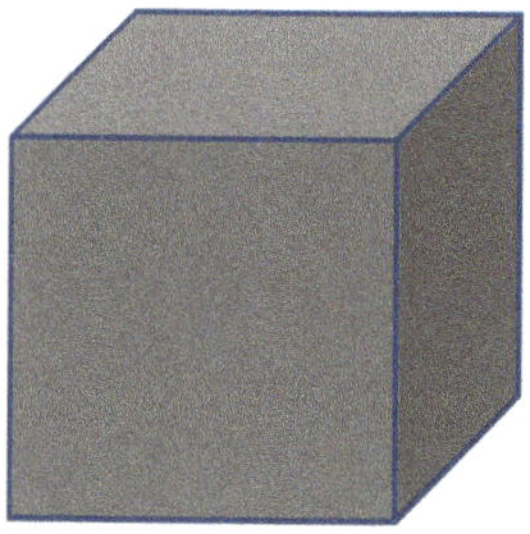

Try to draw different 3-Dimensional Shapes. How would you draw a star? Or a Heart? Follow the same rules when you did the other shapes. On your own, try to make the following shapes

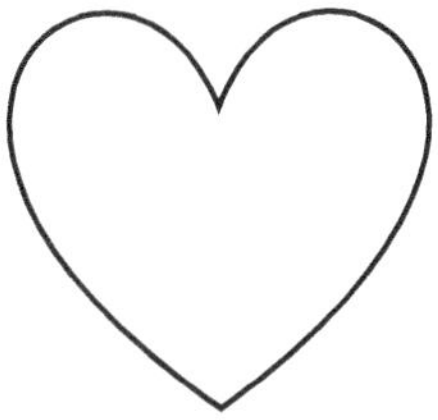

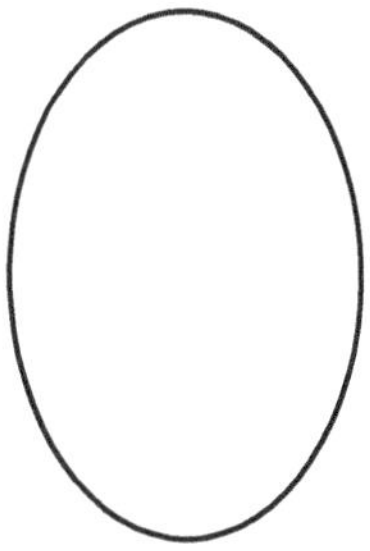

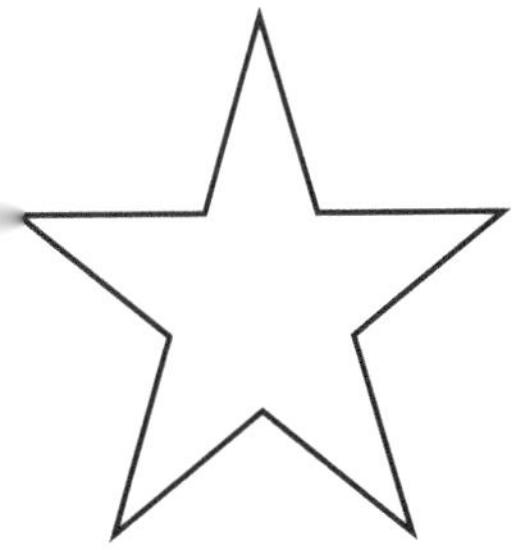

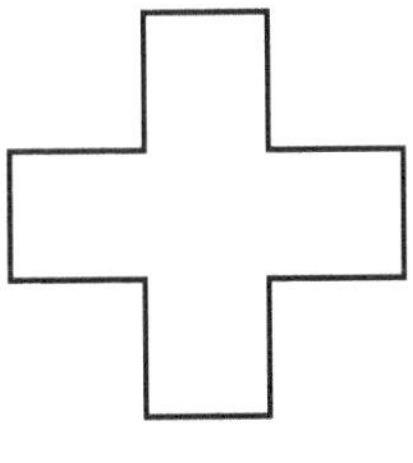

Project 1

Draw you name in 3-Dimensional

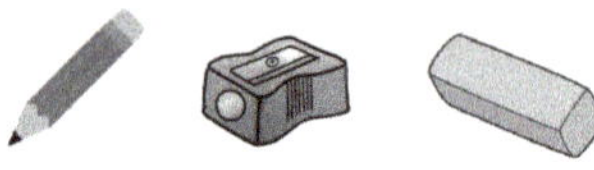

In the space provided, write your name in 3-Dimensional letters like I did. You can color it with markers if you like. Make the front letter lighter and the back part darker

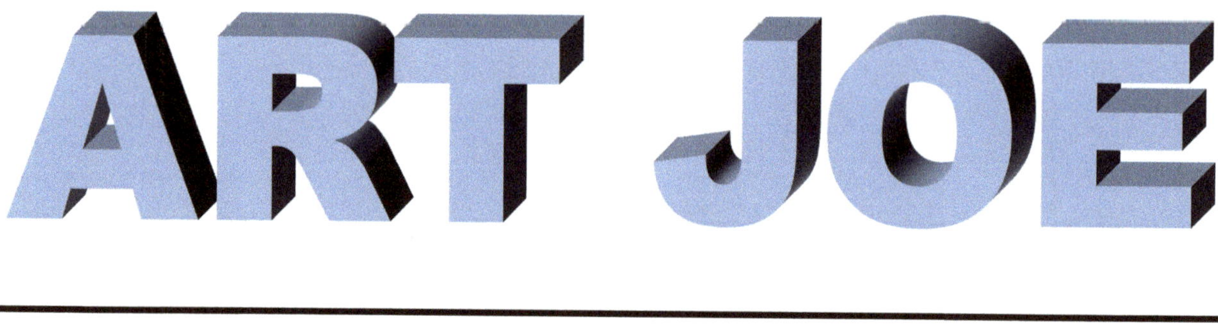

Now we are going to try something new. Instead of having the letter look like a block, we are going to make like it is going all the way back, like this! You can try on the next page

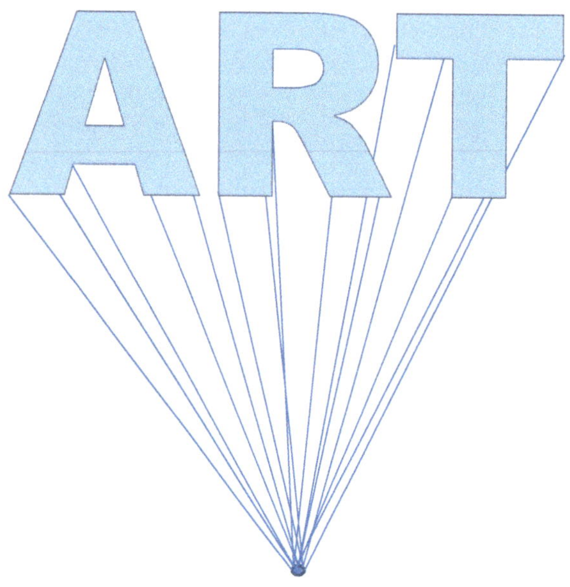

Project 2

Draw you name in 3-Dimensional from single point

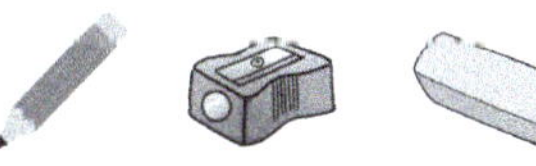

In order to do this, I put a dot at the bottom of the space provided. Draw your name in block letters at the top. Using your ruler, line up the corner of one letter with the dot and draw a straight line. Do this with the corners of each letter. Outline the letter and lines in black marker and color the letters with colored pencils.

You can do this with shapes as well. Practice this on a separate piece of paper.

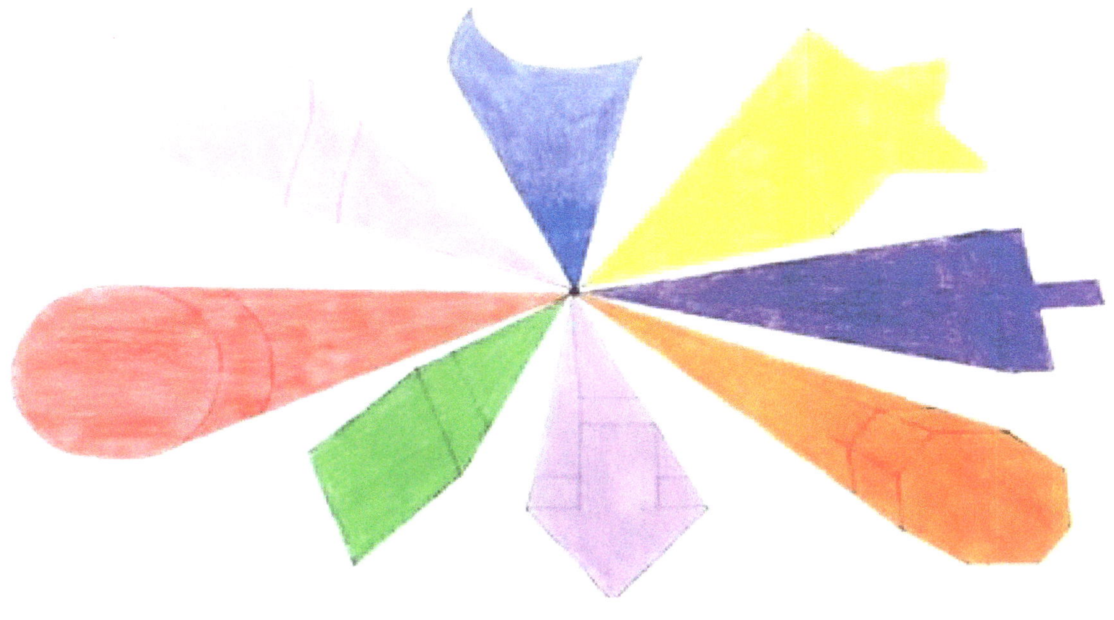

Perspective can also make things seem far away. Below you see two Art Joe's. It looks like one is big and another one is very small. But, If we add perspective to it, like we did to the letters in the previous project, it shows something else.

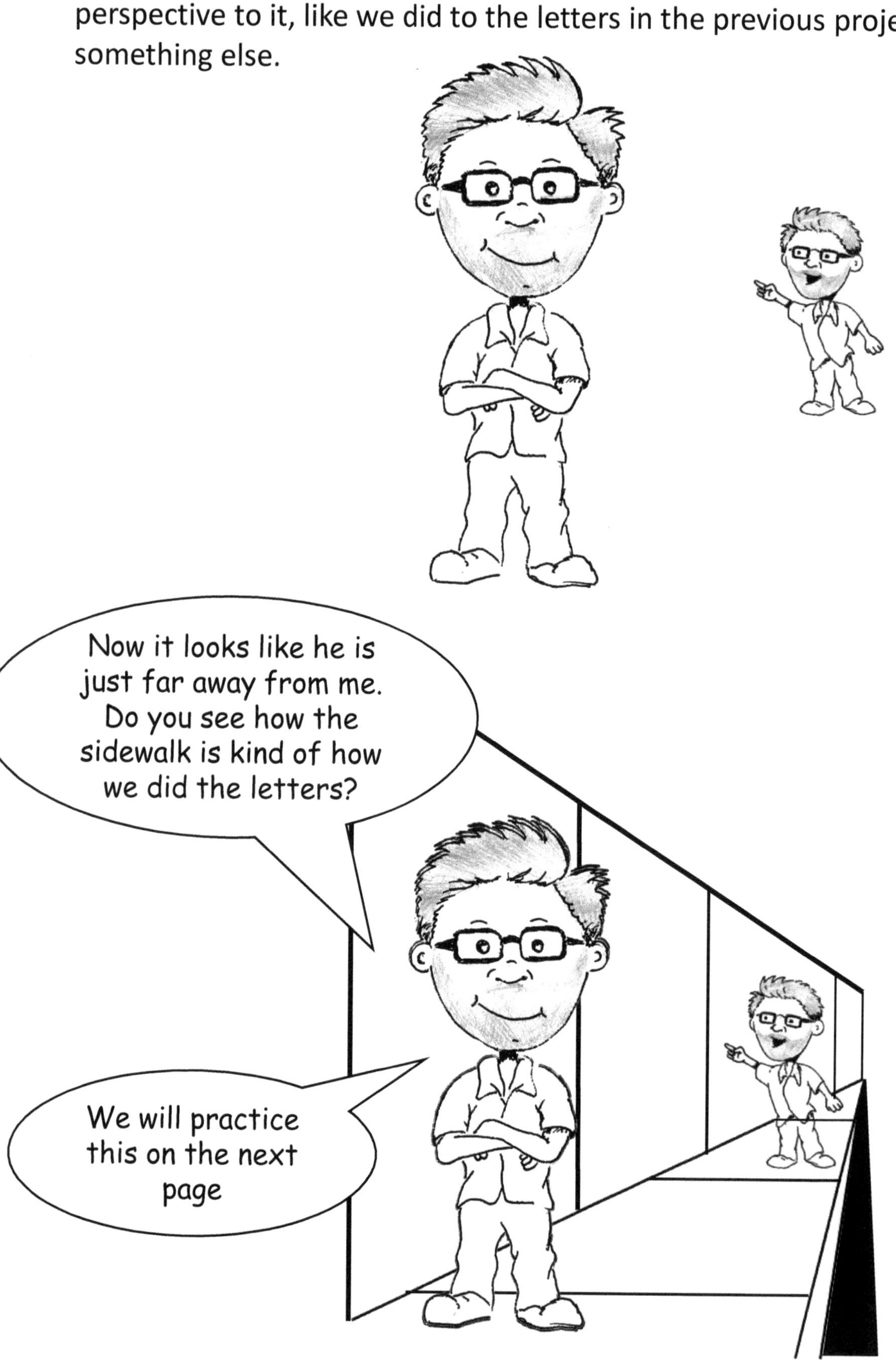

Exercise 2

Draw a picture in perspective 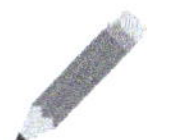 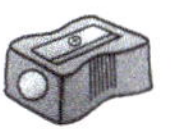 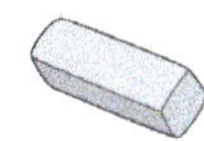

We will draw a scene using perspective. Follow the steps on a separate piece of paper.

Step 1: Draw a straight line across your paper using a ruler

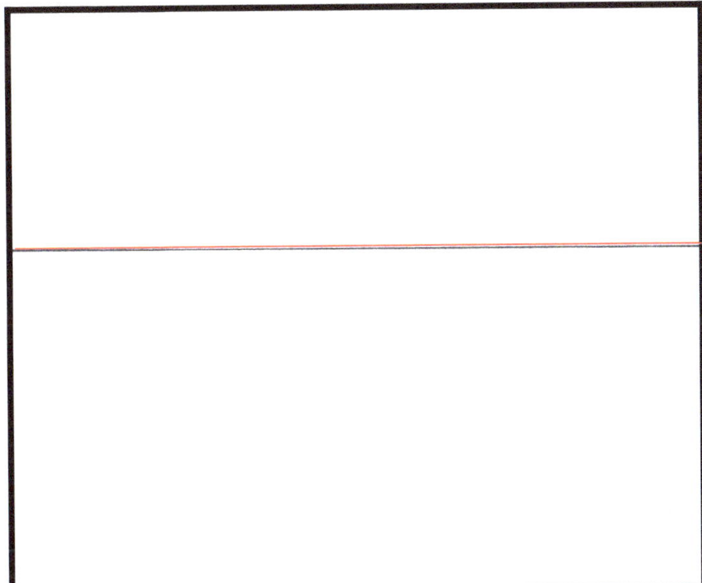

Step 2: Put a dot in the center of the line

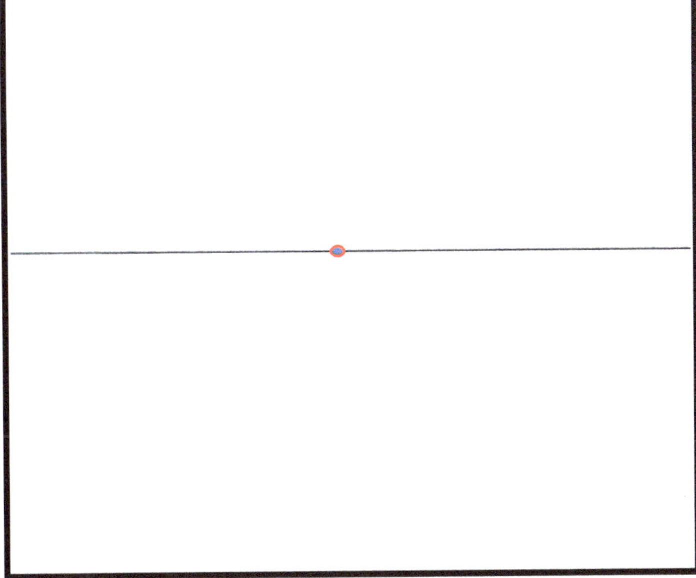

Step 3: Draw two lines at an angle from the dot to the bottom of your page

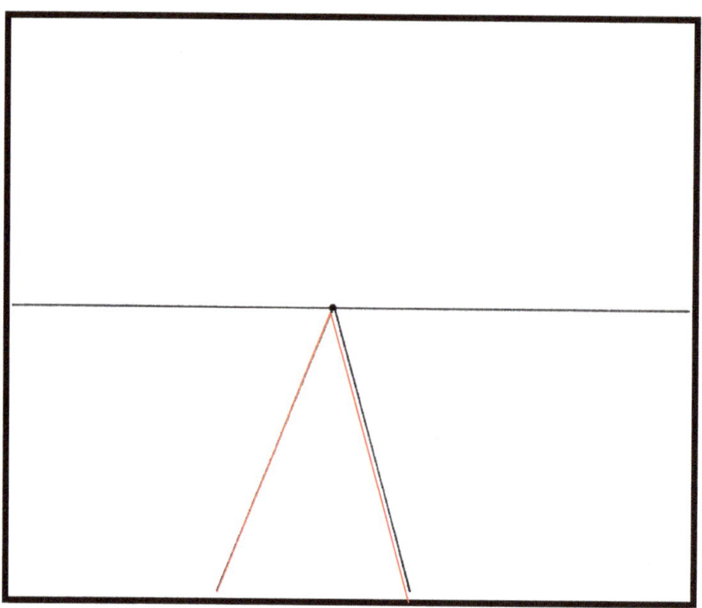

Step 4: Now draw two more lines from the dot about the same distance apart

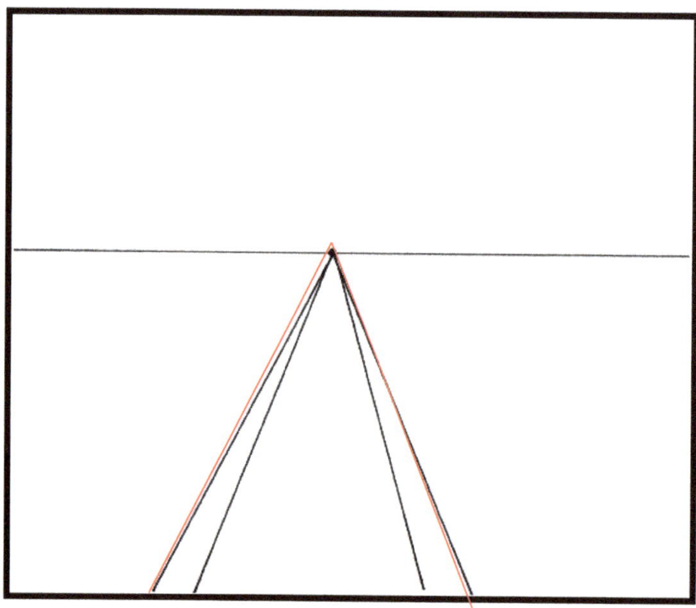

Step 5: Draw two draw two more lines towards the center but only draw part of it. Then, draw straight lines across them as seen below

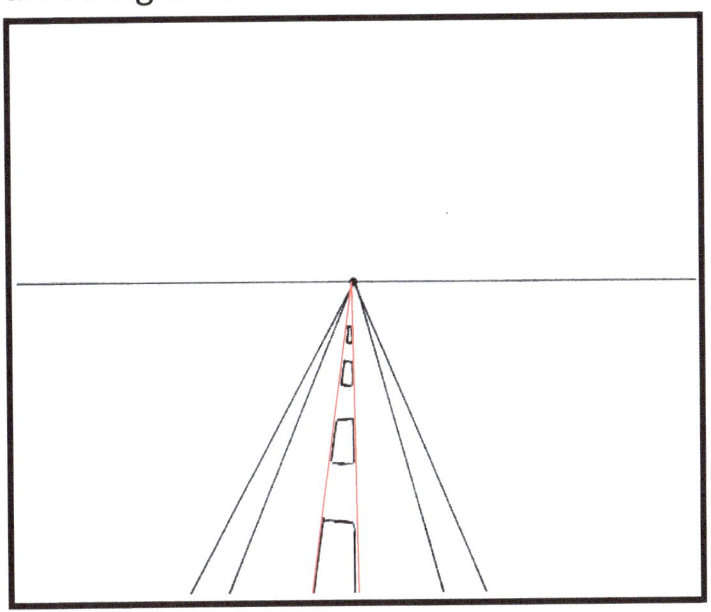

Step 6: Now draw some trees. Do you see how the tops and bottoms of the trees still follow the same lines to the dot. Draw some on the other side as well.

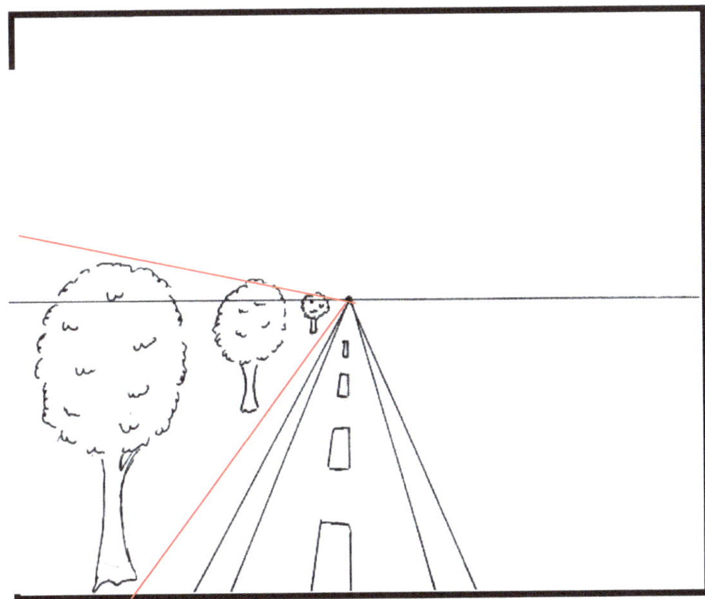

Step 7: Draw some mountains and a sun in the background. When you are finished, erase any lines you don't want such as on the trees. Then color it in.

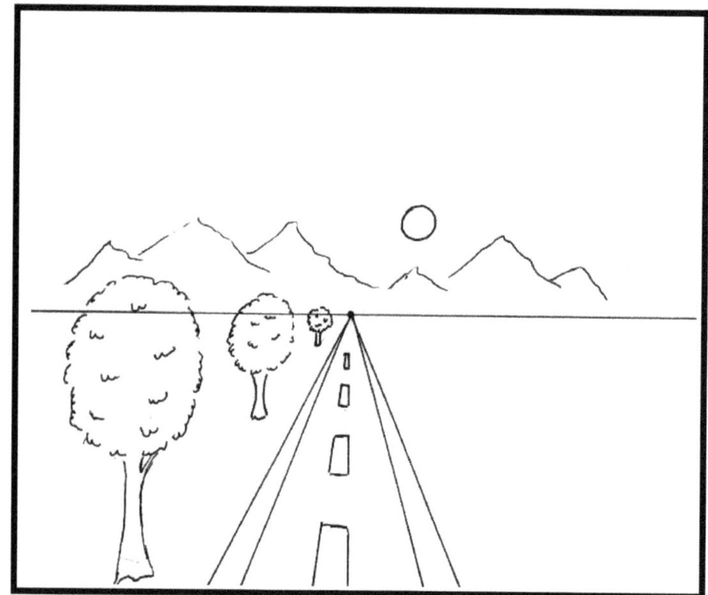

Next, we are going to learn how to make things look round and not flat. But first, something bad happened! A large box fell on Art Joe and he was flattened! Hopefully we can help him out!

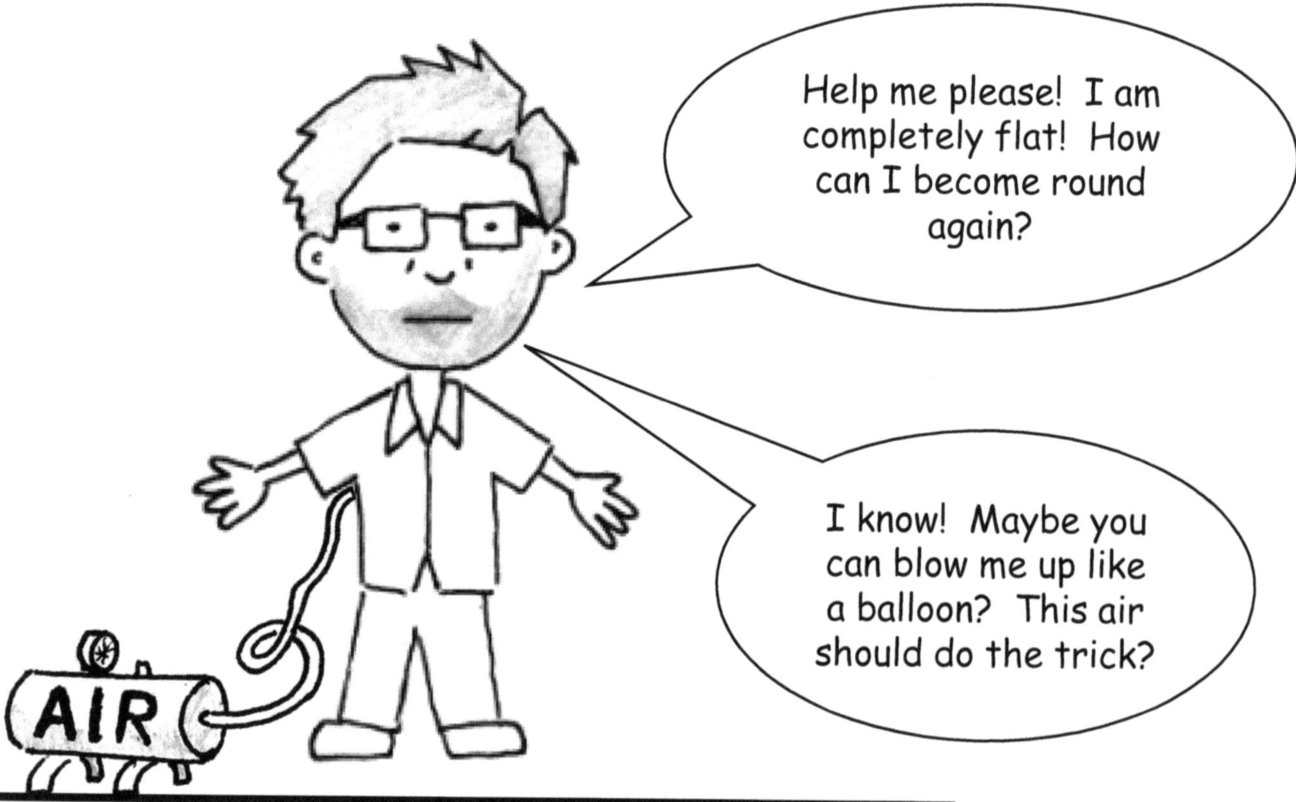

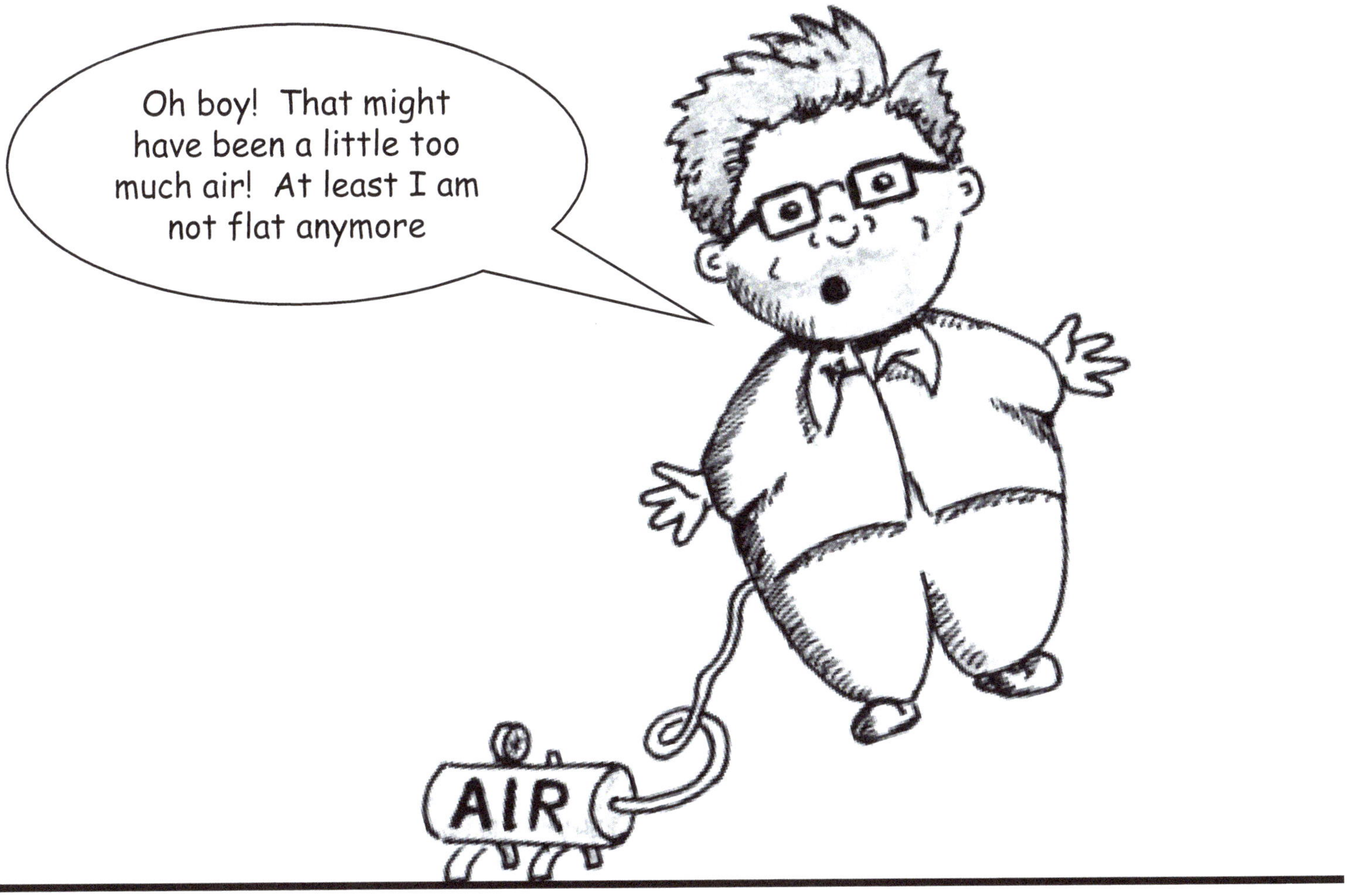

Oh boy! That might have been a little too much air! At least I am not flat anymore

AIR

Aside from being bigger, what are the differences in these drawings of Art Joe?

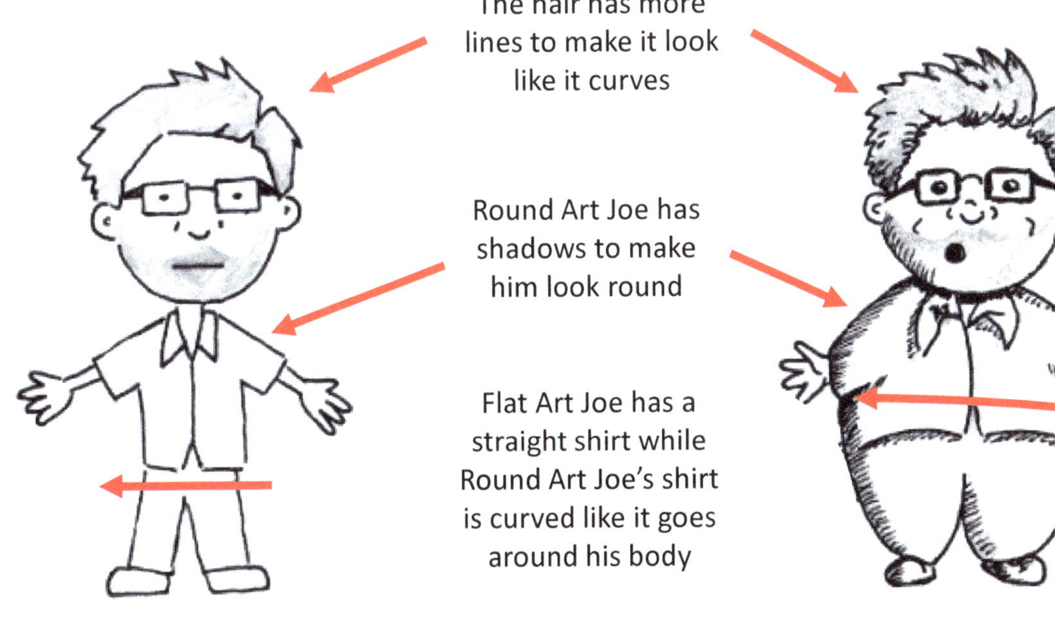

Exercise 3

Draw object that go around something 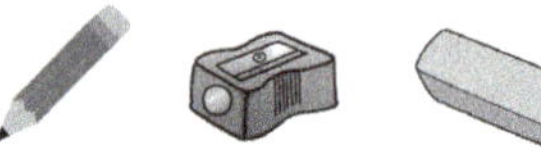

Draw object that look like they are going around something

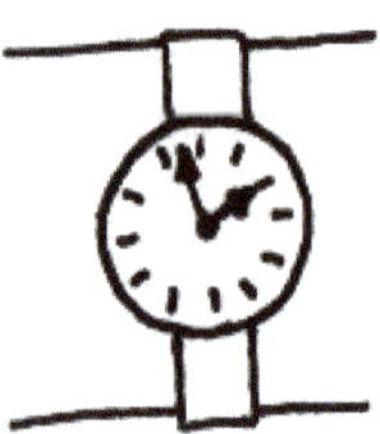

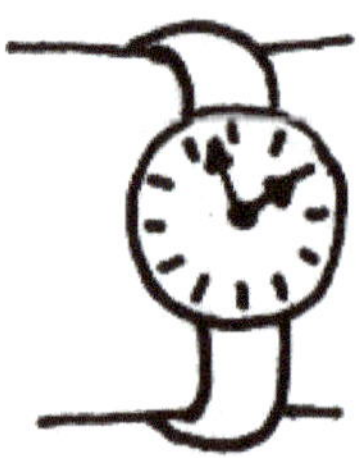

In the 1st image, the watch looks flat. In the 2nd it looks like it goes around the arm

The 1st pencil looks flat. When we curve the lines, the 2nd looks like it is round

---

Put Stripes on this snake

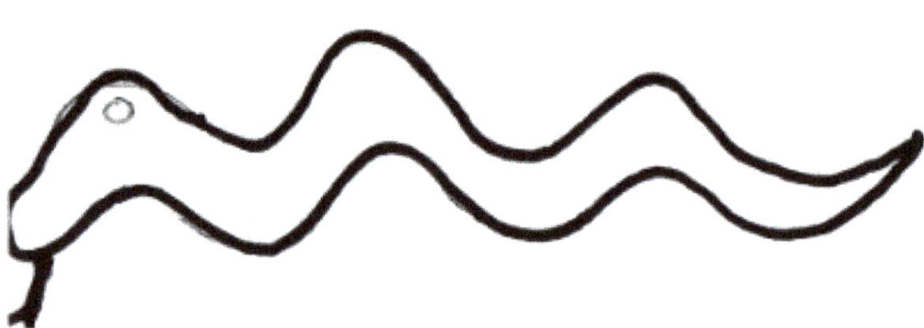

Put a ring on this finger

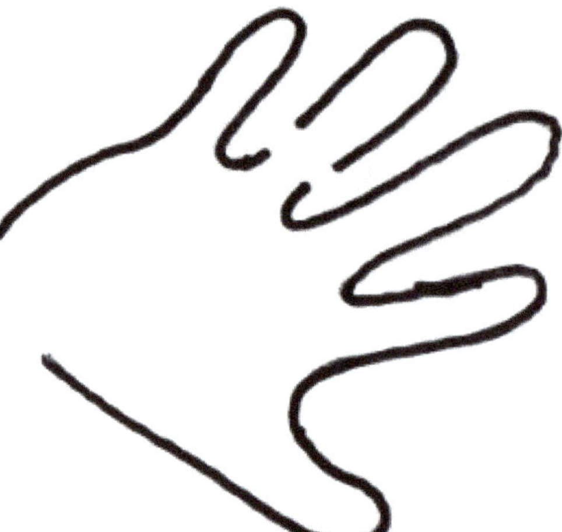

Put bracelets on this arm

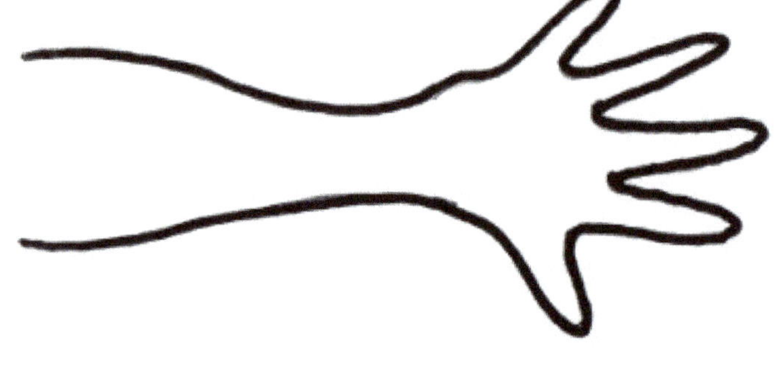

Put a belt on this guy

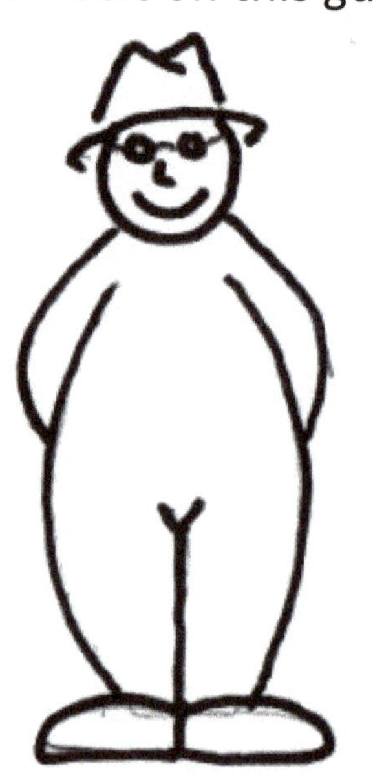

Exercise 4

Draw object that are rounded 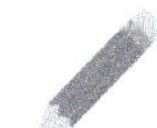 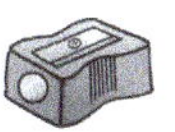 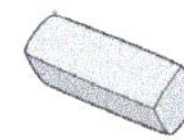

When drawing a rounded object, it should have the same curve at the top and bottom

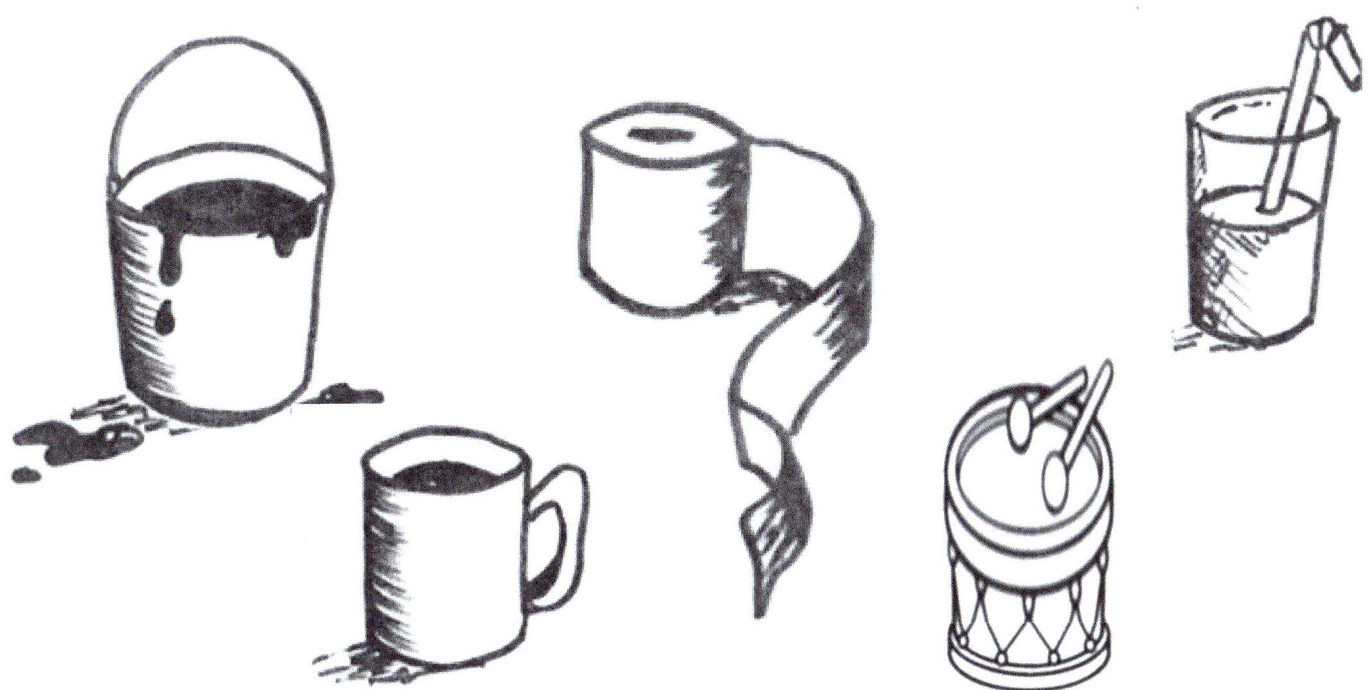

Circle the object that looks like it doesn't have the same curve at the top and bottom.

Now, draw 2 glasses with water in it. Try to get the top of the glass, the water, and the bottom of the glass all to have the same curve.

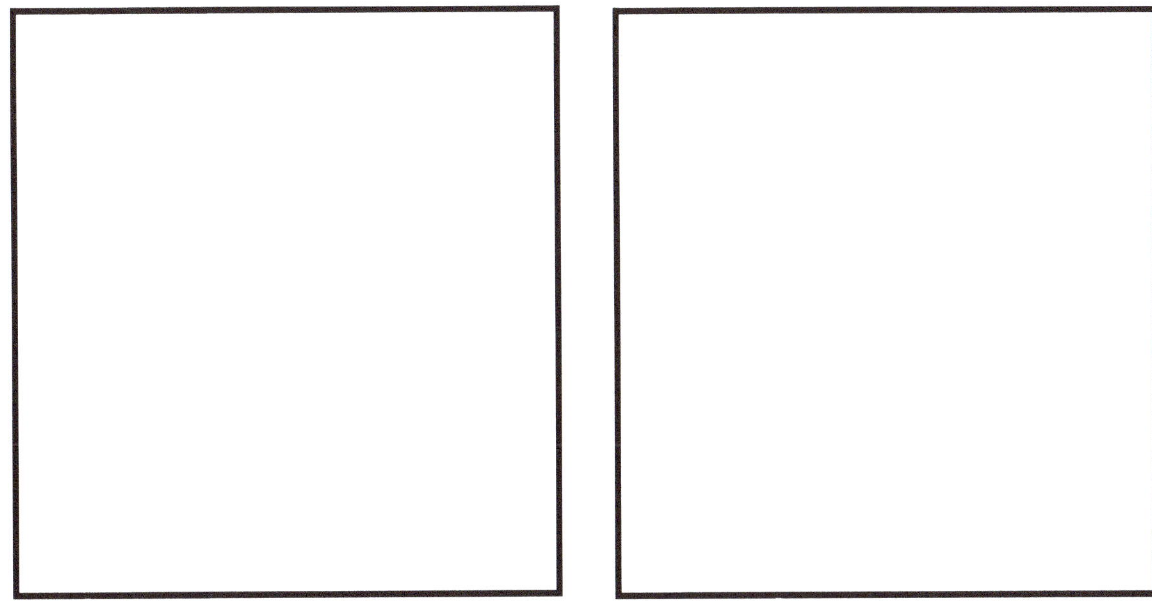

Art History Lesson Seven

Each lesson we will go over some Art History that follow what we have learned in each lesson. During this lesson, we learned about 2-Dimensional and 3-Dimensional objects

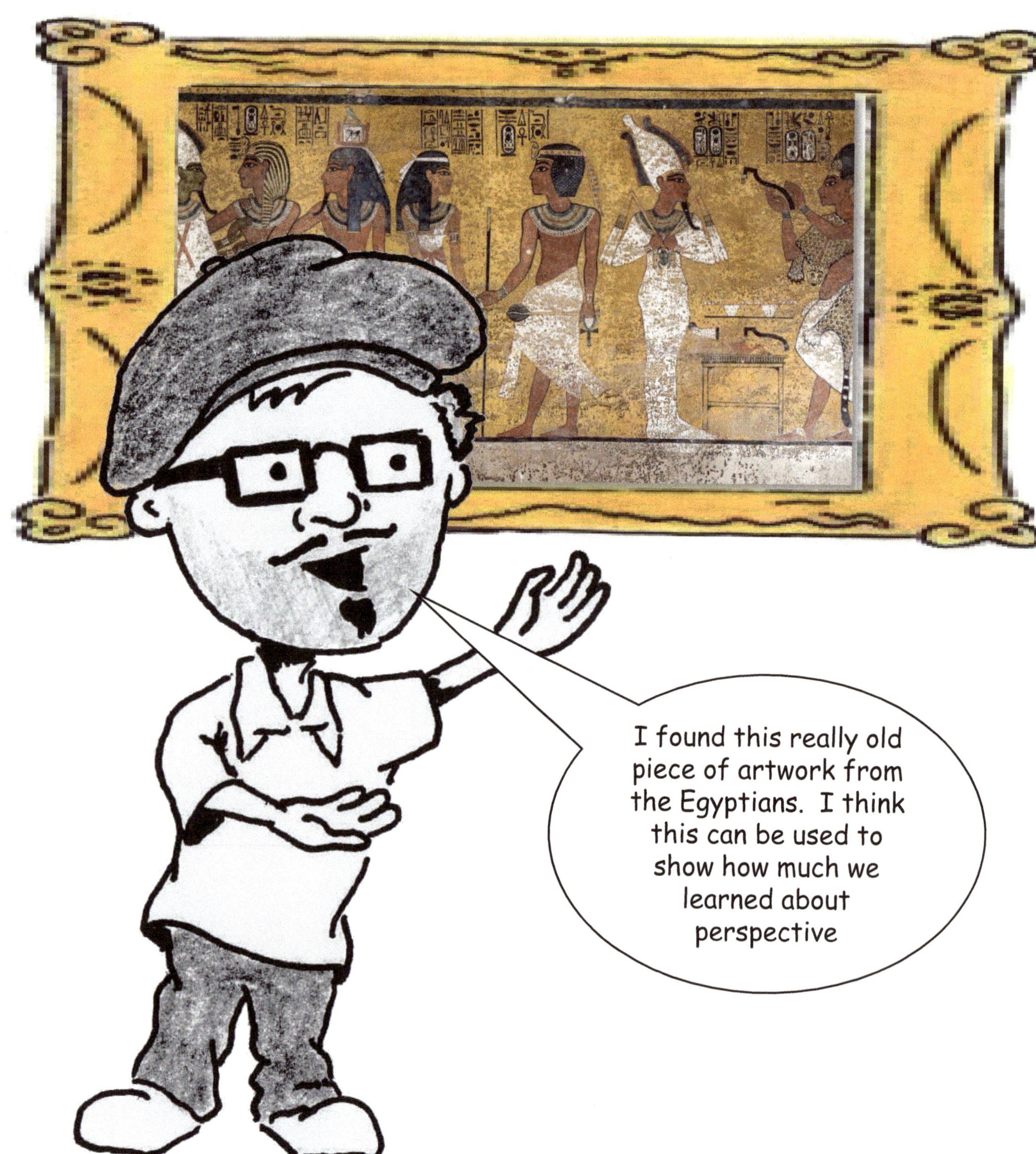

Egyptian Art

Egyptian art is very, very old. Some drawings and paintings like the one below are over 4000 years old. They would draw these to tell a story of what was happening or to show an event that was happening.

They were still learning things about art. One thing they did was make the people very flat. They always showed the chest of the person because it was very important to them.

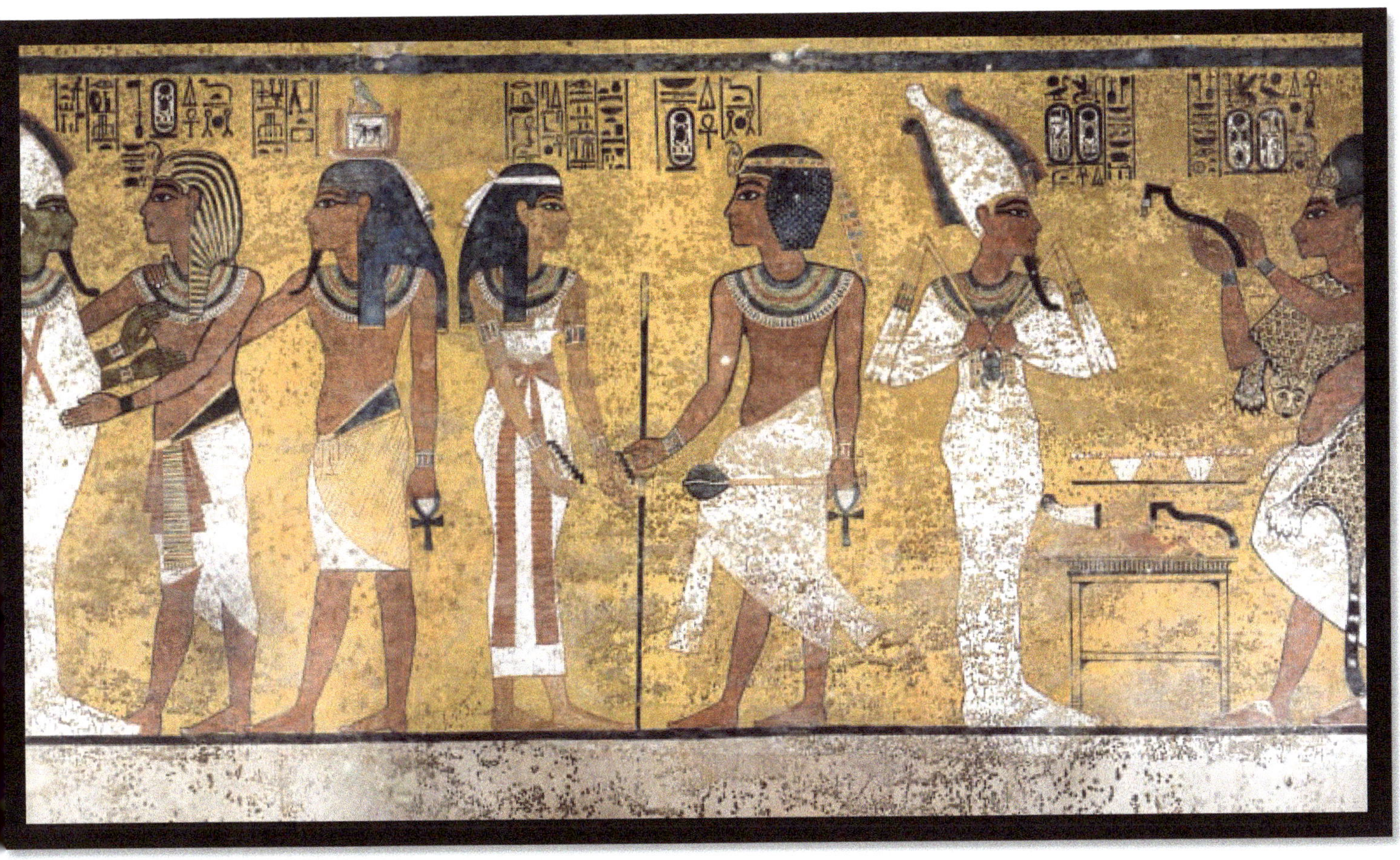

What do you think is happening in this drawing? Who do you think are the important people? Can you tell what they are holding? Try to look at the whole picture and see everything that is going on.

Art History Project

We are going to draw our own Egyptian scene but first, let's learn how to draw how they did. It is almost impossible to stand like this but that is how they wanted to show people.

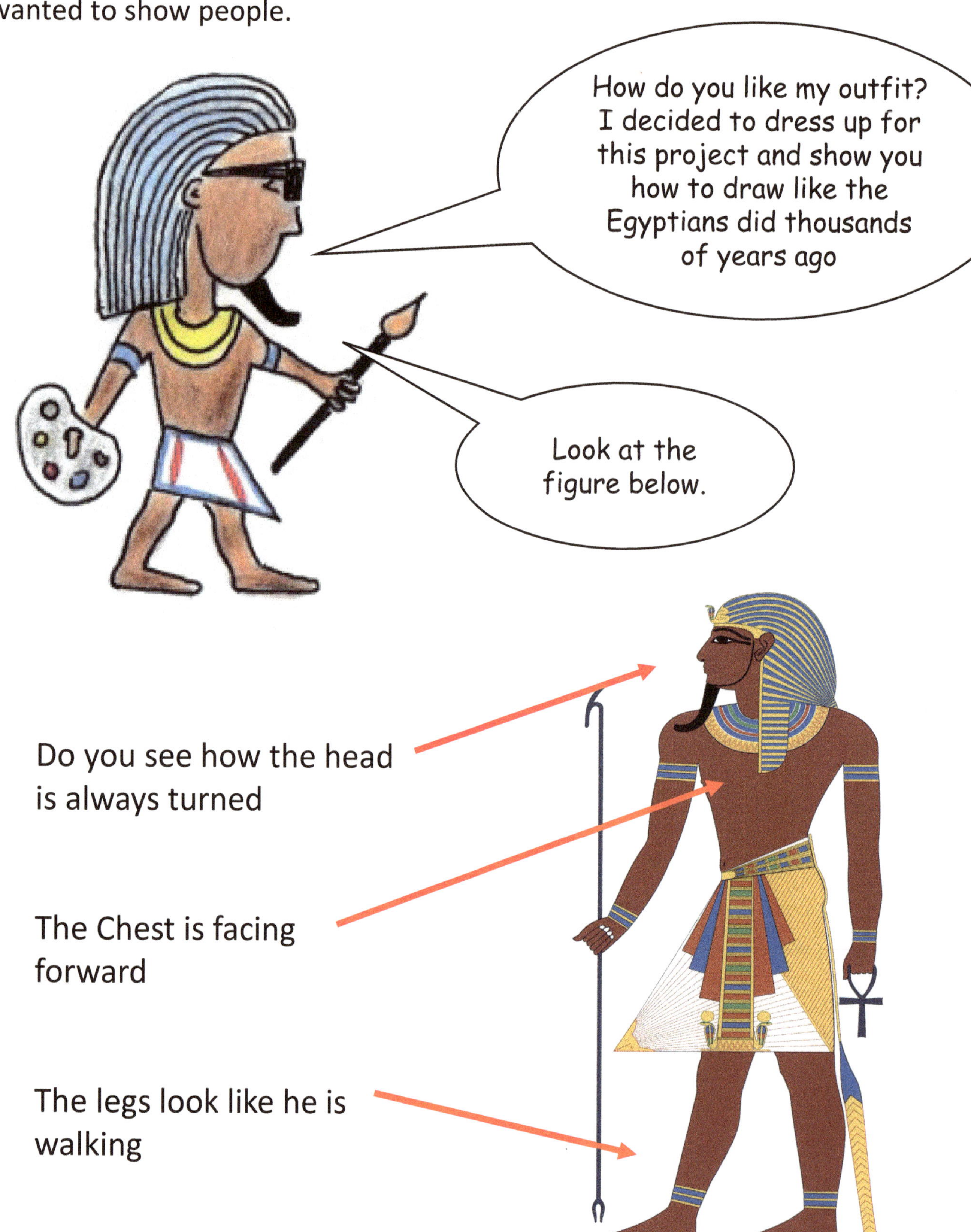

Art History Project

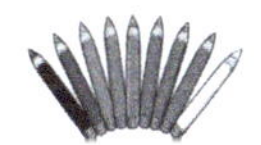

In the space provided, draw a scene similar to the Egyptian art we just looked at. Maybe make your family doing something, or your friends playing a game. Try to draw the people in the picture like we just learned.

Remember to sign your name to your work

Chapter Fun

Uh oh! Art Joe is flat again, but he cannot find the air. Help him find his way through the maze to blow himself up!

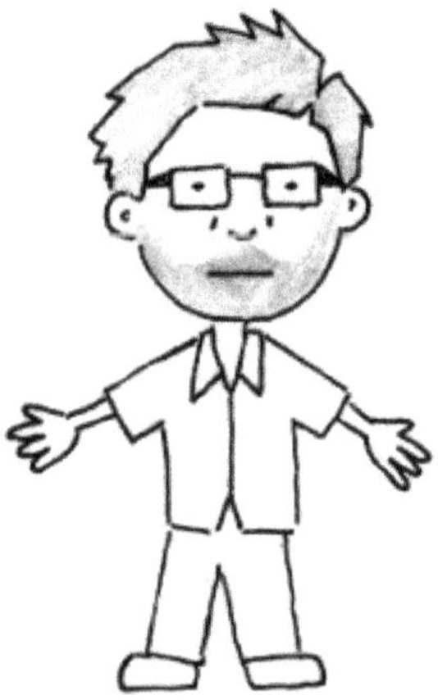

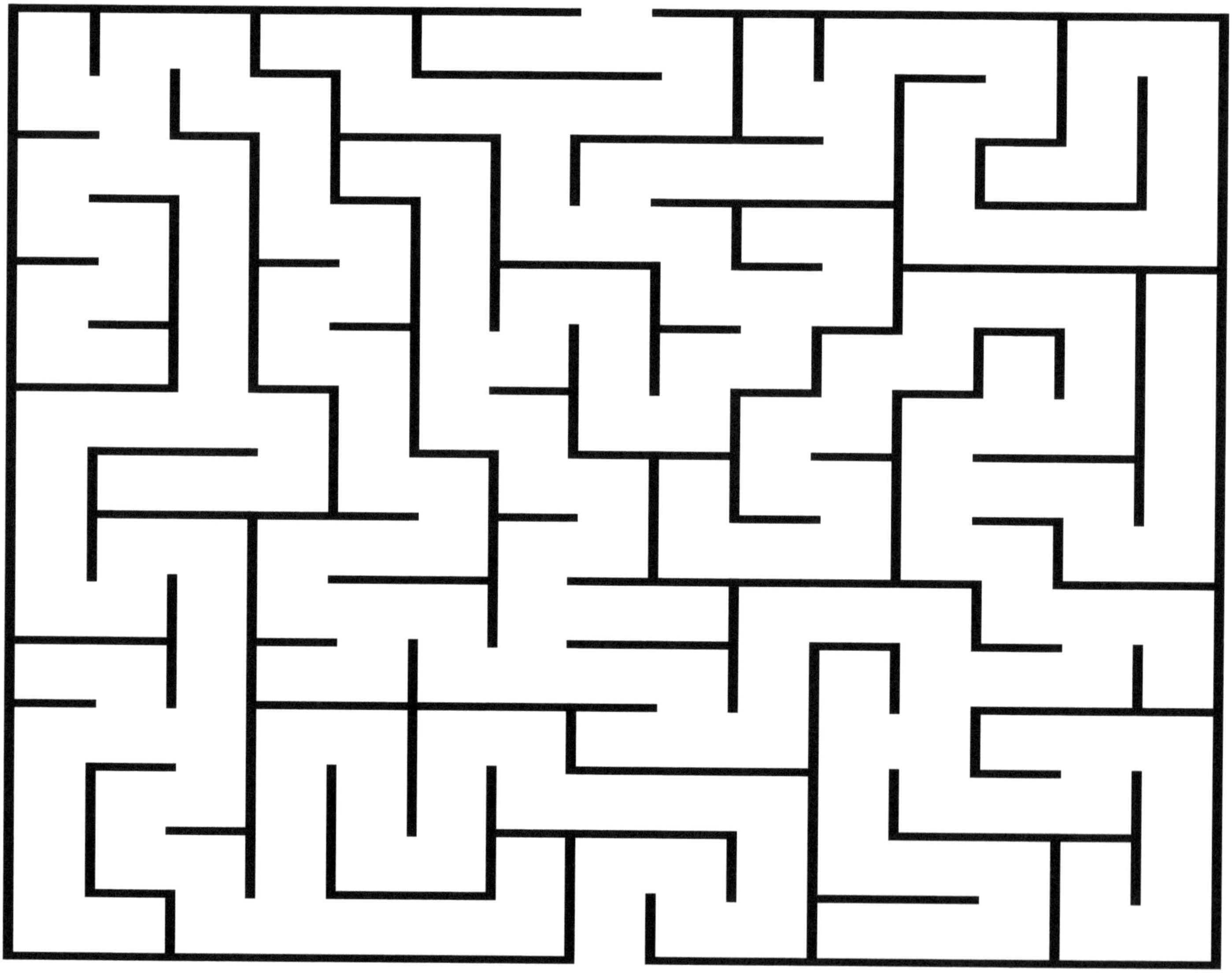

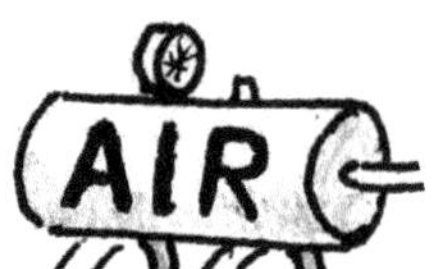

AIR

UNIT 8

Light and Shadow

Lesson 8.1 Light and Shadow

Adding lights and shadows to your drawing can really make a difference. In this lesson, we will begin learning how to add a light source to our drawings and add the shadows accordingly.

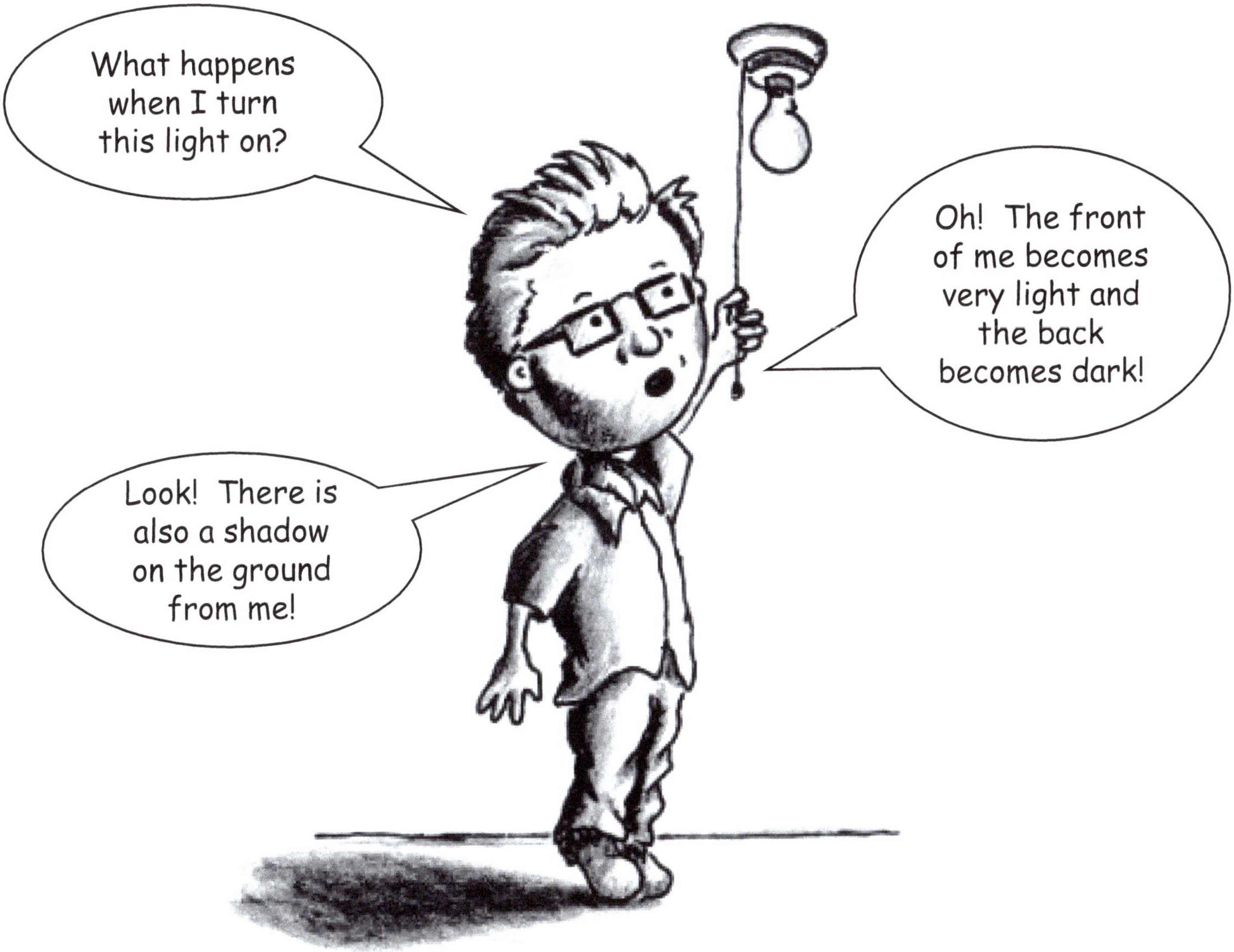

In this lesson, you will need pencils, pencil sharpener, eraser, and colored pencils. Look for the icon next to each project to determine what to use

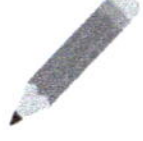
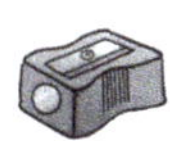
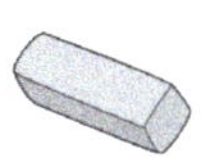
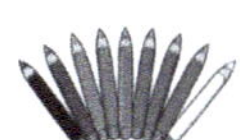

We will start out by learning some basic skills to learn how to shade. When making shadows and shading, you want to make sure you are not pressing too hard with your pencil.

To practice this, we are going to draw a line. At first, press your pencil down hard to make a dark mark. Then, as you move your pencil across the line, press lighter and lighter until you barely see the mark.

Press hard -------------→Press softer-------------→And Softer---------→Until you barely see it

Try it on your own a few times

Now try it the other way. Start off really soft and press harder and harder

Now that we practiced how to draw softly, let's talk about shadows. There are some rules to follow when drawing shadows.

First, shadows should follow the shape of the thing that's causing the shadow. If it is a round object, the shadow should be rounded as well. If it is shaped like a triangle, the shadow should be triangular as well.

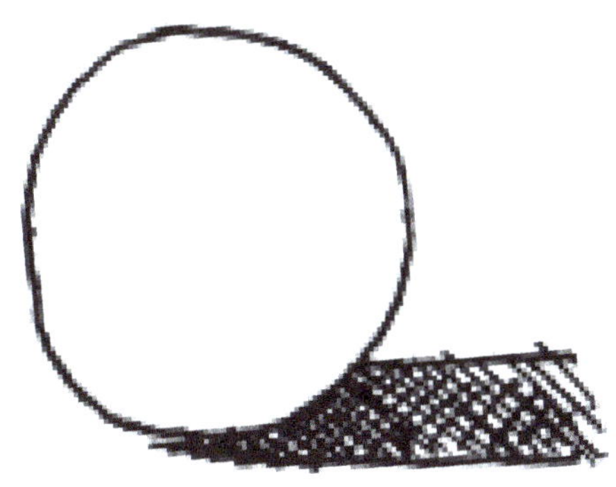

This ball should not have a square shadow

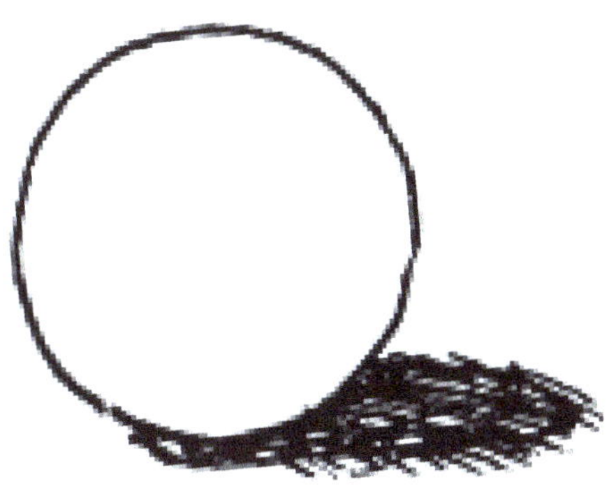

It should have a rounded shadow like this

The shadow should not be too big for the object. It will usually be smaller than the object.

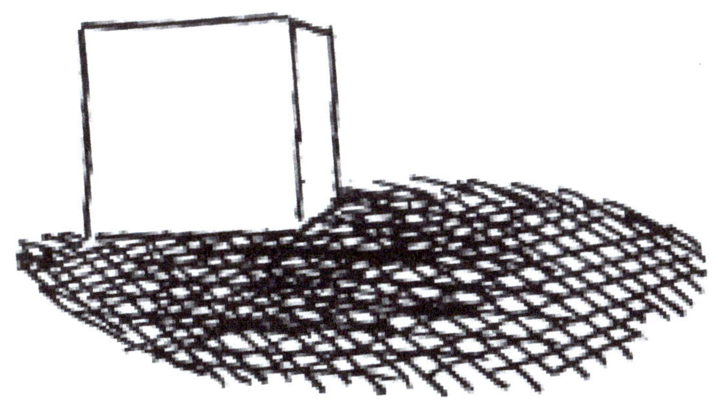

This shadow is way too big

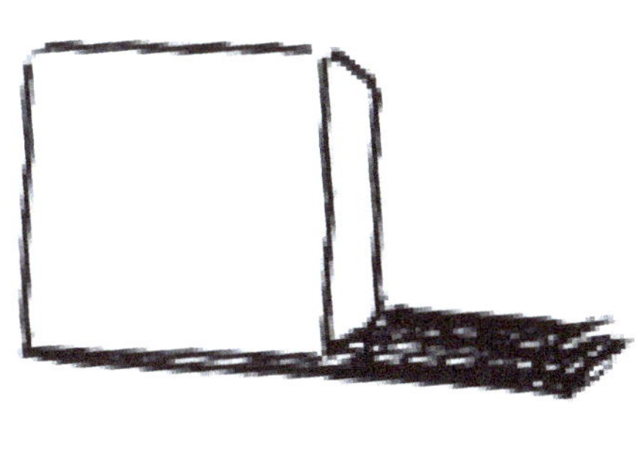

It should be smaller, like this

Exercise 1

Finding where the light is coming from

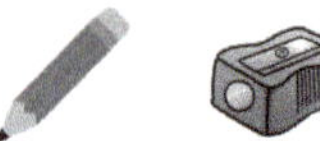
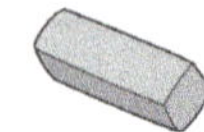

Look at the shadows from each object and figure out where the light is coming from. Draw a lightbulb or sun where the light is.

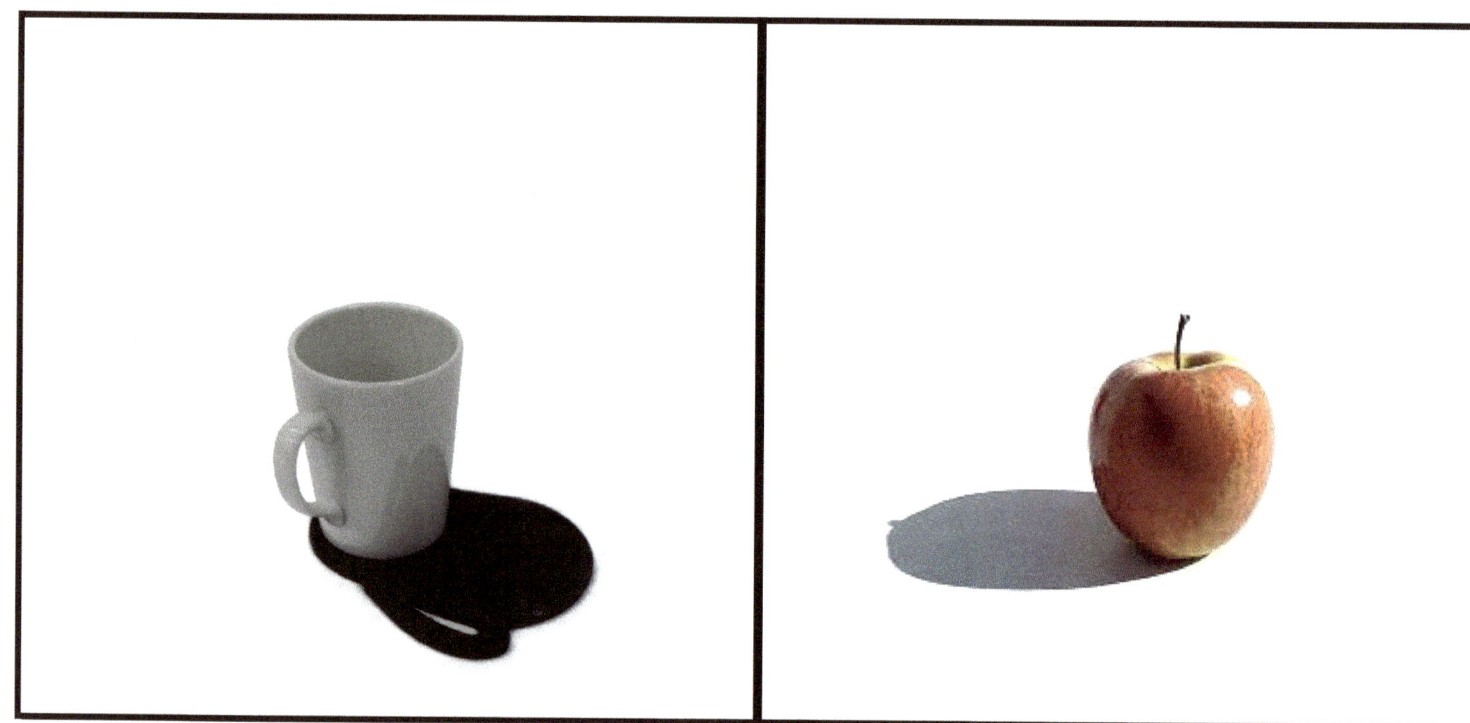

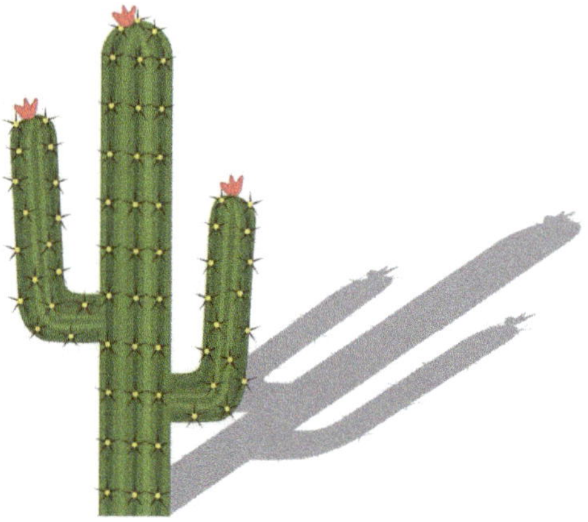

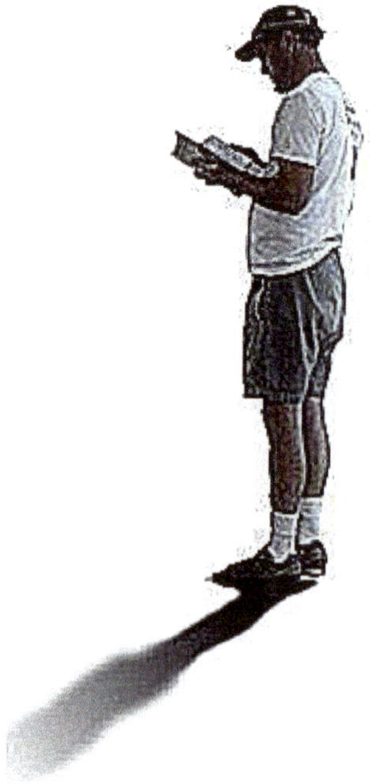

Exercise 2

Practice drawing Shadows from different objects 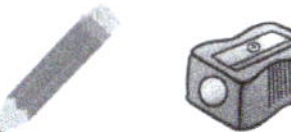 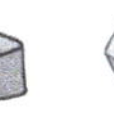 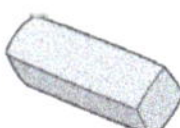

Draw the shadow for each object. Look where the light bulb is so you know where the shadow should go.

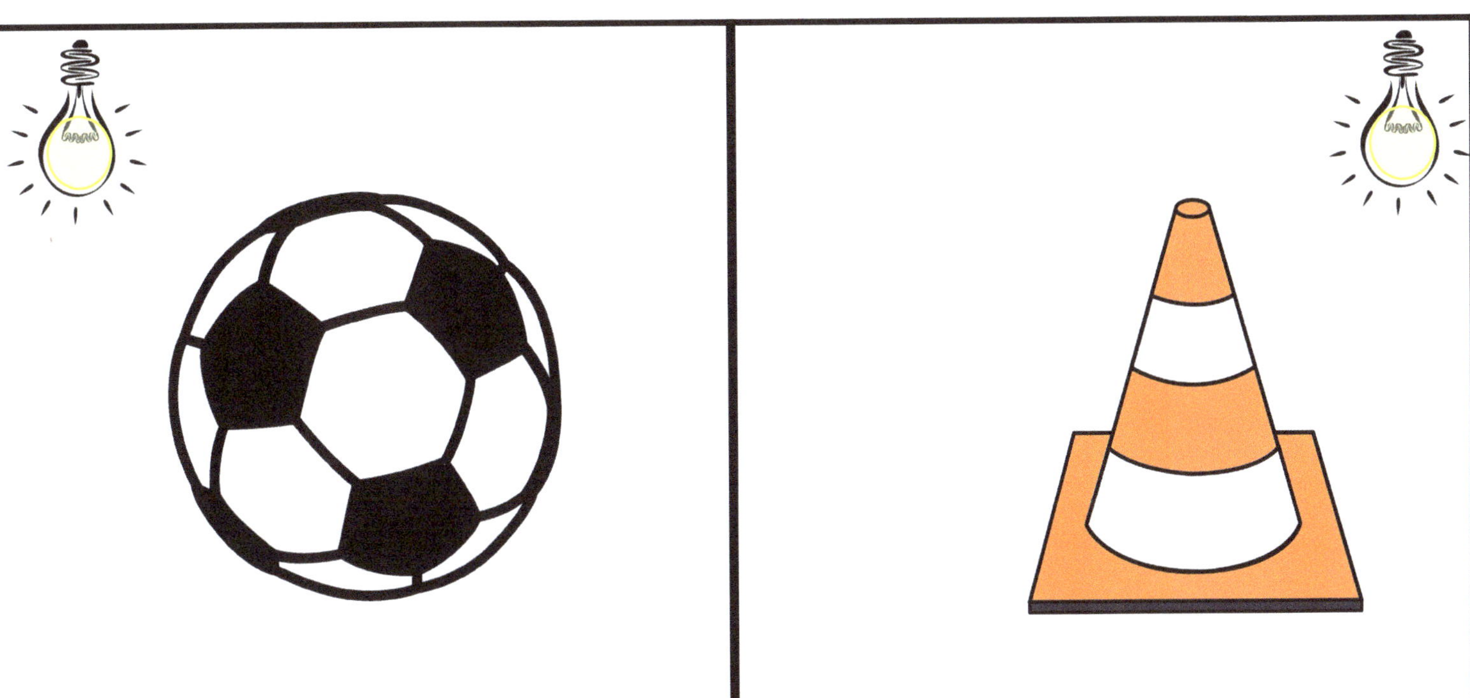

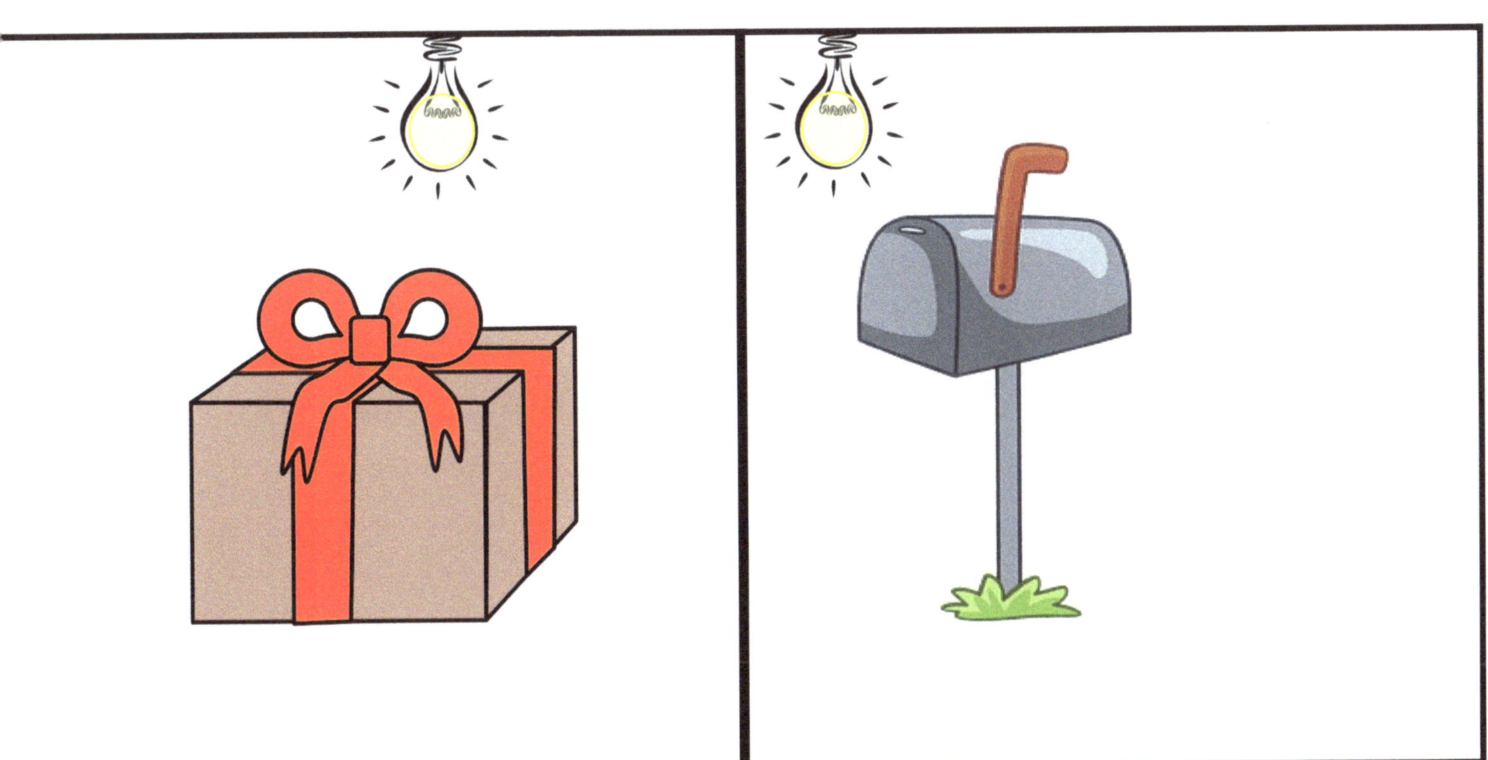

What if you have a couple objects. The shadows will all go in the same direction

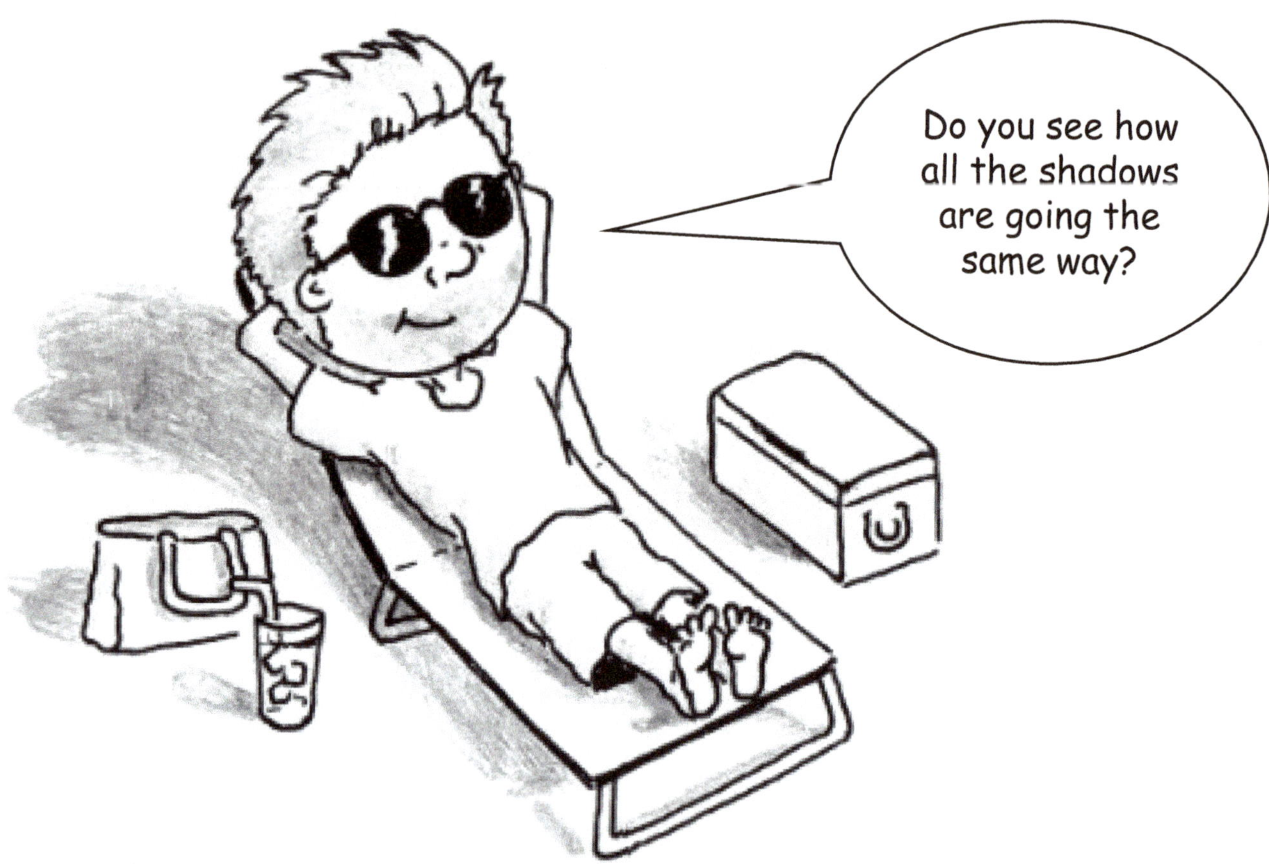

Draw a couple simple objects like boxes or balls and draw the shadows for each item. I provided the light but make sure your shadows go in the same direction

Think of light as a bunch of sun rays coming down. Wherever the sun hits, there will be light and where the sun gets blocked, it will be shadows.

Look at the picture below. Do you see the sun rays coming down? Where is it hitting the tree? Do you see how the tree is blocking some of the rays?

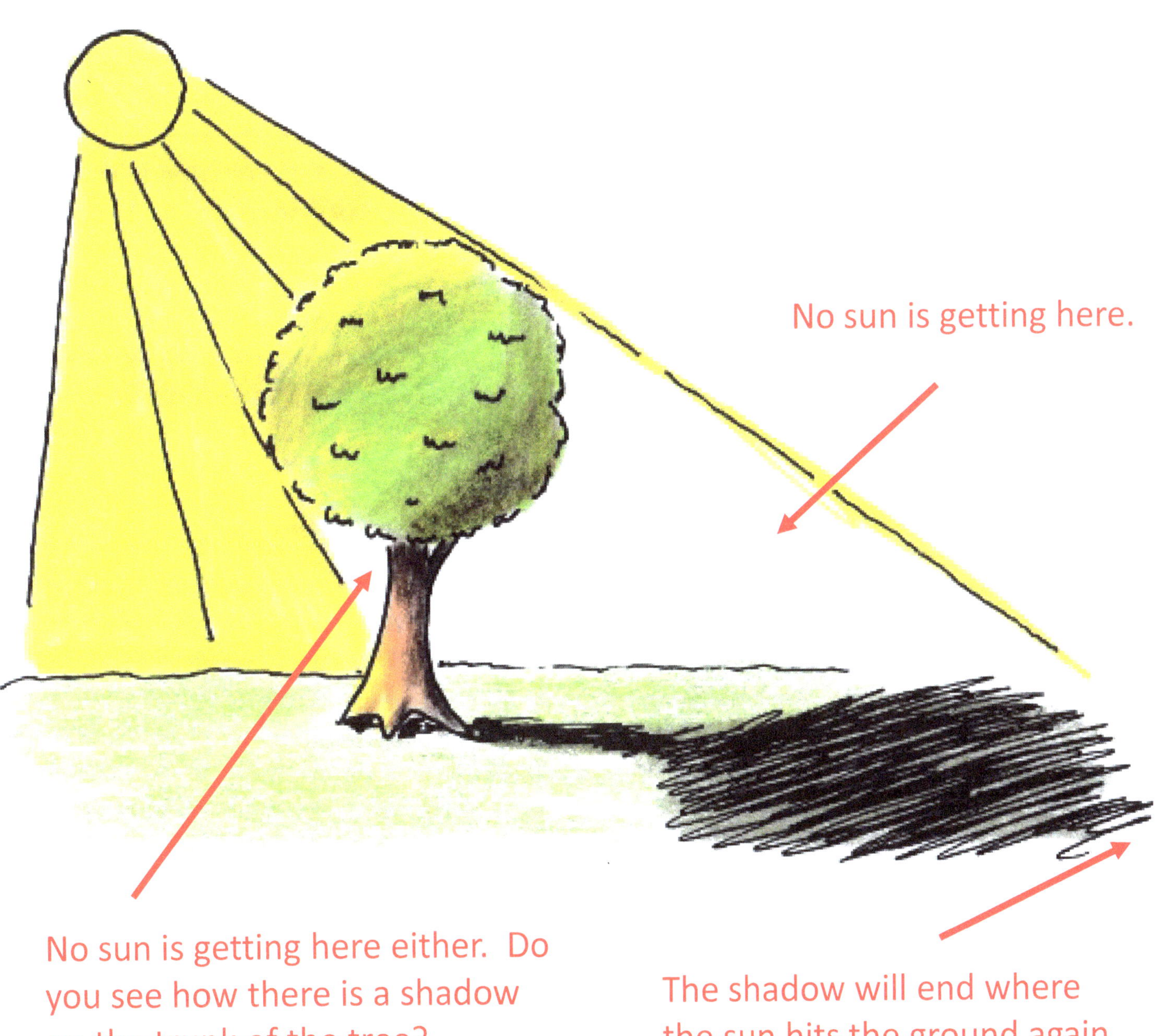

On the next page, try to draw the light and shadow on the tree provided.

Exercise 2

Practice drawing Shadows when the light is higher or lower 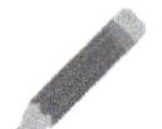 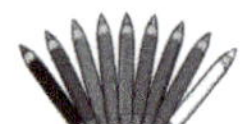

Art Joe is standing in the grass. The sun is high in some scenes and lower in other. Draw the shadow of Art Joe from the sun in each scene

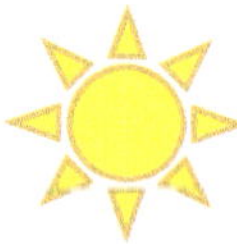

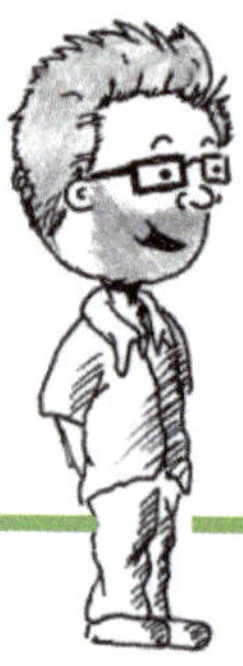

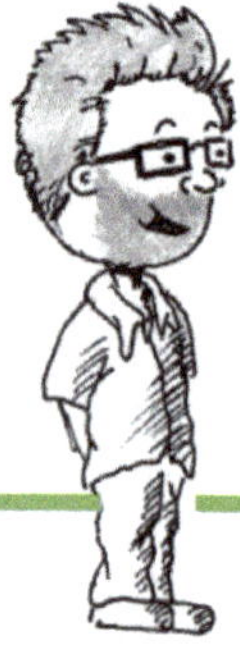

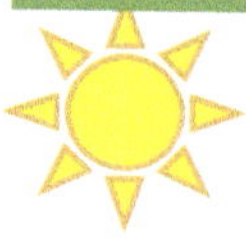

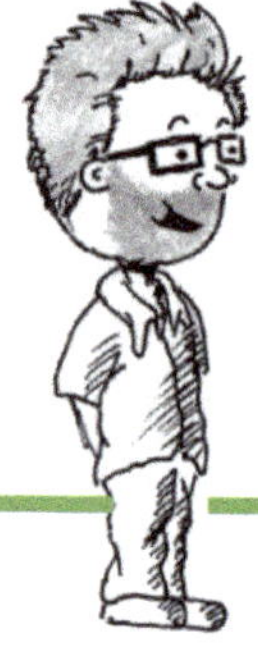

Project 1

Adding light and shadow to a tree

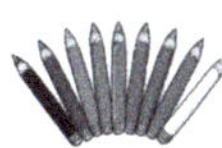

Draw where the light will hit the tree and where the shadow will be.

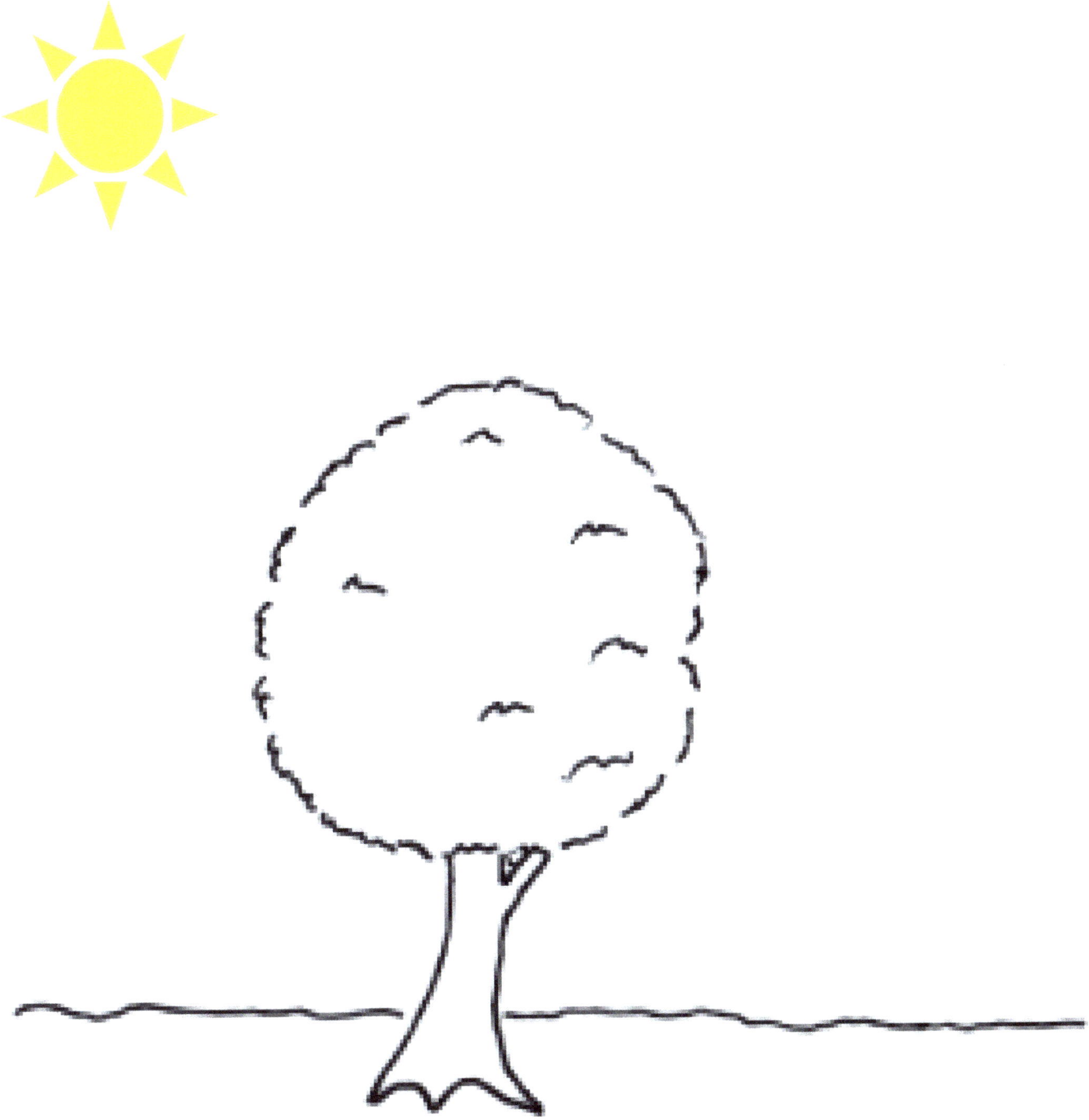

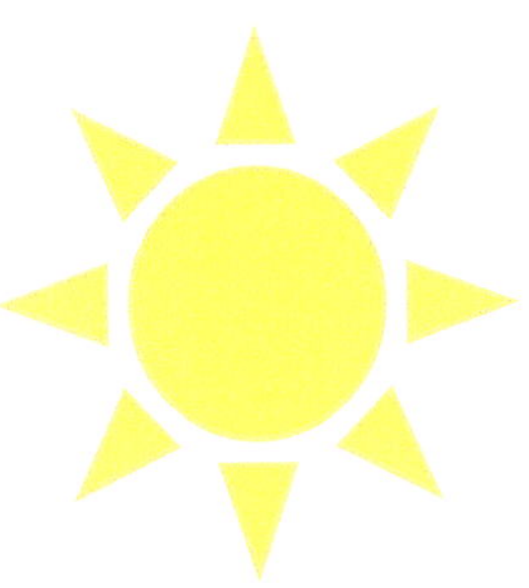

We will now learn how to use colors to add lights and shadows. We will practice with this pear now. Follow along with the pear on the next page. You can use your Pastels or Colored Pencils, but Pastels might work the best.

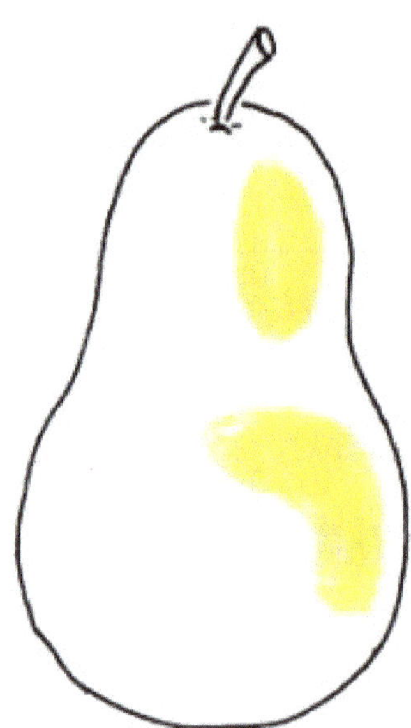

Step 1: Find where the light is coming from and color it a bright color (yellow)

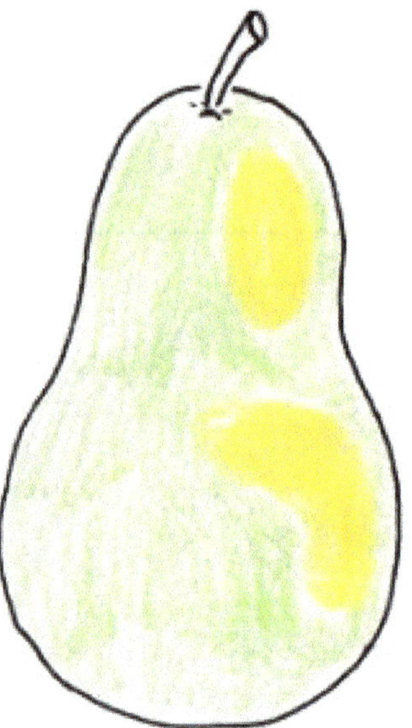

Step 2: Now, softly color the rest of the pear a light green.

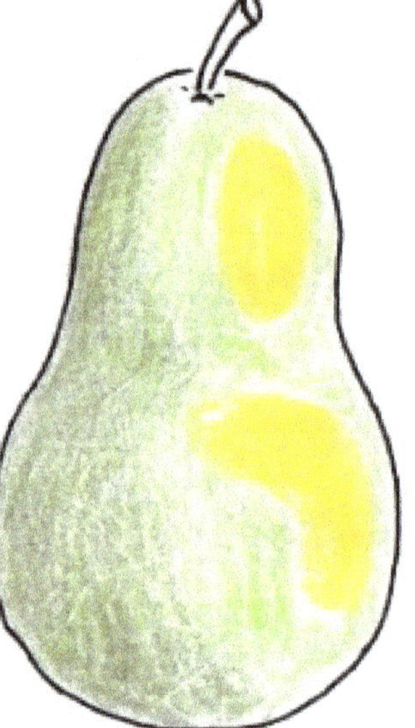

Step 3: Color the edge that isn't lit, a darker green

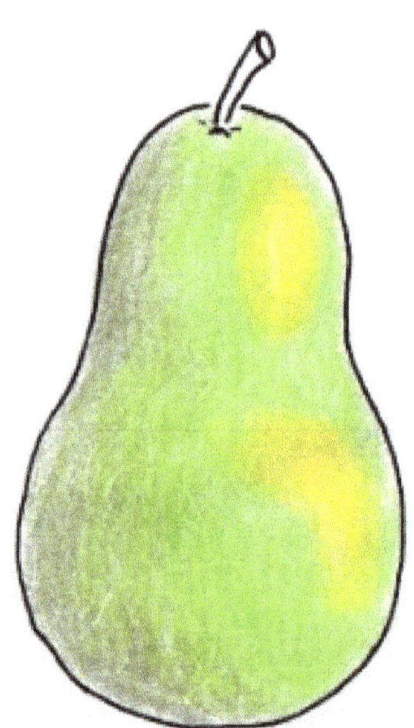

Step 4: Use the light green and color the whole pear darker. Leave some of the yellow though.

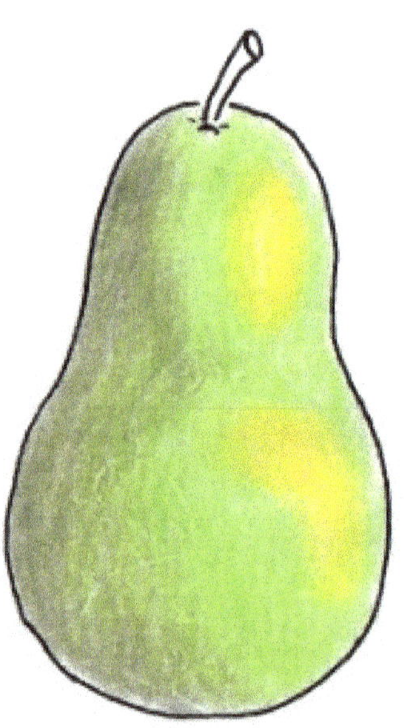

Step 1: Now color the dark edge with the dark green again but harder to make it dark.

Exercise 3

Practice Coloring a Pear

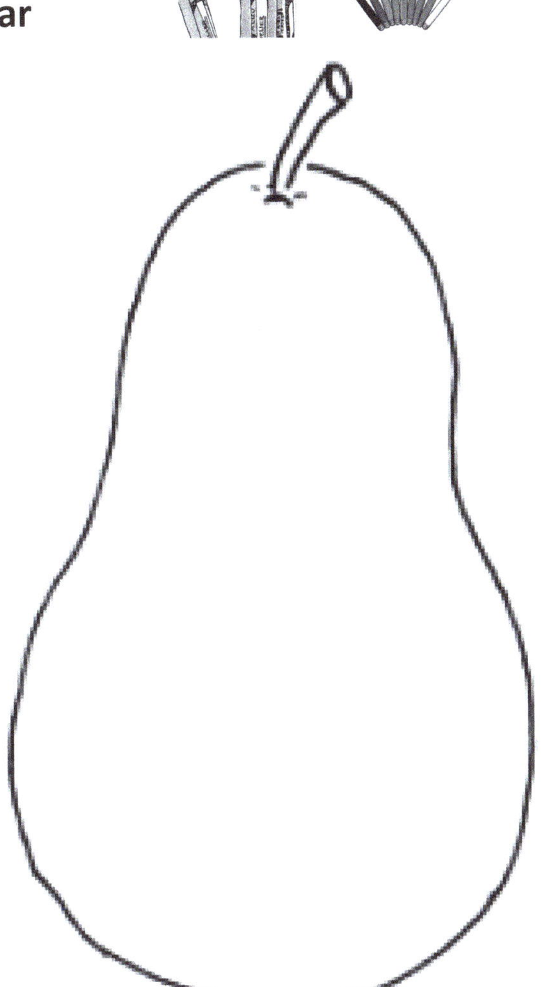

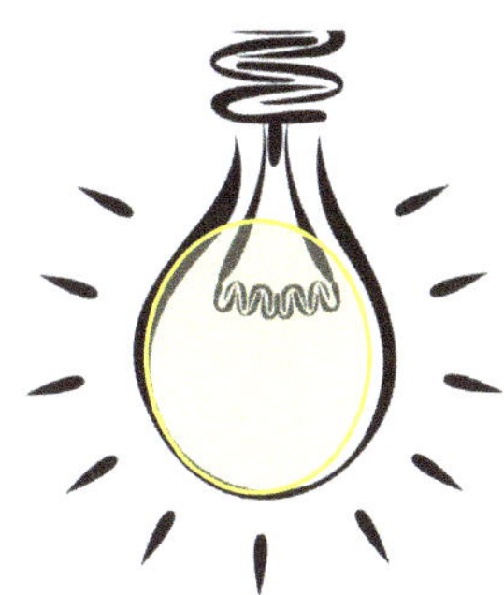

Step 1: Find where the light is coming from and color it a bright color (yellow)

Step 2: Now, softly color the rest of the pear a light green.

Step 3: Color the edge that isn't lit, a darker green

Step 4: Use the light green and color the whole pear darker. Leave some of the yellow though.

Step 5: Now color the dark edge with the dark green again but harder to make it dark.

On the next page, color the other items with pastels or colored pencils. Watch where the light is coming from and don't forget the shadows.

Project 2

Color the light and shadows of these objects with pastels

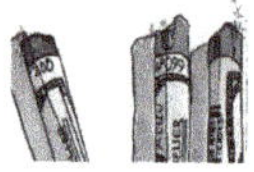

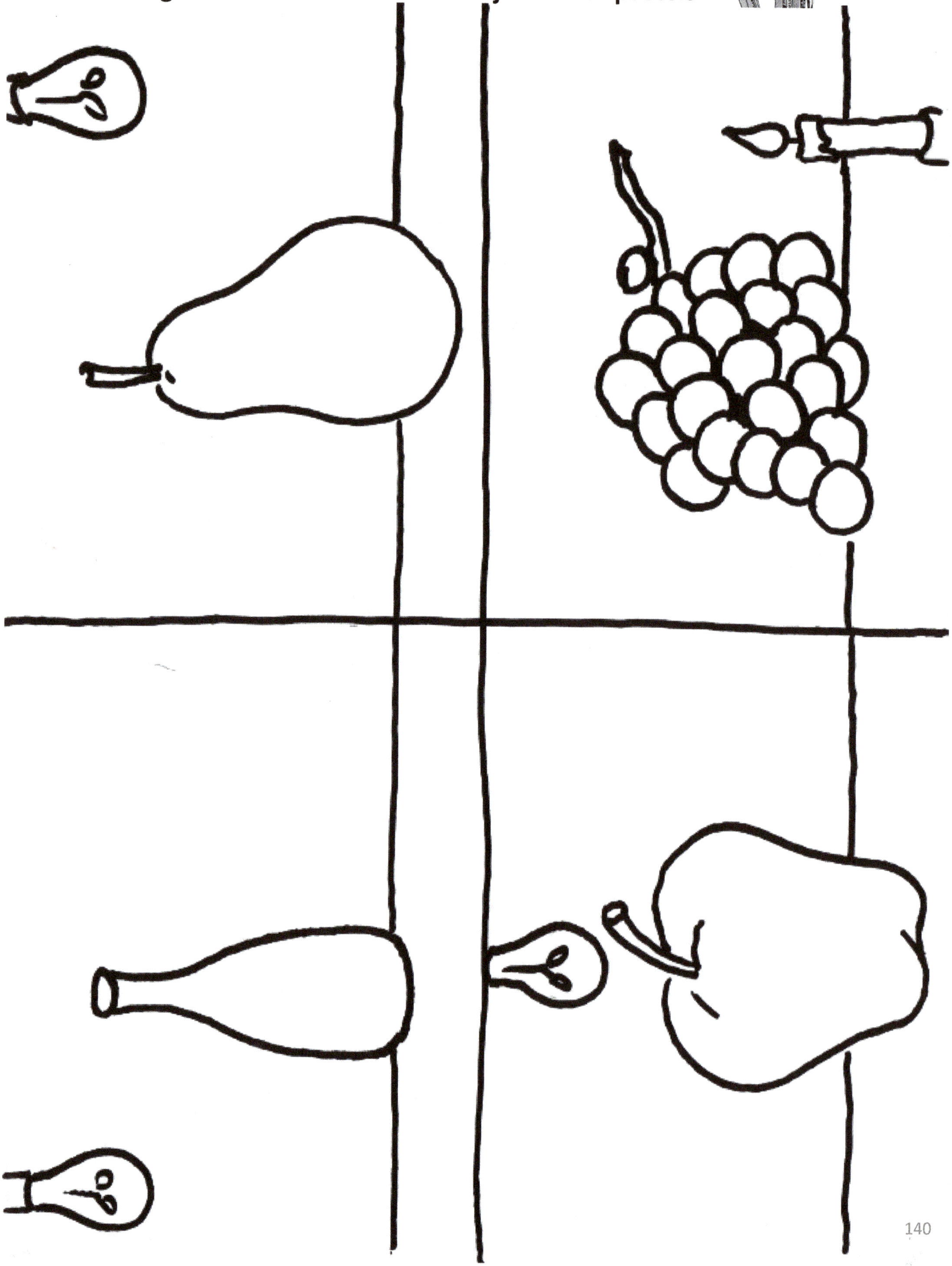

Project 3

Draw and color an object with the light and shadow

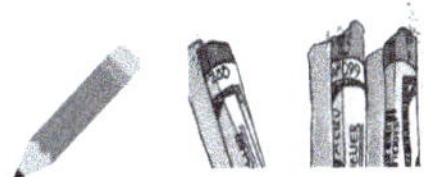

Find an object around your house. Have it close to a light so you can see the shadow. Then color the object with the light and shadows with pastels.

Remember to sign your name to your work

Art History Lesson Eight

Each lesson we will go over some Art History that follow what we have learned in each lesson. During this lesson, we learned about light and shadows

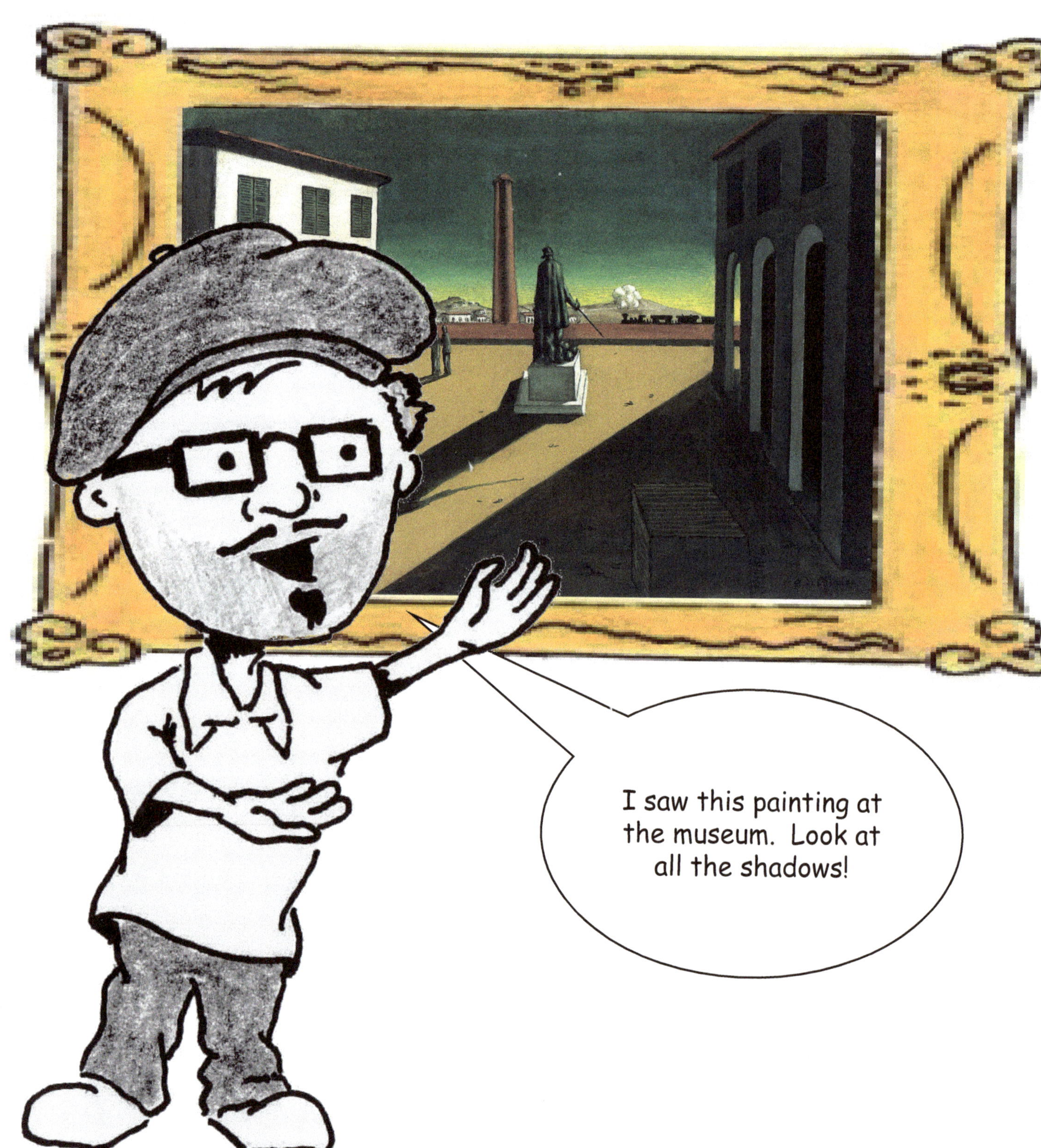

Giorgio de Chirico

Giorgio de Chirico was an Italian painter in the 1900's. He painted a lot of Roman type buildings that had very long shadows. Here are a couple examples of his paintings. The first is titled "Plaza" and the second painting is called "Piazza d'Italia" or Plaza in Italy. Do you notice how long his shadows are? Where do you think the sun would be?

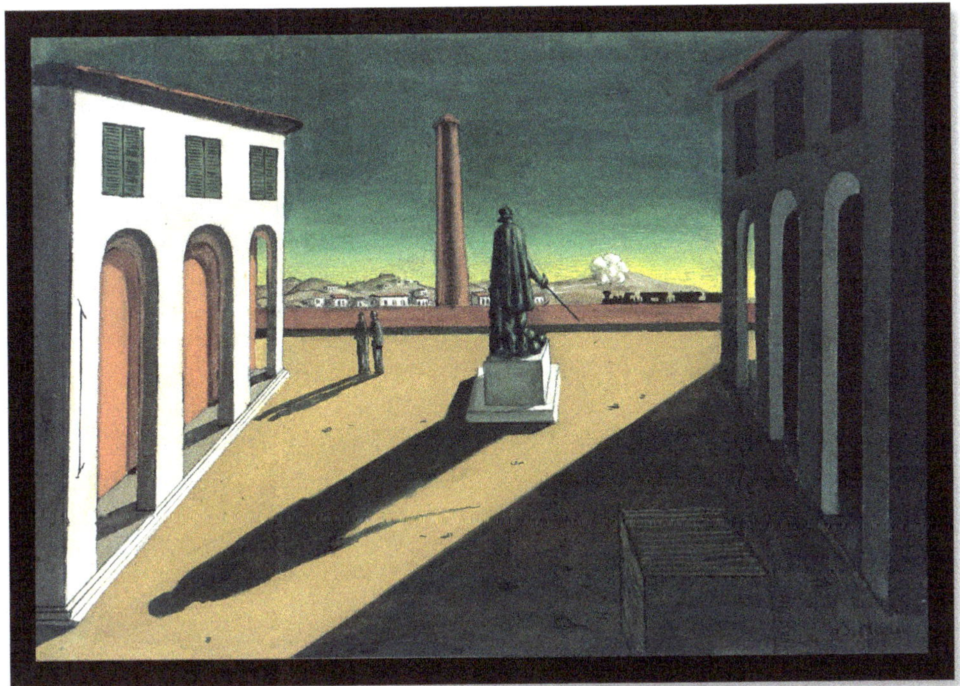

Do you notice how long his shadows are? Where do you think the sun would be?

Do the pictures look real? Or do they seem like a dream? What do you think of them?

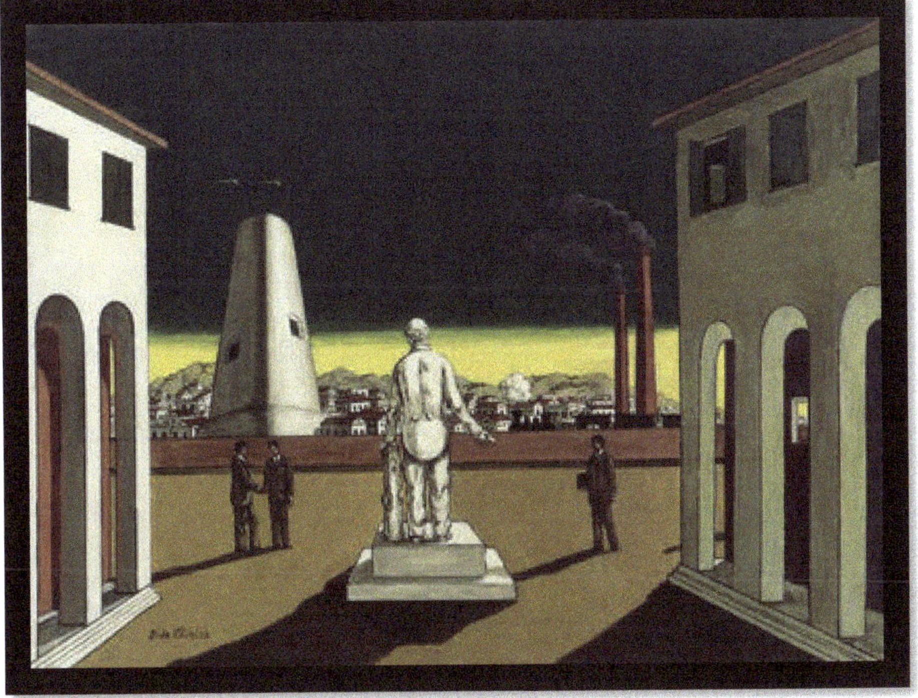

Art History Project

We will add some shadows to one of Giorgio de Chirico paintings. Look at his other paintings and see how he put in the shadows and try to do the same. Remember, the shadows will go in the same direction and don't forget to add shadows to everything, the people, buildings, and statue.

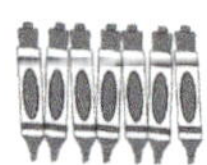

Use a brown marker for this

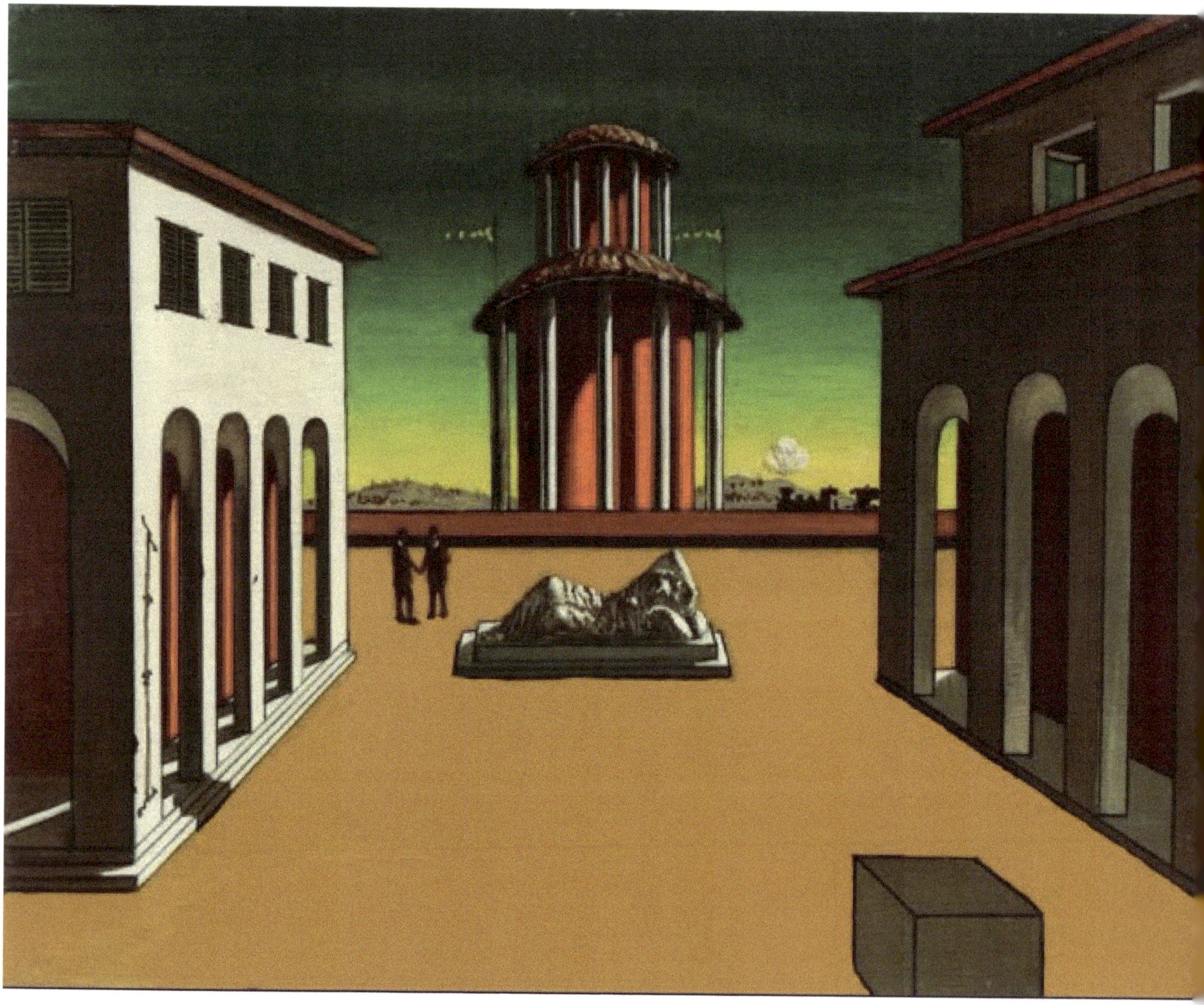

Chapter Fun

Oh dear, the shadows for these animals got all mixed up. Match the correct shadow with the correct animal

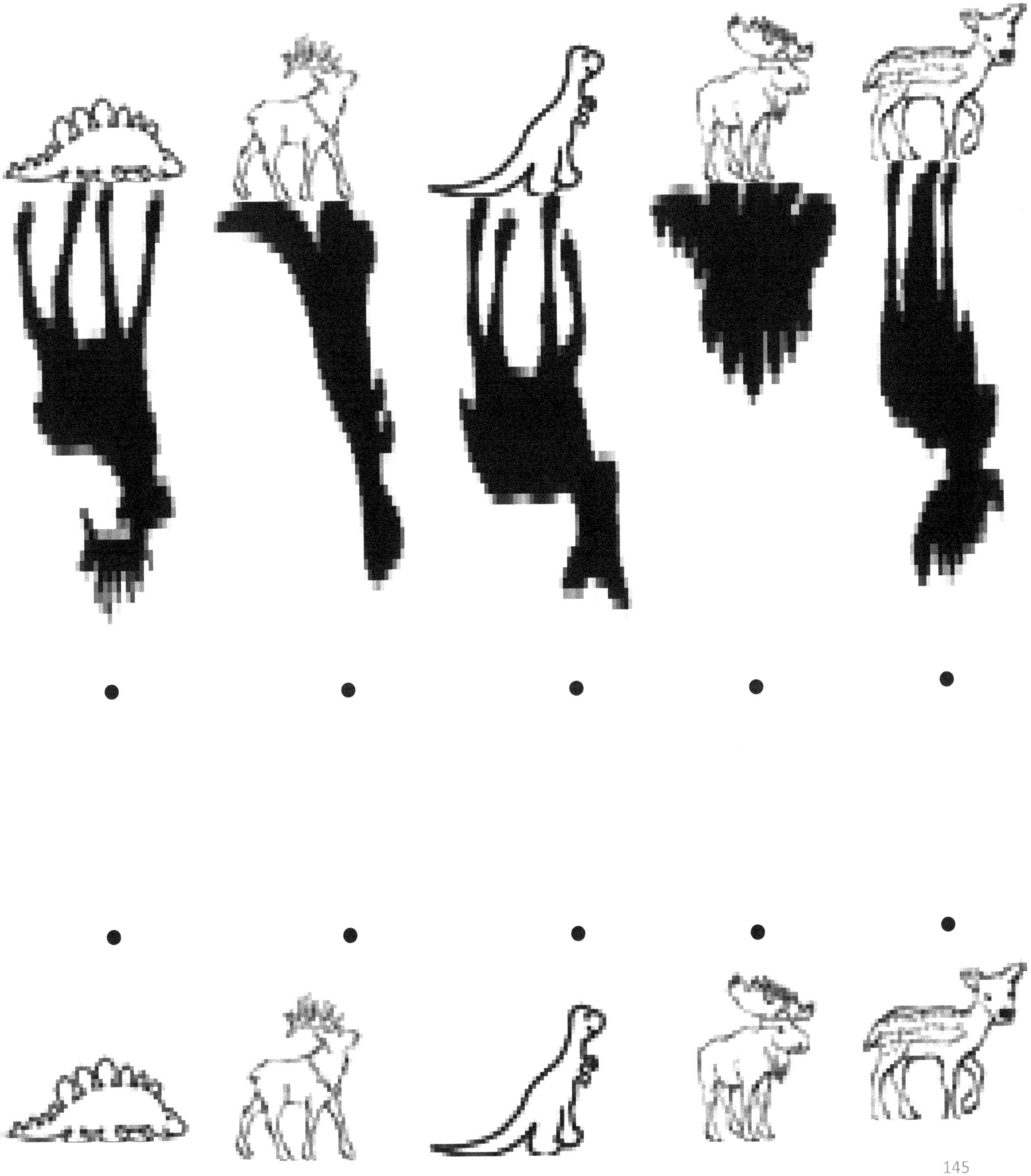

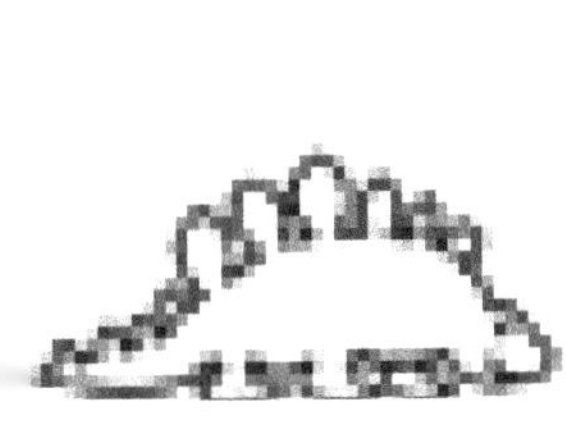
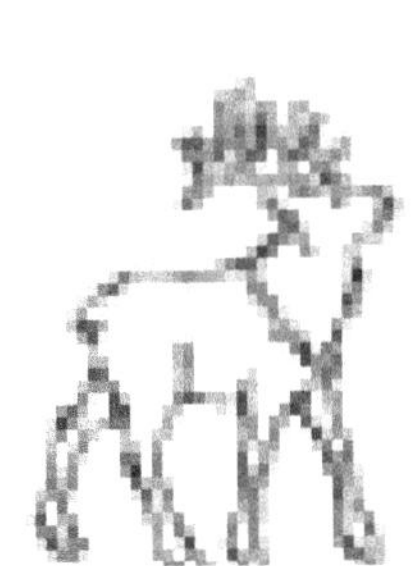
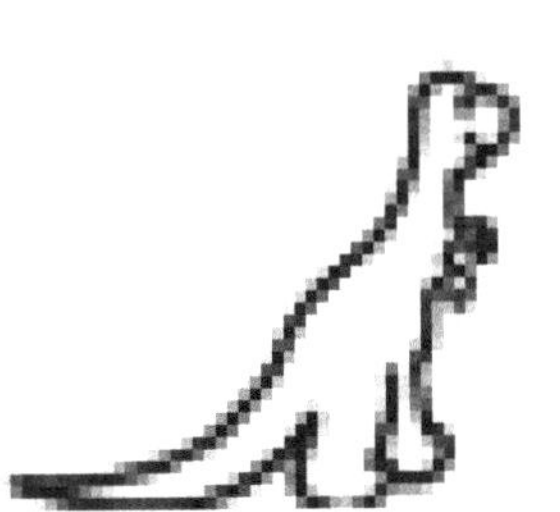
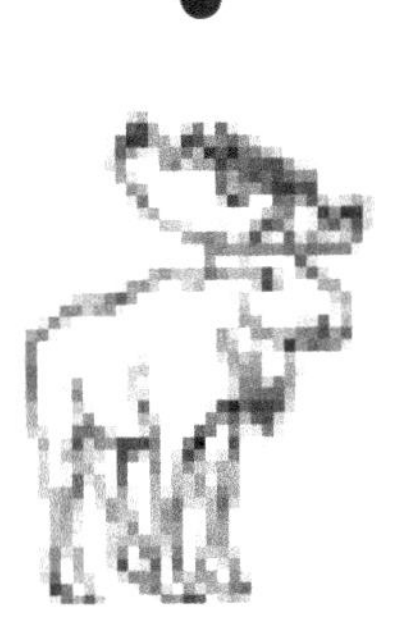
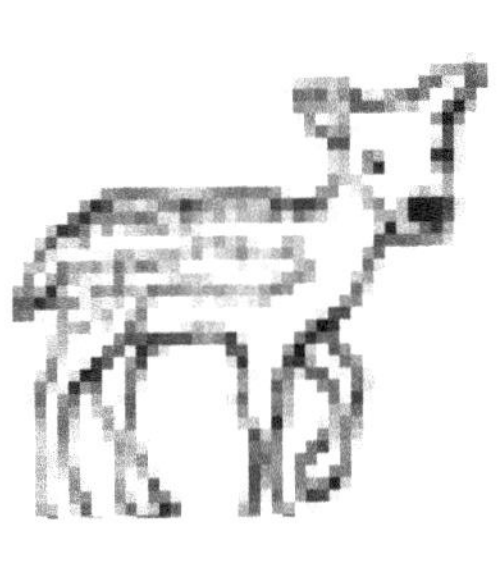

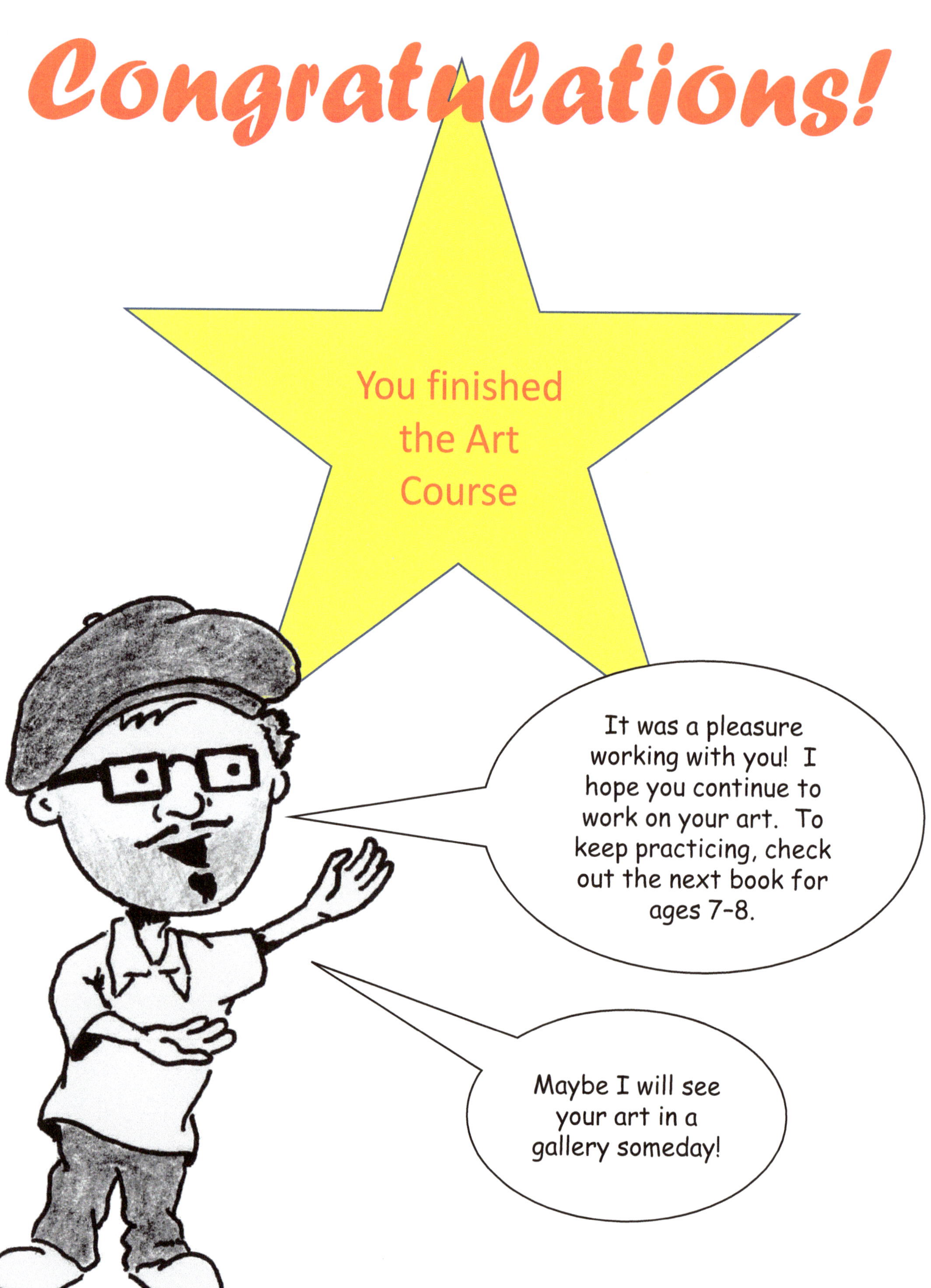
Congratulations!
You finished the Art Course
It was a pleasure working with you! I hope you continue to work on your art. To keep practicing, check out the next book for ages 7-8.
Maybe I will see your art in a gallery someday!

Lines for practicing letters from Unit 2.

Extra **easy** Graph from Project 1 of Unit 2

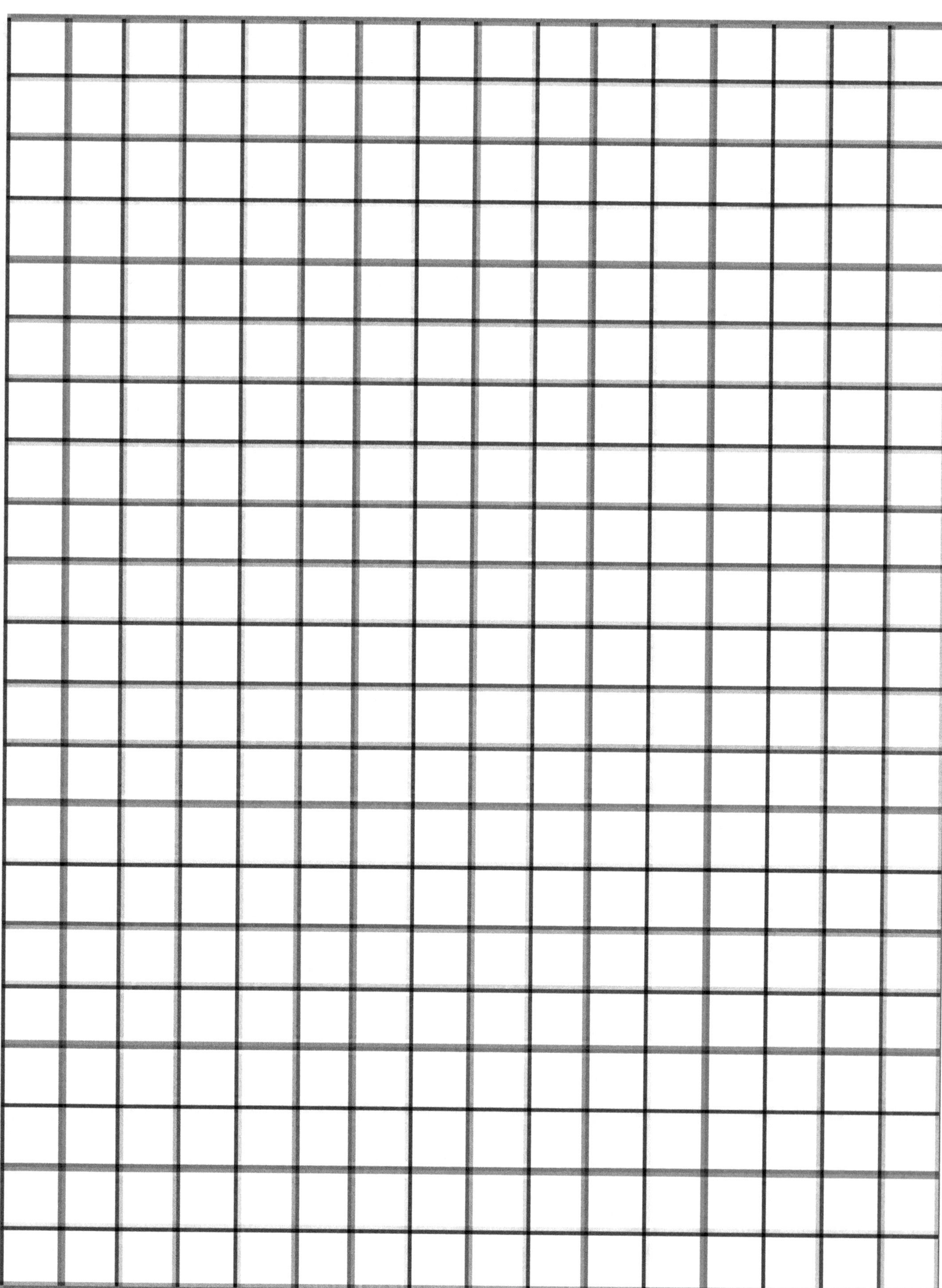

Extra **difficult** Graph from Project 1 of Unit 2

Extra **difficult** Graph from Project 1 of Unit 2

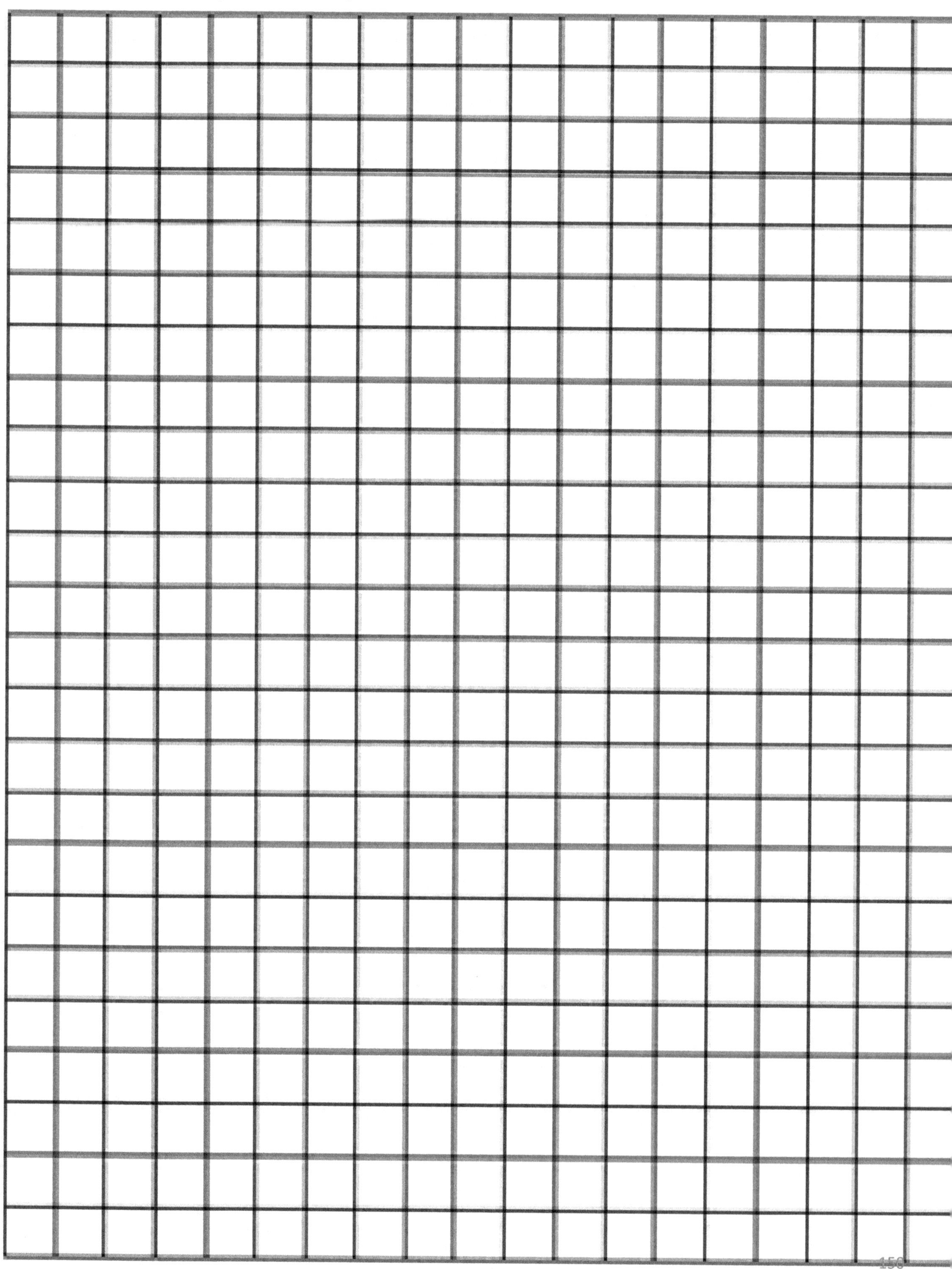

Large Color wheel from Unit 3.

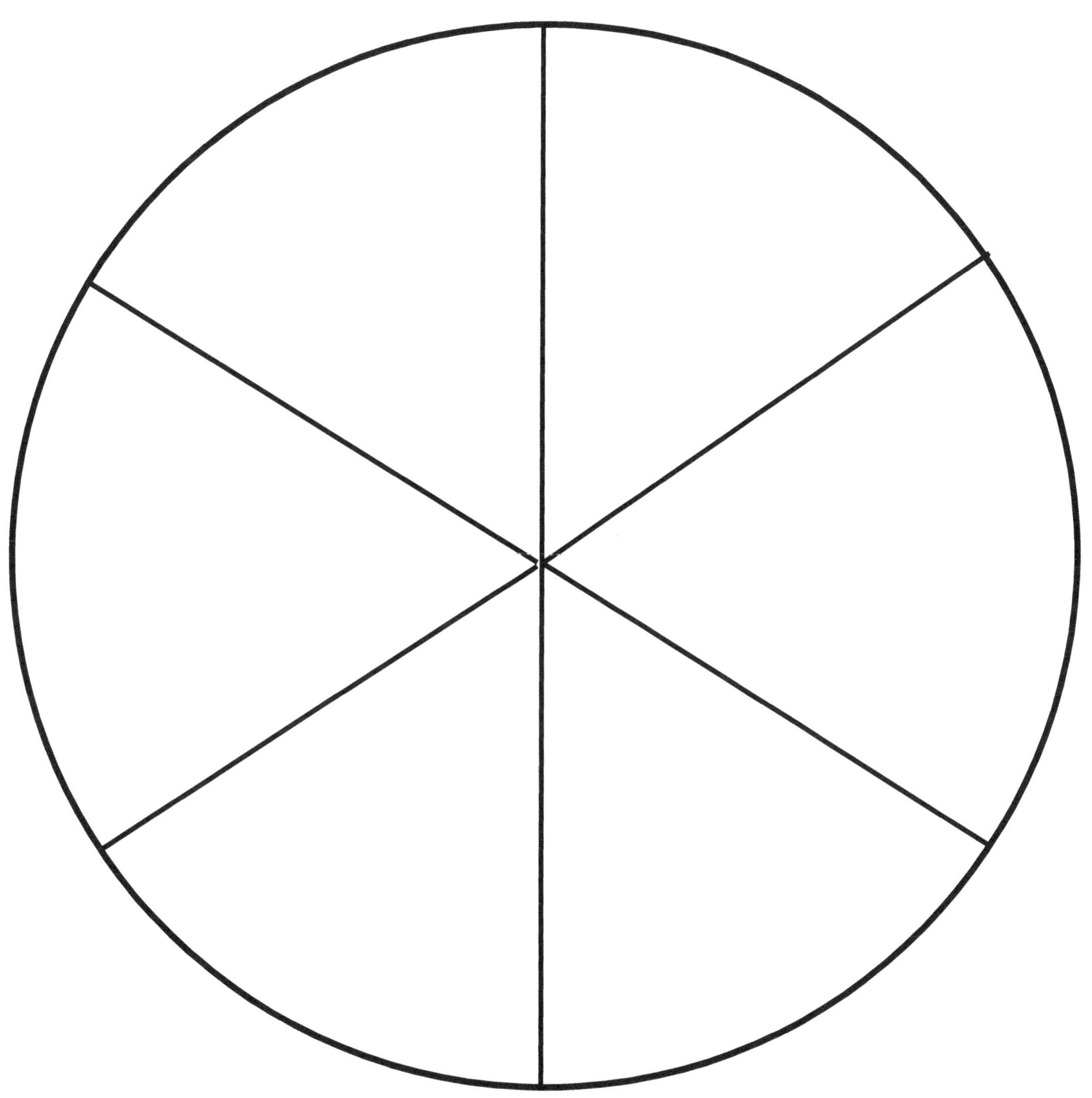

Small Color wheel from Unit 3.

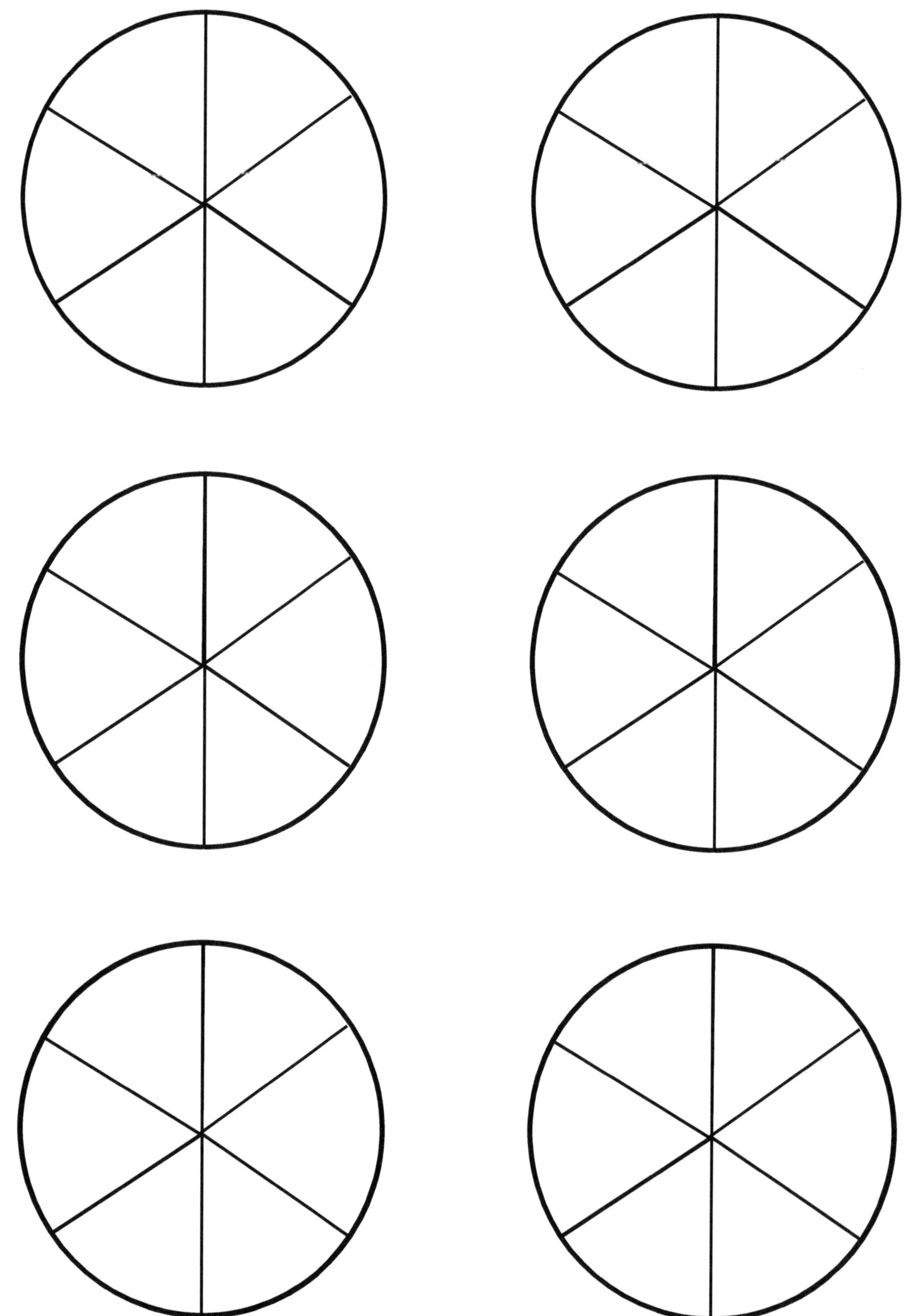

Cut outs for M.C. Escher Art History Project from Unit 5.

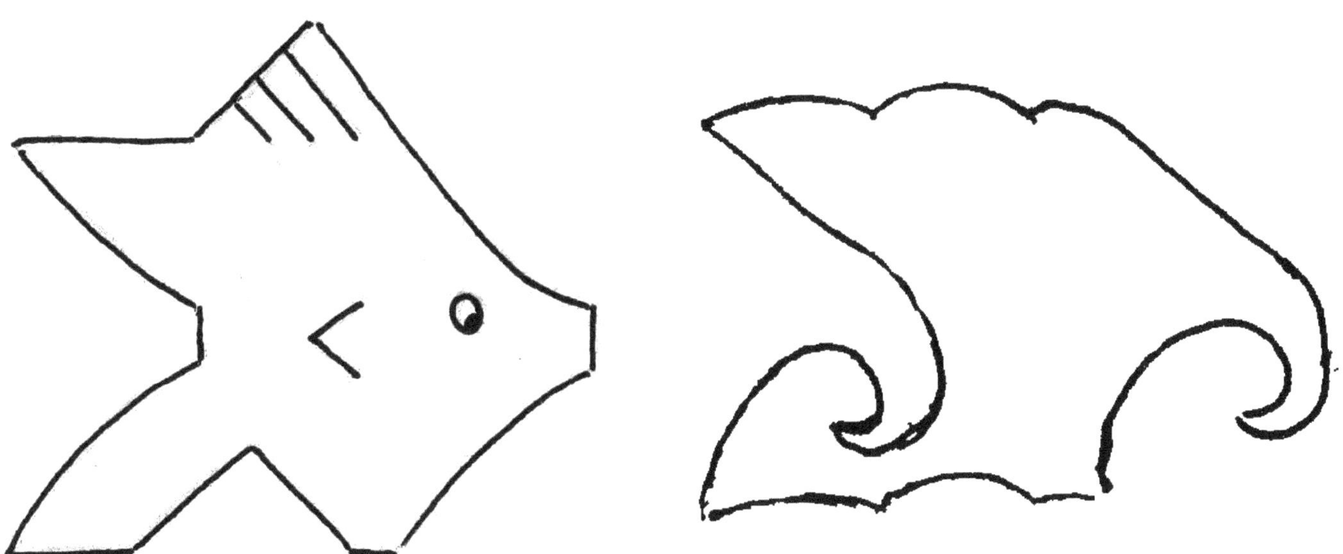

Face outlines from Unit 6.

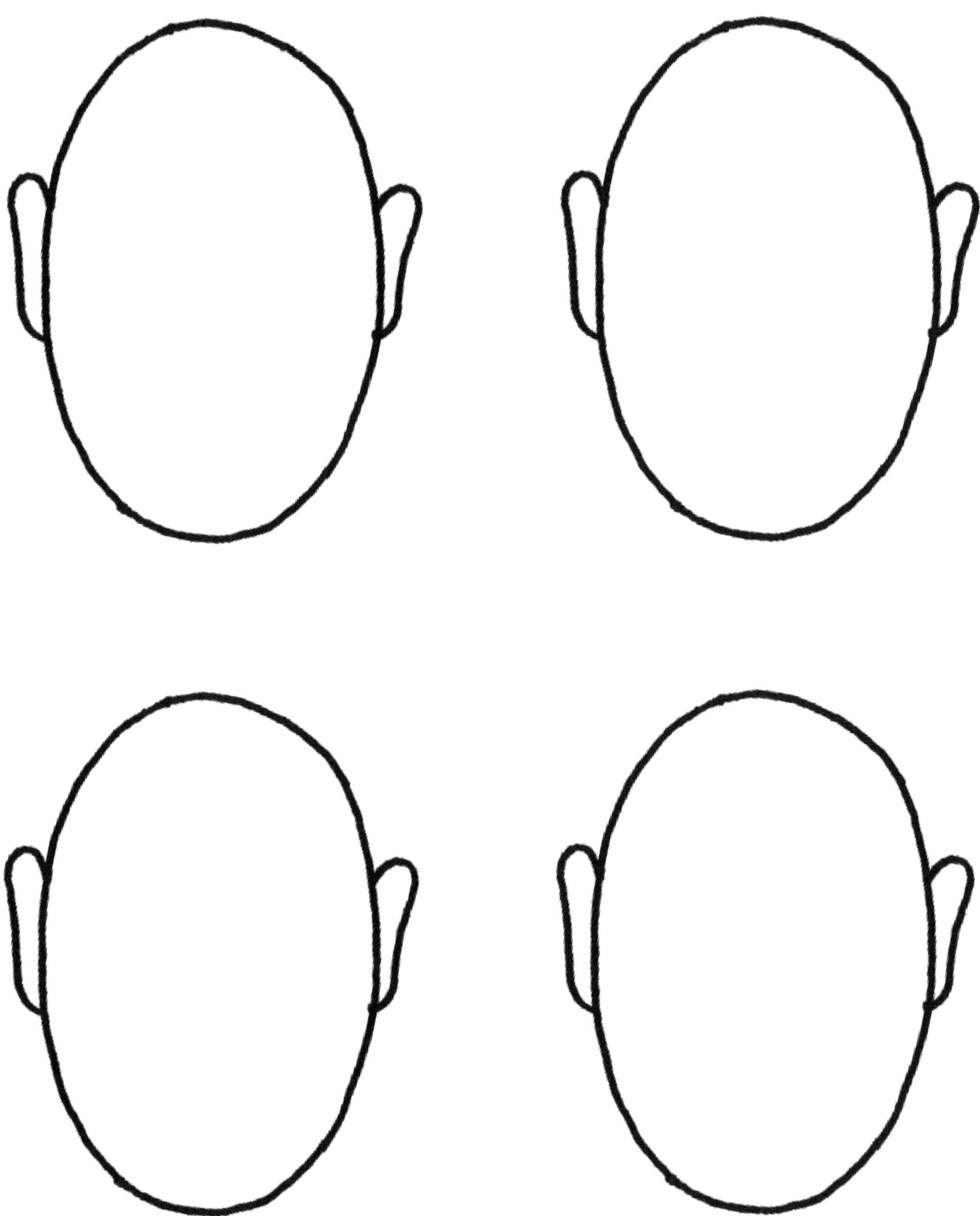

Face outlines from Unit 6.

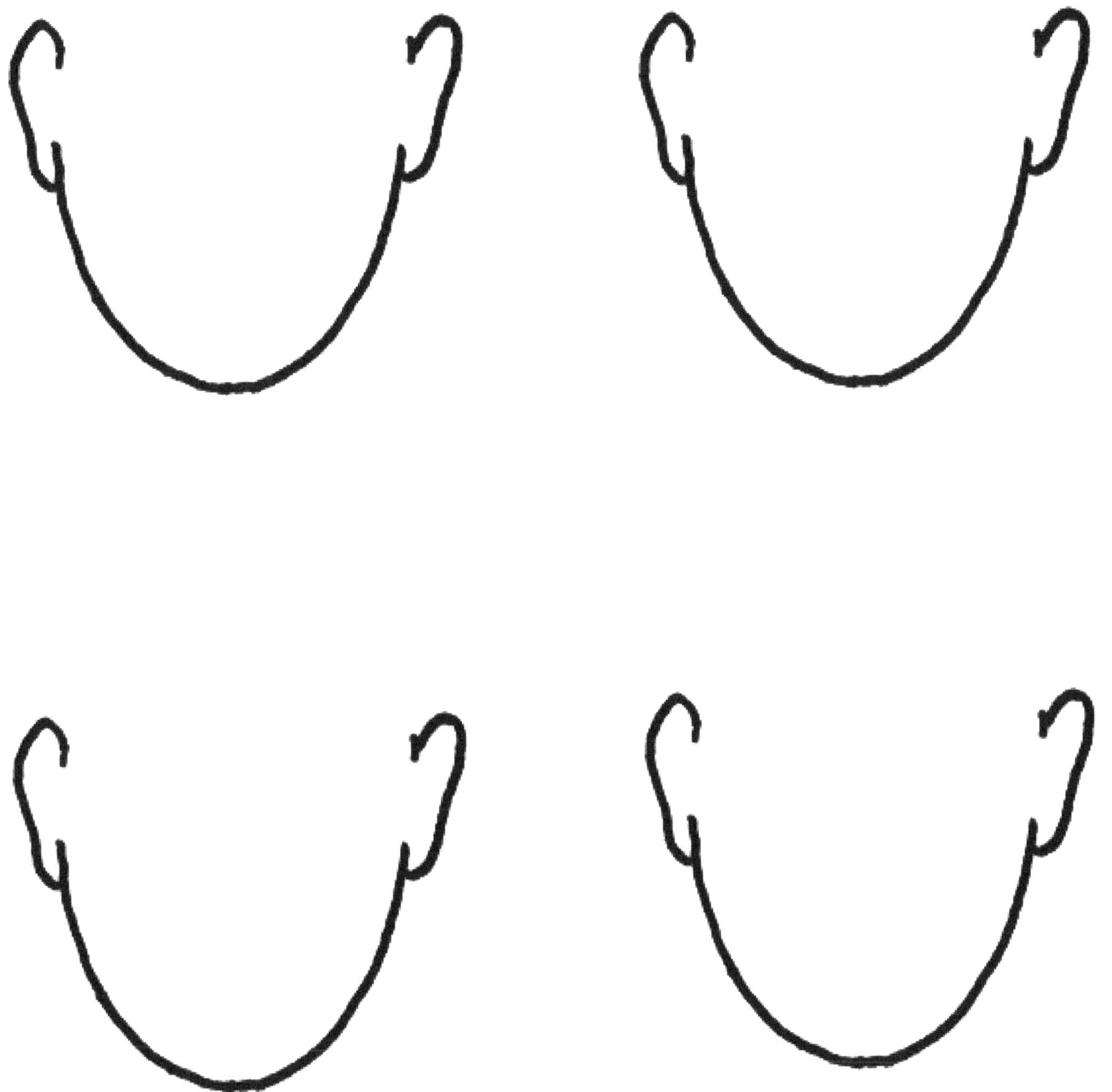

Face outlines from Unit 6.

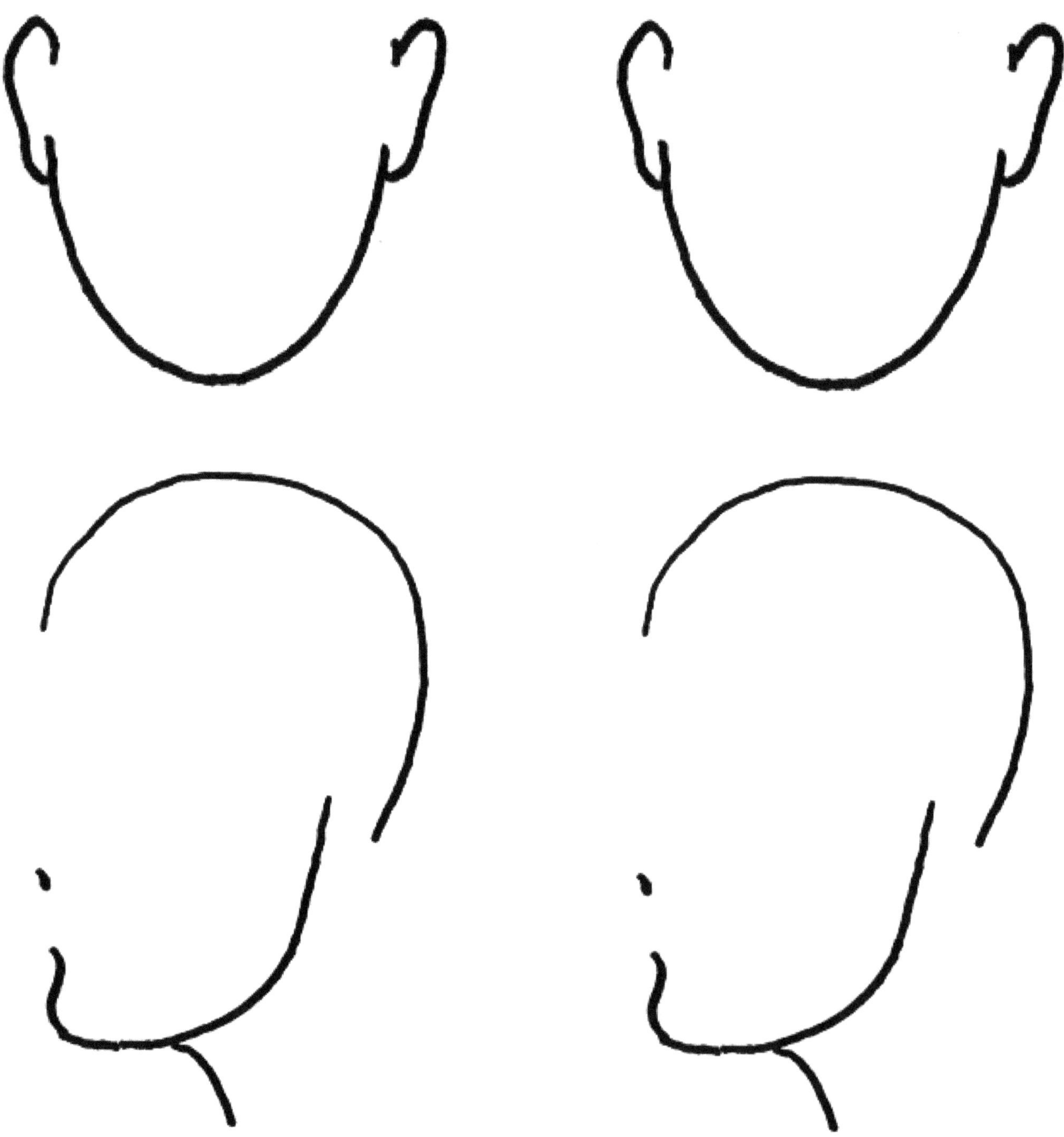

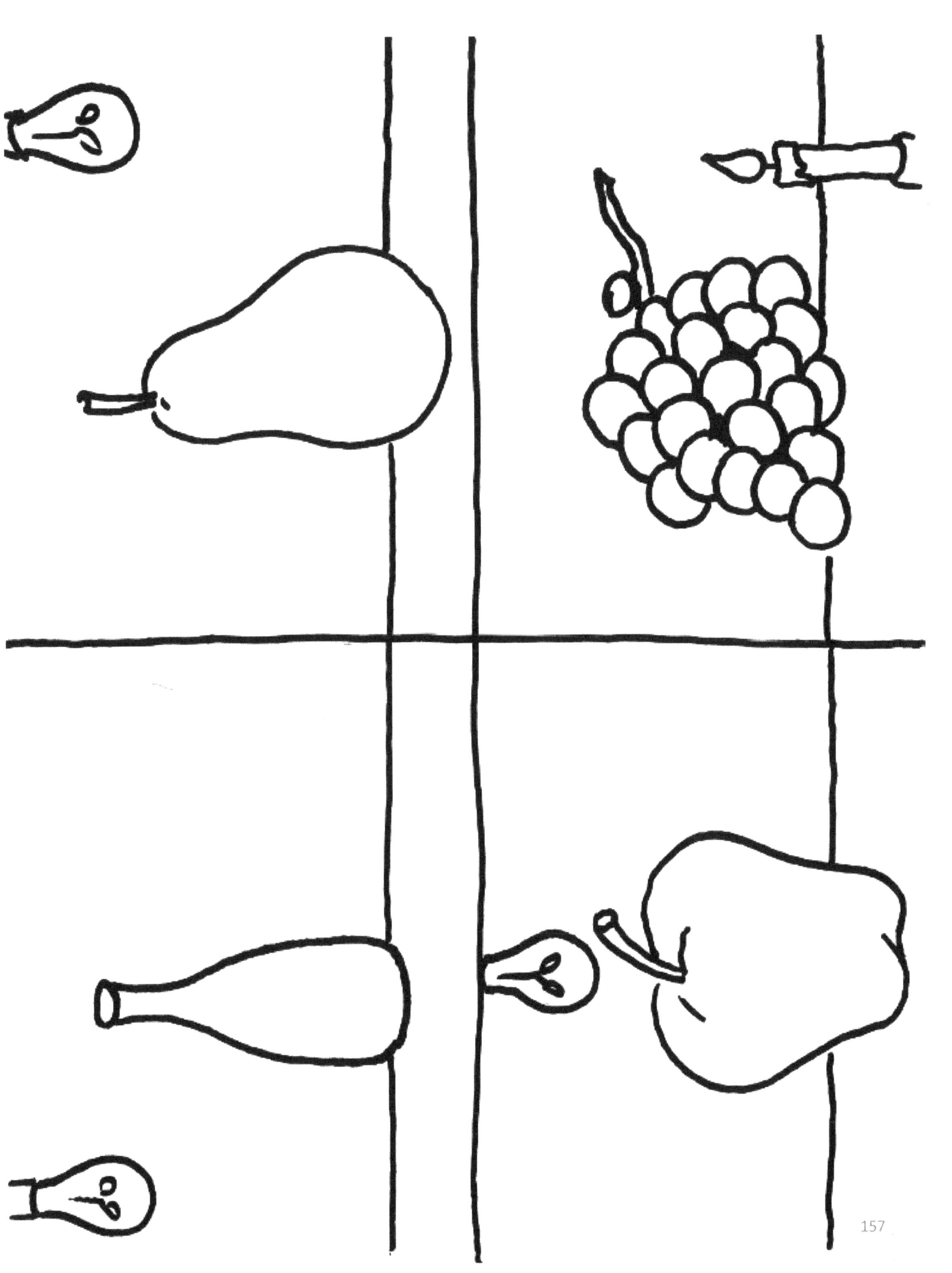

www.ingramcontent.com/pod-product-compliance
Ingram Content Group UK Ltd.
Pitfield, Milton Keynes, MK11 3LW, UK
UKHW062000290726
14090UKWH00021B/1314